the corporate finance handbook

the corporate finance handbook

3rd edition

consultant editor
jonathan reuvid

forewords by
sir edward george *governor, the bank of england*
david irwin *chief executive, small business service*

TENON

LEE CROWDER
Solicitors

ROYAL & SUNALLIANCE

KPMG

KOGAN PAGE

Publisher's note

Every possible effort has been made to ensure that the information contained in this handbook is accurate at the time of going to press, and the publishers cannot accept responsibility for any errors or omissions, however caused. All liability for loss, disappointment, negligence or other damage caused by the reliance on the information contained in this handbook, or in the event of bankruptcy or liquidation or cessation of trade of any company, individual or firm mentioned, is hereby excluded.

This third edition published in 2002

Kogan Page Ltd
120 Pentonville Road
London N1 9JN
www.kogan-page.co.uk

British Library Cataloguing in Publication Data
A CIP record for this book is available from the British Library

ISBN 0-7494-3626-3

Contents

Foreword

I am very happy once again to contribute this Foreword to *The Corporate Finance Handbook*. The Bank of England continues to take a close interest in the availability of finance to firms of all sizes and this falls squarely within one of the Bank's three core purposes – that of seeking to ensure the effectiveness of financial services in the United Kingdom. Naturally, our other core purposes – maintaining the integrity and value of the currency and maintaining the stability of the financial system – also play a vital role in creating an environment in which businesses can plan confidently for the future.

During the late 1970s and early 1980s, the Bank published its own guide to sources of finance for businesses, *Money for Business*. More recently, we have produced regular reports on the financing of small firms generally, as well as focusing on the position of particular categories of small firms (particularly ethnic minority and high-technology small firms). A recurrent theme of our work has been the importance of ensuring that finance is not only available but is also appropriate to firms' particular needs. I believe that there has been considerable progress in this direction in recent years, but businesses still need to know where to look for what they require.

This third edition of *The Corporate Finance Handbook*, which covers the full range of types and potential sources of finance for small, medium-sized and large firms, makes a valuable contribution towards meeting that demand. Indeed, I hope that it will help businesses to access the finance they need for their growth and development.

Sir Edward George
Governor, Bank of England

Foreword

I am pleased to have been invited once more to provide a Foreword to *The Corporate Finance Handbook.*

The Small Business Service is now well into its second year of operation and has made substantial progress towards its aim of making the United Kingdom the best place in the world in which to set up and run a business. The revamped Business Link network in England is now complete, providing a simple route to information and advice for small businesses through a single access point. The other elements of the gateway are also now in place – including a call centre, website and knowledge base. In developing these, the SBS has called upon expert knowledge contained in publications such as *The Corporate Finance Handbook.*

For this edition, the SBS has provided details of the initiatives it is taking forward in the area of SME finance. Alongside its well-established national programmes, such as the Small Firms Loan Guarantee Scheme and the Smart scheme, the SBS has created a UK High Technology Fund and Regional Venture Capital Funds – the latter should start making investments in growth businesses in the regions later in the year. The SBS is also taking forward measures aimed at helping small businesses to better understand the financing options available and to be better prepared to take on an investment. Further details of these initiatives are provided in Chapter 1.3.

David Irwin
Chief Executive, Small Business Service

About the Contributors

Bertoli Mitchell

Established in 1994, Bertoli Mitchell is an M&A boutique specialising in the publishing sector.

Christopher Gasson is a corporate financier and financial journalist, and an associate at Bertoli Mitchell. He is author of *Media Equities: Evaluation and Trading*, published by Woodhead Publishing.

Judy Brown

Judy Brown has advised corporate financiers and boards of directors on HR issues in corporate acquisitions and management buy-outs for many years. A Fellow of the Institute of Chartered Accountants in England and Wales and a Fellow of the Chartered Institute of Personnel and Development, she combines a financial approach and regulatory awareness with an understanding of HR strategy and best practice.

Forward Trust

Forward Trust Limited is one of the UK's leading providers of asset-based services and finance, employing some 1,200 people. From vehicle fleet management to complex asset financing for major projects, Forward Trust has the experience and expertise to provide solutions for commercial organisations.

A wholly owned subsidiary of the HSBC Group – one of the world's largest banking and financial services organisations – Forward Trust has assets in excess of £5bn.

Forward Trust operates brands within three strategic market sectors: rail, cars and commercial vehicles; and their respective related services. Forward Trust has a strong commitment to providing added value services. The need to differentiate and generate a competitive edge through the quality of customer service is a key priority.

KPMG Corporate Finance

KPMG Corporate Finance provides financing and investment banking advice to quoted and private companies and public sector bodies. It acts as lead adviser and deal manager on the full range of corporate transactions including M&As, disposals, structured and project finance, leveraged buy-outs, public securities offerings, privatisations and valuations.

Stephen Craik is a partner and head of private equity for KPMG Corporate Finance in the Midlands. He was named overall winner in the latest Sunday Times Rainmaker Awards.

Charles Milner is a partner and UK head of private equity at KPMG Corporate Finance.

Tony Sharp is a partner with KPMG Corporate Finance based in Leeds.

Mike Stevens is vice-chairman and UK head of mergers & acquisitions at KMPG Corporate Finance.

Lee Crowder

Lee Crowder is one of the Midlands' most dynamic and forward-thinking legal practices. It represents a wide range of organisations and individuals throughout the UK and overseas and has provided a first class legal service for nearly 250 years. Its service is client focused and it appreciates the need to understand its clients' businesses, enabling it to provide commercially aware, quality legal advice.

Lloyds TSB Development Capital (LDC)

Lloyds TSB Development Capital (LDC) is the Venture Capital arm of Lloyds TSB Group plc. It invests between £0.5m and £10m in unquoted companies with a turnover typically in excess of £5m.

It makes investments in a full range of equity products including ordinary shares, preference shares, convertible preference shares and loan stock. It invests money from the bank's balance sheet, so it does not suffer the same pressure as some other venture capital funds to seek a rapid return of its money.

LDC has invested in over 350 businesses in its 20-year history across a wide variety of industry sectors, of which IT forms a large proportion of its portfolio. It invested £115 million in 2001.

LDC is now ranked as one of the top two mid-market private equity houses in the UK.

Michael Joseph is managing director of Lloyds TSB Development Capital.

NMB-Heller Limited

NMB-Heller is a unique provider of structured finance for businesses. The company's products include: Invoice Finance, to which can be added Credit Control, Credit Protection, Stock Finance, Trade Finance, Term Loans and Treasury Management. Used alone or in combination, these are designed to offer flexible working capital solutions for changing circumstances such as periods of rapid growth; a planned acquisition; possible refinancing; or MBO/MBIs. In conjunction with its associates, working capital finance can be made available throughout Europe.

NMB-Heller Ltd is a wholly owned subsidiary of NMB-Heller Holding, a company jointly owned by ING Group and Heller Financial Inc., a wholly-owned subsidiary of the Fuji Bank.

Old Mutual Securities

Old Mutual Securities' Corporate Finance team specialises in advising smaller and medium-sized quoted companies with growth aspirations. It is stockbroker to over 80 fully listed companies and financial adviser to a considerable number of these. It is also Nominated Adviser and stockbroker to 30 AIM listed companies. The Corporate Finance team is particularly experienced in advising and preparing companies for flotation and other services include secondary equity issues, acquisitions, mergers, disposals, public takeovers and defences, reorganisations and restructurings. The team's success in the smaller and medium-sized companies market is attributed to its members achieving a clear understanding of clients' needs in order to work closely with them in seeking to achieve their goals.

Old Mutual Securities is a member of the London Stock Exchange and is regulated by the FSA. Old Mutual Securities is a recognised sponsor for the London Stock Exchange's Official List and is a listed Nominated Adviser for AIM.

Adrian Piper

Adrian Piper is head of the Investment Directorate of the Small Business Service. He joined it on secondment from the Bank of England where as

Acting Head of the Domestic Finance Division, he had responsibility for producing the bank's reports on finance for small firms.

Jonathan Reuvid

Jonathan Reuvid is consultant editor and part-author of a series of international business books and of titles relating to the finance and business management of UK small and medium sized enterprises, all published by Kogan Page.

Royal & SunAlliance

Royal & SunAlliance has recently launched Management Assurance, a packaged product providing specialist insurance protection with bespoke cover to suit the needs of each and every business, whether public or private. Directors & Officers Liability insurance can be taken out individually, or combined with other up-to-the-minute covers such as Employment Practices Liability insurance, Crime, Kidnap Ransom & Extortion, Pension Scheme Liability insurance, Professional Indemnity insurance and Libel insurance. The product includes unique value-added services designed to help insureds avoid distracting and time-consuming losses and ultimately support the insureds in managing their future with confidence.

Keith Baxter is worldwide practice leader, Credit & Bonds, Royal & SunAlliance ProFin.

RPS Group plc

RPS is the largest independent environmental consultancy in Europe, providing commercial and practical advice to both business and the public sector. With teams of environmental auditors based in London, Frankfurt, Paris, Rotterdam, Edinburgh and Dublin, RPS has specialised in advising on cross-border transactions in Europe and the US. Dr David Hockin is responsible for the development and co-ordination of environmental due diligence for the RPS Group plc.

Russam GMS Ltd

Charles Russam is chairman of leading Interim Management provider Russam GMS Ltd with offices in Birmingham, Bristol, Dunstable, Leeds and Manchester.

Tenon Group

Tenon is the first company of its kind in the UK, a quoted accountancy based business.

Accountancy and related business advisory services have always been fragmented in the UK. The idea behind Tenon was to give businesses integrated, flexible services at a local level. Tenon offers genuine depth and breadth of service by giving its local offices access to experts in many different financial and business fields. For the entrepreneur or business owner, Tenon represents the perfect way to access the range of advice normally offered only to very large organisations. That includes help with highly specialised areas of business where expertise is critically important.

The structure of Tenon is one of strong and established accountancy based practices – practices that are knowledgeable and trusted within their local communities. With Tenon clients can develop a long-term relationship with a local advisor, secure in the knowledge that they are also accessing national expertise. Tenon's main focus is on UK privately owned businesses and their owners and growth has been rapid with around 1,800 staff operating from 35 different UK offices.

Tenon Corporate Transactions offers integrated, strategically focussed corporate finance advice to mid-market and SME businesses, with the emphasis on supporting a broader strategy, rather than focussing on transaction execution alone.

Shiju Varghese is a director of strategic development and corporate finance based in Tenon's City of London offices. He has over 10 years' experience in strategic management and corporate finance work associated with the implementation of strategies, including structuring and launching business development and expansion initiatives. He can be reached by e-mail at Shiju.Varghese@tenongroup.com or by telephone on 020 7448 8120.

Nick Jones is a director of corporate finance based in Tenon's City of London offices. Nick has a wide range of corporate finance experience including advice on management buy-outs, raising equity finance from private providers, sales and acquisition of businesses. He can be reached by e-mail at nick.jones@tenongroup.com or by telephone on 020 7448 8117.

Maurice Fitzpatrick FCA ATII is a taxation director and head of economics at Tenon. If the former role, he is particularly interested in inheritance tax, capital gains tax, employee share schemes, and the tax efficient structuring of corporate deals. In the latter role he is frequently quoted in the media on a wide variety of fiscal and economic issues. He can be reached by e-mail at Maurice.Fitzpatrick@tenongroup.com or by telephone on 020 7448 8125.

Jay Sanghrajka is head of taxation services for the London region of Tenon and has wide experience of the taxation aspects of corporate finance including restructuring groups, MBOs, sale of business, ES financing and advising on sale and purchase documentation. He can be reached by e-mail at jay.sanghrajka@tenongroup.com or by telephone on 020 7448 8104.

TMG Corporate Finance

David Houghton is a director at TMG Corporate Finance, based in Manchester. TMG specialises in the owner-managed business sector, advising on all corporate finance matters including M&As, MBOs, MBIs and development funding assignments.

Introduction

This third edition of *The Corporate Finance Handbook* is intended for the directors and owners of businesses whose continuing prosperity and growth depend upon putting in place and maintaining an appropriate balance of external funding.

Within the spectrum of small and medium-sized enterprises (SMEs), and after excluding those businesses that are sole traders or self-employed, the Department of Trade and Industry has estimated that there are some 264,000 UK companies, described as 'middle-sized businesses', which generate almost one-third of all the money earned by British business and account for one-quarter of all employees. All of these companies have external financing requirements and it is to their senior management that the six sections of this book are addressed.

Part One describes the current corporate finance environment in general terms and provides background to the more specialised sections that follow. In Chapter 1.3, Adrian Piper, Investment Director of the Small Business Service (SBS) launched in 2000, gives a lucid account of the agency's operations and the interface between this new government initiative, Business Links and the networks of formal and informal venture capitalists. Chapter 1.4 is devoted to the special financing issues of technology-based small firms (TBSFs).

Part Two focuses on the different types of debt finance available to businesses at varying stages in their development. Authors from leading institutions have updated their contributions to the previous edition. For the first time, a chapter on foreign trade finance is included.

In Part Three, the book turns to private equity – the heart of corporate financing. The introduction of external equity investment is possibly the single issue of most concern to boardroom strategy-makers. The role of formal and informal venture capitalists is addressed, as are the preparations for attracting private equity and the legal aspects of equity transactions.

Part Four will be of interest chiefly to those readers whose companies have reached the level of trading at which flotation on a public stock market has become a realistic option. The motivation for 'going public' is discussed objectively against the alternative of a trade sale as a means of releasing shareholders' capital. The key legal and taxation issues that arise in the course of preparing for an Independent Public Offering (IPO) are identified and their implications for directors are examined. Finally, the phenomenon of public to private transactions is discussed.

In Part Five the processes of buying businesses and selling your business are highlighted including the key issue of valuation. The realities of management buy-outs are questioned in Chapter 5.4. Taxation aspects of purchasing and selling private companies and their businesses and legal due diligence issues are further discussed.

Finally, Part Six offers guidance on some of the key management issues that emerge in most growing businesses and are brought to the fore at the time of negotiating external funding, particularly of an equity nature, in connection with flotation or merger and acquisition (M&A). Of particular interest to directors will be Chapter 6.3 which describes the new opportunities for rewarding management with a stake in the business through the Enterprise Management Incentive (EMI) schemes, which recent government taxation changes have generated.

The principal sponsors and authors of *The Corporate Finance Handbook* are three leading firms of professional advisers who are engaged in providing services to corporate clients at all stages in the development of their external financing. KPMG Corporate Finance has contributed chapters on key topics in each of the private equity, public equity and M&A sections of the book. The Tenon Group has provided guidance on taxation in Parts Four, Five and Six, on corporate strategy in Part One and on the processes of raising venture capital and generating investment in Parts Three and Six. Lee Crowder, the Birmingham-based corporate law firm has contributed all the chapters on legal issues in Parts Three to Six.

The publishers express their thanks to Sir Edward George, Governor of the Bank of England, and to David Irwin, Chief Executive of SBS, for their Forewords to the book. Our appreciation is due to all the individual authors who have written with knowledge and clarity on their specialist subjects.

Although the UK business outlook for 2002 remains uncertain, it is unlikely that the appetite for corporate finance will be much diminished. More challenging financial markets will raise the demand for expert advice in managing external corporate finance. Hopefully, this book will make a contribution towards a better understanding of the issues involved.

Jonathan Reuvid
London, December 2001

Part One

The Corporate Finance Environment

1.1

Strategic Considerations – Making the Right Choice

Shiju Varghese
Managing Director, Strategic Development and Corporate Finance, Tenon Corporate Transactions

The nature of corporate finance

Corporate finance is the broad heading given to the process of transacting and managing certain activities of companies, including the raising of funds and the realisation of value through a sale or listing. These include raising funds for the purpose of financing existing activities, developing new activities or investing in new fixed assets, buying other companies or businesses and selling the whole or part of companies, or even selling certain specific assets. At its most basic level it could be arranging a simple loan for the purchase of a piece of machinery, or agreeing an overdraft facility to meet cash needs during a seasonal slow down. Alternatively, it could be a hugely complex deal involving the issue of complex instruments to financial institutions and the public.

There are numerous methods by which any of the above activities can be financed and structured by any of the parties to a transaction, but ultimately whatever means is adopted will be classified as either debt or equity. Debt will eventually have to be repaid and will almost certainly have to be serviced until then, whereas equity is effectively permanent capital. Activities where equity is the primary consideration include the listing of shares on stock markets, introduction of venture capital or private equity into a business and funding management buy-outs and buy-ins. In merger and acquisition (M&A) activities both equity and debt are likely to feature prominently. Debt-focused transactions include overdrafts and term loans, leasing, factoring, guarantees, asset and trade finance, and bond issues.

Providers of capital, whether debt or equity, will expect to make a return on the funds provided, with the level of return expected linked to the perceived risk attached to either the entity receiving the funds or the project for which the funds are earmarked.

The providers of finance can be shareholders in the business, both pre-existing and those who become shareholders as a result of the transaction, and the funds thus provided are classified as equity. If the provider of funds does not become a shareholder in the business the funds can be classified as debt, although in certain circumstances debt may take on the characteristics of equity.

Despite the wide range of funding options available to businesses – or perhaps because of it – decisions on which form of finance to introduce, or structure to adopt, are often taken reactively in response to short-term needs or what is on offer from bankers or other institutions currently supporting the company, and not in relation to a longer-term strategy for growing shareholder value. This is a crucially important issue to consider as in any free market economy enhancement of shareholder value has to be the primary objective of business activity, even if there will also be other important goals. Therefore, at the very least, any decision must at least preserve current shareholder value and ideally should enhance it over time. Sadly, it is often the case that shareholder value is actually eroded as a consequence of having made the wrong or not completely appropriate decision. Clearly, it is not possible to ensure that no decision will ever turn out to be inappropriate, but it should be possible to minimise risk and maximise the chances of success, barring totally unforeseen circumstances.

Corporate finance practitioners, including bankers, accountants, lawyers and other professionals, whether working in-house or within external advisory organisations, should be able to assist in the planning and execution of transactions. Although in many cases advisers merely execute transactions in tried and tested ways, sometimes they create innovative new ways of structuring things.

Whatever the skills of any particular set of advisers, they should be able to add real value to the process by not only advising their clients on the best options, but also by negotiating the best terms, particularly on price and flexibility, whether the deal involves buying or selling, debt or equity. In addition to assistance when new deals are being done, corporate finance advisers should be able to assist in the restructuring of the existing capital structure of a business should that be appropriate.

The need for strategic thinking

Any planning that is formulated in a strategic vacuum or based on unsound strategic thinking invariably comes unstuck. Whether the decision is to buy or sell a business or to expand into new activities, while accepting that it is impossible to predict the future, it can be very useful to consider the effect of things not going as anticipated.

A timely example would be the fate of Marconi. The former GEC put all of its eggs into the telecommunications basket and went from having one of the largest cash piles in British industry to a mountain of debt and the threat of catastrophic collapse in the space of barely two years. While no one could have forecast all the events that conspired against Marconi, one must wonder if the company's management and its many advisers truly considered all the risks inherent in its dramatic change of business direction. Marconi can be contrasted with Royal Dutch Shell, which has always employed the technique of 'scenario planning', and which has helped it to weather many storms including the severe downturn in oil prices in the 1970s.

Although the two examples quoted above are large listed companies, the issue of strategic thinking and planning is no less relevant to the smallest private business. Often, all that is needed is for a contrary approach to be taken in the planning process to try and anticipate how the business would cope with things not turning out as planned. The issue is not that an accurate scenario is forecast, but rather that the possibility of things not turning out as planned is seriously considered and factored into the decision-making process. Sadly, the planning process in many companies all too often concentrates on the possible up-side only. Another very current example is the position in which many companies that went public in the last few years on the crest of the bull market wave now find themselves. With the decline in the markets, many of those companies are finding that their listing is now actually a handicap and are beginning to consider going private again.

Naturally, not all decisions made can be judged on the basis of hindsight alone, but a process of strategic thinking in the context of corporate finance may lead to better decision making, with the ability to respond to changing circumstances in an orderly and structured manner. Such an ability can be borne of the understanding that a sale may be better delayed, for example, or that it may be better to borrow rather than dilute equity, or that the only way to secure the right level of funds may be to give up equity.

Acquiring capital to implement strategies

Determining an appropriate mix of debt and equity in a firm's capital structure can be vital to successful strategy implementation. In theory, a business should have enough debt in its capital structure to boost its return on investments by applying debt to activities that earn more than the cost of debt. However, this must be balanced with the need to service fixed debt obligations regardless of low earning periods. While equity does not usually carry with it fixed service obligations, issues such as dilution of ownership and the need to share future earnings with new shareholders must be considered. In times of depressed share prices, debt may prove to be the most suitable alternative both in terms of cost and demand. However, if interest rates are high, issuing equity becomes more attractive.

Another consideration is flexibility. As an organisation's capital structure changes, so does its flexibility for considering future capital needs. Using all debt or all equity today may impose fixed obligations, restrictive covenants or other constraints that could severely reduce a firm's ability to raise additional capital in the future.

Issues of control can be an overriding concern in owner-managed companies where dilution of equity affects the decision-making power of majority shareholders. Even for listed companies this can be a serious concern in an environment of mergers, acquisitions and hostile takeovers.

The corporate finance adviser as strategy consultant

Corporate finance advisers need to be responsive to changes in the wider business environment and help their clients review and adjust their forward business strategies accordingly. Even in the absence of significant changes to the business environment, company owners and managers should be encouraged to step back and revisit the fundamentals of their business thinking.

A good place to start may be the motivations, aims and objectives of the shareholders and/or directors for the future development of the business. If the company is unlisted, perhaps the intention is to build it up for eventual sale or for a stock market flotation. If the business is family controlled and managed, perhaps there is a succession problem that can be solved only by introducing and motivating new management. If the company is listed and its share price is languishing, perhaps it should consider going private again. Alternatively, if a company has particularly high-performing shares it may wish to initiate an acquisition strategy using its shares as currency.

Turning to the business itself, the management and their advisers need to be satisfied that there has been sufficient research to identify the position of the company in its market place. Each element in a thorough SWOT (strengths, weaknesses, opportunities and threats) analysis needs to be examined thoroughly and analysed. If the evidence is insufficient or inconclusive, additional research should be performed. The following are some of the critical issues on which the management must reach a clear understanding:

- environment analysis – the overall attractiveness of the industry; industry lifecycle; buyer segments; competitor analysis;
- competitive strategy – buyer needs; value chains; positioning the firm;
- organisational implications – achieving differentiation; achieving cost leadership;
- organisation analysis – structure and systems; culture and values; skills and resources;
- corporate and global strategy – restructuring? diversification?

In terms of the company's own capability for success, the directors need to make an objective evaluation of the quality, depth and breadth of the company's management, its structure, business systems and, where relevant, manufacturing systems. Another key issue is the company's ability to introduce new products successfully into existing and new markets – a critical factor in any decision to expand regionally or globally from local markets.

These investigations and the self-questioning process will enable the board and its advisers to formulate a strategic plan for, typically, the next five years ahead. The strategic plan becomes the framework within which the company will develop its more detailed business plans and the financing plan with a choice of financial instruments.

Inevitably, the process is reiterative: formulation, implementation, review and feedback. Typically, the planning loop would be of six months' duration. As the strategic planning routines become implanted in management culture, so the process will become more intensive and self-critical.

The role of the adviser within this process is to maintain an objective external viewpoint, act as a facilitator and source of expertise, and guide the client as required to the realisation of their plans.

1.2

Financial Market and Business Conditions for SMEs

Jonathan Reuvid

In the present economic conditions of the last quarter of 2001 both the financial market and business outlook for SMEs are in a state of uncertainty. Even before the terrorist outrages of September 11, it was evident that the brave assertions made at the beginning of year by the European Central Bank (ECB) and finance ministers of leading Eurozone member countries that the EU economies would be little affected by a prolonged US downturn had proved to be overconfident. The economists' axiom that 'when America sneezes, the rest of the world catches a cold' has been revalidated. It remains to be see whether September 11 and the continuing threat of terrorism or worse will cause the 'cold' to develop into a more severe attack of economic 'influenza'.

At first sight, economic indicators suggest that business in the United Kingdom is holding up rather well. Real GDP year over year growth has declined from 2.8 per cent in the third quarter (Q3) of 2000 to 2.2 per cent for Q3 (2001), while the retail price index (January 1987=100) rose from 170.9 to 174.0 over the same 12-month period. The unemployment rate continued to fall from 3.5 per cent in Q3 (2000) to 3.1 per cent for Q3 (2001), but rose marginally in October. However, the most recent reports of the Purchasing Managers Institute (PMI) released in the first week of November provide gloomier reading.

For manufacturing, although there was a surprise increase of 1.4 per cent in output in August, the year on year growth rate remained negative at –2.0 per cent with further declines in output signalled. In October, new orders weakened for the sixth month running and export orders fell back sharply for the second month in succession to the lowest level for nearly three years. In its latest quarterly survey, the Confederation of British Industry (CBI) reported export optimism at a 20-year low.

For service-sector companies, the PMI reported that business activity contracted in September 2001 for the first time since February 1999. New orders have weakened across all sectors, with many companies deferring the placement of new contracts while the hotels and restaurants and transport sectors all reported widespread cancellations of new business. No doubt the Bank of England's Monetary Policy Committee will be closely monitoring how effective the interest rate cuts since September 11 will be in restoring confidence.

These weakening international and domestic conditions are reflected in mergers and acquisitions (M&A) activity in 2001 involving UK companies. The *Thomson Financial Datastream* third-quarter data released on 6 November (www.ntc-research.com) clearly shows the depressed condition of financial markets. In 2000, UK companies made 587 acquisitions of other UK companies worth almost £107 billion, but this activity dropped to 221 transactions during the first half of 2001. In 2000, there were 557 overseas acquisitions by UK companies worth more than £18 billion, but overseas acquisitions in the first six months of 2001 fell to 170 transactions worth £26.5 billion. Similarly, acquisitions in the United Kingdom by foreign companies fell from 227 worth £64.6 billion in 2000 to only 79 transactions worth £15.7 billion in the first half of 2001.

The implications of all these trends and indicators for SMEs are hardly encouraging. In the absence of further traumatic events, the most likely outlook is that consumers and businesses will continue to cut their debts and, in the case of the latter, strengthen their balance sheets.

Types of corporate finance available to SMEs

Debt finance

In the eighth edition of its report, *Finance for Small Firms* (March 2001), the Bank of England points out that, in total, SMEs have become markedly less reliant on external finance in recent years. For those that do raise external finance, traditional bank loans and overdrafts remain the primary source of funding. Bank lending to SMEs rose rapidly in 2000 after several years of decline, with term loans accounting for 72 per cent of lending as at the end of September 2000 and the maturity profile remaining stable. A slight shift towards variable rate loans (nearly 70 per cent of total bank lending at 30 June 2000) was discernible, while asset-based and receivable finance remains significant (see Chapter 2.2).

The Bank of England's report reveals that at mid-year 2000, approximately 37 per cent of SMEs throughout Britain had loans of less than five years outstanding totalling £39,400 million, of which £28,100 million was in term borrowing. The banks were operating on a nationwide average lending margin of 2.7 per cent. The total stock of lending to SMEs reached a record high of £42.5 billion in September 2000, an increase of more than 14 per cent year over year.

The specific financing issues that technology-based small firms (TBSFs) encounter are described in Chapter 1.4, but another category of small firms with special needs is that of businesses in deprived communities. The reasons why these firms are disadvantaged are easy to understand:

- The availability of external finance is crucial because those who set up businesses in deprived areas are less likely to be able to draw on internal funds than those in more affluent areas.
- Businesses in deprived areas tend to lack business experience as well as collateral and personal equity.
- Business tends to be concentrated in sectors subject to higher failure rates; they suffer from remoteness, small and localised markets and high crime rates.

Data collected by the Bank of England indicated that the major UK banks currently lend some £1.5 billion to small businesses in some of the most deprived areas, but that the proportions of overdrafts to term loans and fixed to variable rate loans are almost the same as for the country as a whole. However, the average lending margin charged to SMEs in deprived areas is significantly greater at 4.1 per cent, which is attributable to the increased lending risk. From the data available, the default rates of small businesses in deprived areas may be over three times as high as the nationwide average.

Equity finance

Although the UK venture capital industry is the largest and most developed in Europe, it currently invests little more than 5 per cent of funds in start-ups and early-stage finance, compared with 20 per cent in expansion capital and as much as 75 per cent in management buy-outs/management buy-ins (MBOs/MBIs). Moreover, the figures for average deal sizes suggest that the opportunities for SMEs, including TBSFs, to raise formal venture capital of under £500,000 are fairly limited.

Research shows that the majority of SMEs have never accessed either private equity or public equity finance. Private equity finance comprises the two distinct markets of formal and informal equity. Formal private equity is sourced from banks, special investment schemes (some of which are described in Chapter 1.3) and private equity and venture capital firms. The term 'private equity' is commonly used in the United Kingdom in place of 'venture capital', which is reserved for a subset of private equity involving the smaller, earlier-stage and often more risky deals. The British Venture Capital Association (BVCA) has acknowledged this tighter definition by extending its logo to include 'Representing British Venture Capital and Private Equity'. The comments that follow on SME financing reflect the narrower definition of venture capital.

Essentially, venture capital involves the long-term commitment of external equity to enable businesses not listed on any public stock exchange to grow and prosper. In becoming an equity partner, the venture capitalist will place more emphasis on realising the final capital gain than regular cash flows. Typically, investments last for three to seven years, although exits are generally anticipated within five years. Typically, the venture capitalist will also provide expertise, experience and contacts to help nurture the business and the capital gain will be realised either as the result of an independent public offering (IPO) or through a trade sale.

Alternative sources of venture capital

In addition to formal venture capital described above and elsewhere in this book, there are other sources of financing that play their several parts in funding the development of SMEs.

Bank equity products

The main clearing banks, which also promote reputable 'business angels', have designed and offer a range of equity products for smaller companies. Prominent among the funds on offer from the clearing banks are the nine HSBC Enterprise Funds, operated by HSBC, which provide investments from £5,000 to £250,000 specifically orientated to start-ups and small businesses. HSBC has committed £18.75 million to these funds since 1992. HSBC has also leveraged in money from other sources (including the European Investment Bank (EIB)), which have committed over £45 million to the Enterprise funds and a separate fund for technology-based companies, of which some £27 million has already been invested in 203 companies. The average investment value is just £133,000. In addition, HSBC Ventures, the bank's venture capital arm, specialises in investing equity sums of between £250,000 and £2 million.

Separately, the Bank of Scotland contributes to a number of Scottish-orientated funds, such as the Dumbartonshire Fund and the West Lothian Venture Fund; the Bank also participates with other clearers as an investor in the Scottish Equity Partnership. Barclays, HSBC, Lloyds TSB, and RBS-NatWest together support the National Business Angel Network (NBAN), which relies on a regional presence to match business angels with appropriate investment opportunities.

Informal venture capital

This market consists of high-net-worth individuals – 'business angels' – willing to invest risk capital in small unquoted companies. In addition to capital, business angels are able to provide expertise and advice to assist the investee company in return for their equity stake. They play an important role in filling the gap between debt finance and the formal venture capitalists whose attention is focused on larger deals. With a lower cost base and different objectives, business angels are more comfortable investing smaller amounts and are more orientated towards start-up or early-stage funding.

With its comparatively low visibility, business angels' activity is probably underestimated. The 1999–2000 edition of the BVCA directory lists 48 business angel networks and research by Southampton University,[1] which the BVCA commissioned, concluded that 280 registered business angels invested £20 million in 1998–99 through 192 investments in 185 companies. Based on the limited sample of BVCA registered angel networks, the same survey found that 51 per cent of business angel investments were for amounts of less than £50,000 and only 24 per cent of investments were over £100,000,

1 BVCA, *Sources of Business Angel Capital 1999/2000* (2000).

compared with 86 per cent of formal venture capital investments. Some 60 per cent of the business angel network investments were focused on start-ups and early-stage financing and only 11 per cent on MBO/MBI investments. It was estimated in 1999 that the United Kingdom had approximately 18,000 business angels and that they invest about £500 million annually.[2] If this is true, the informal market would appear to provide some £300 million each year to start-up and early-stage finance, which puts it on an equal footing with the formal market in the provision of such funds.

Business angels bring other benefits to the businesses in which they invest. In particular, they can generate additional financing; banks are said to contribute to 86 per cent of businesses receiving finance packages from business angels, and venture capitalists to 25 per cent. Business angels that play an active part in advising or managing the companies in which they invest tend to act as magnets to more formal investors and give credibility to an enterprise among its customers and suppliers. Indeed, through the media of the banks and the Small Business Service (SBS), encouragement is being given to business angels and formal venture capital funds to co-invest in SMEs.

Overview of external finance sources for SMEs

The different forms of debt and equity finance up to public flotation are discussed in detail in Parts Two and Three of this book, but Charts 1.2.1 and 1.2.2 help to put into perspective the relative contributions which each make to the provision of external finance for SMEs.

Perhaps the most striking conclusion from a first glance at the charts is the very small contribution that formal venture capital makes to the overall financing requirements of SMEs. Given the present economic environment and confidence levels, it seems unlikely that this contribution will be raised from the 1997–99 level of 1 per cent in the foreseeable future.

The second significant point is that the proportion of SME external finance provided by the banks rose from 48 per cent over the period 1995–97 to 61 per cent in the period 1997–99, and, as the absolute value for bank lending in September 2000 indicates, appears to be rising

2 Mason, C and Harrison, R.: 'Public Policy and the Development of the Informal Venture Capital Market: UK Experience and Lessons for Europe', in K. Cowling (ed), *Industrial Policy in Europe* (1999).

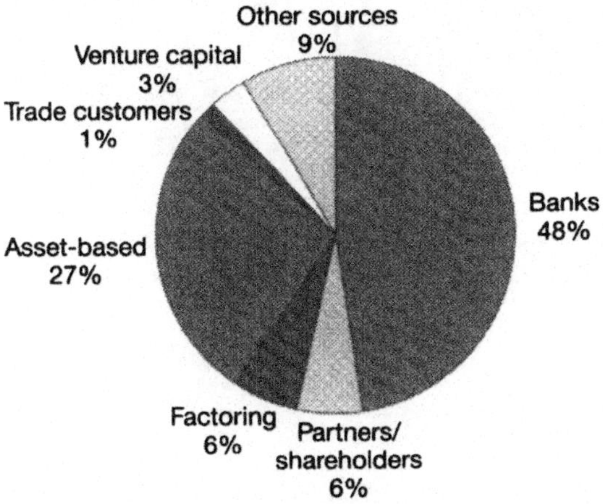

Figure 1.2.1 Sources of external finance for SMEs 1995–97
Source: ESRC Centre for Business Research Cambridge

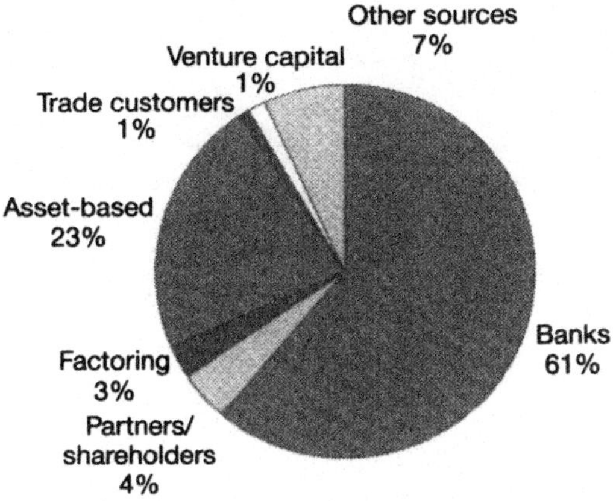

Figure 1.2.2 Sources of external finance for SMEs 1997–99
Source: ESRC Centre for Business Research Cambridge

further. However, it is possible that the survey on which the charts are based has magnified the extent of any recent shift to traditional bank finance, because the database contained a disproportionately high element of expanding firms seeking finance and fewer sole traders and partnerships.

Acknowledgements to the Domestic Finance Division of the Bank of England for access to their March 2001 publication 'Finance for Small Firms – An Eighth Report', from which much of the content for this chapter was sourced.

1.3
Small Business Service (SBS) and SME Finance

Adrian Piper
Investment Directorate, Small Business Service

Small Business Service (SBS)

The Small Business Service (SBS) was formally launched on 3 April 2000 and is the sole government agency responsible for business support in England. Its goal is to build an enterprise society in which all small businesses thrive and achieve their potential. The SBS provides business support, advice and access to appropriate expertise through the Business Link network. It also manages a number of national services.

Role of SBS Investment Directorate

The role of the SBS Investment Directorate is to identify any market weaknesses in the provision of finance to SMEs and to decide whether and how these might be addressed.

Small Business Investment Taskforce (SBIT)

The 2000 Budget report announced the creation of a Small Business Investment Taskforce (SBIT) to advise David Irwin, SBS chief executive, and through him the Government, on how best to stimulate the operation of markets providing finance for SMEs. The SBIT also advises on SME finance issues generally, including how best to intervene in venture capital markets.

Formed in September 2000, with an expected term of three years, the SBIT is made up of 18 members who represent a wide cross section of venture capitalists, 'business angels', micro-finance practitioners, financial and business advisers and banks and other providers of debt finance. All have significant, relevant knowledge and experience, which ensures the credibility of the SBIT within the finance sector and associated industries. The SBIT chairman is Sir David Cooksey.

Smart

The Smart scheme in England provides grants to help individuals and small businesses research and develop technologically innovative products and processes, or to buy external consultancy to improve their use and exploitation of technology. The scheme offers support under five elements:

- Technology reviews help a business assess its use of technology against best practice in the sector. A grant up to a maximum of £2,500 is available to cover external review costs if a business expends the equivalent of the grant in terms of its own effort. Projects must involve at least one day's paid consultancy.
- Technology studies for an in-depth look at a business's use of technology help it to identify technological opportunities that may lead to innovative products and processes. A grant of 75 per cent of external study costs, up to a maximum £5,000, is available if the business expends the equivalent of the study costs in terms of its own effort. Projects must involve more than one day's paid consultancy.
- Micro project awards are 50 per cent of eligible costs, up to a maximum grant of £10,000, for the development of simple, low-cost prototypes of new products or processes that involve technological advance and/or novelty. The minimum project size supported is £5,000.
- Feasibility study awards are 75 per cent of eligible project costs, up to a maximum grant of £45,000, for a technical and commercial feasibility study into highly innovative technology. The minimum project size supported is £30,000.

- Development project awards are 30 per cent of eligible project costs, up to a maximum grant of £150,000 (including any grant received for a feasibility study), for the development up to pre-production prototype stage of a new product or process that involves a significant technological advance. The minimum project size supported is £60,000. (A very small number of exceptional development projects may receive up to £450,000 at a negotiable rate not exceeding 30 per cent.)

For a technology review, technology study or development project, applicants must have fewer than 250 employees; for a feasibility study, fewer than 50 employees; for a micro project, fewer than 10 employees.

Debt finance

The banks are by far the most important source of external finance for SMEs in the United Kingdom and are likely to continue to be so. The majority of bank finance consists of term lending and overdrafts, although recent years have seen an increase in other bank products, such as asset-based finance and factored debt. However, the banks continue to place a heavy reliance on security for lending. This, in itself, creates a market gap weakness affecting those businesses that have no security to offer.

Small Firms Loan Guarantee Scheme (SFLGS)

The Small Firms Loan Guarantee Scheme (SFLGS) offers guarantees on loans to small firms with viable business proposals that are unable to obtain conventional finance because they lack security to offer against a loan. By providing a guarantee against default, the scheme encourages lenders to lend where they would not otherwise do so.

Loans over periods of between two and ten years are provided by participating banks and other financial institutions that take responsibility for commercial decisions affecting borrowers. For established businesses that have been trading for two years or more at the time of application, the SBS provides an 85 per cent guarantee on loans of up to £250,000. For other businesses, including start-ups, the guarantee is 70 per cent on loans of up to £100,000. In return for the guarantee, the borrower pays a premium to the agency. For loans with a fixed rate of interest the premium is 0.5 per cent per year on the outstanding loan amount, while for loans with a variable rate of interest the premium is 1.5 per cent per year on the outstanding loan amount.

Loans of up to £30,000, from some of the approved lenders, are subject to simplified administrative procedures which enable the lender to approve applications without first referring them to the SBS, thus speeding up the lending decision.

Applications are made direct to one of the approved lenders who will consider whether to lend the money, and whether it should be by way of a conventional loan or overdraft or the SFLGS. The lender will apply to the SBS for a guarantee covering 70 per cent or 85 per cent of the loan.

Since the launch of the scheme in June 1981, over 76,000 loans, valued at over £2.7 billion, have been guaranteed.

Equity

Risk, or equity, finance, in a variety of forms and from a range of sources, is an increasingly important source of finance for SMEs in the United Kingdom. While it currently accounts for only a small proportion of total SME financing in the United Kingdom, risk capital plays an important role in financing higher-growth small firms. Since the mid-1990s, there has been substantial growth in the supply of risk capital to enterprises from both formal venture capital funds and informal individual 'business angel' investors.

Venture capital investment in the United Kingdom rose to £1,503 million in 1999 (up from £580 million in 1995) involving some 800 companies. Of this total, £347 million was invested in early stage ventures involving 260 companies.

Business angel investment is also increasing rapidly. Although data on this market is much less comprehensive, the supply of UK business angel investment is estimated at around £500 million per year, from some 18,000 actual and potential business angels, investing in some 3,500 businesses.

However, it is widely accepted that raising equity capital in the amounts appropriate to smaller businesses can be particularly difficult due to the high costs and relatively high risk of such investments.

The SBS is taking forward a number of initiatives aimed at increasing the supply of equity finance to SMEs. These include the setting up of Regional Venture Capital Funds; the creation of a UK High Technology Fund; the stimulation, through the National Business Angels Network (NBAN), of the business angel market and proposals for early growth funding.

Regional Venture Capital Funds

There is a current market weakness in the provision of equity finance in amounts below £500,000 for SMEs with aspirations to grow. The Government is establishing a minimum of nine regionally based, commercial funds that increase the amount of 'equity gap' venture capital available to the SME market. These funds are seeking to:

- increase the amount of equity finance available to growing SMEs, to enable them to realise their growth potential;
- ensure that every region in England has access to a viable regionally based venture capital fund, making equity-based investments in amounts below £500,000 in SMEs; and
- demonstrate to potential investors that robust returns can be made by funds investing in the 'equity gap'.

The Regional Venture Capital Funds are:

- commercially focused;
- managed by experienced fund managers with appropriate FSA authorisations; and
- able to raise significant private-sector investment.

Following state-aids clearance, the Government has announced:

- agreement in principle to invest up to £60 million by the European Investment Bank's venture capital arm, the European Investment Fund;
- seed funding by the Government of up to £80 million;
- indicative targets for each region:
  (a) £30 million for the North West
  (b) £20 million for the East of England
  (c) £30 million for the South East
  (d) £25 million for the South West
  (e) £25 million for Yorkshire and Humberside
  (f) £15 million for the North East
  (g) £20 million for the West Midlands
  (h) £20 million for the East Midlands
  (i) £50 million for London.

UK High Technology Fund

Research continues to emphasise the significance of technology-based businesses for future growth in a modern economy and the difficulties they can face in raising early-stage finance. There has also been a reluctance on the part of UK institutions to invest in venture capital funds focused on early-stage high-technology investments. The UK High Technology Fund is a 'fund of funds' that has been set up to address these issues as follows:

- Westport Private Equity Ltd was appointed to manage the 'fund of funds'.
- The fund manager has exceeded the fundraising target, securing commitments of £106.1 million from private-sector investors alongside government investment of £20 million. The co-investors are institutions that are not currently investing in early-stage high-technology venture capital.
- Westport has already made commitments to invest in underlying funds.
- Investments in sectors being supported by the Fund include software, pharmaceuticals, communications, Internet technologies and biosciences.

National Business Angels Network (NBAN)

Informal investors, or 'business angels', play an important role in providing smaller amounts of risk capital to businesses with growth potential, particularly start-up and early-stage businesses. Recent years have seen a significant increase in the level of business angel activity. However, research shows that there are still insufficient mechanisms to distribute information on investors and investment opportunities.

The SBS is therefore jointly supporting the National Business Angels Network (NBAN), with a number of clearing banks and other sponsoring organisations. NBAN is working with the local Business Angels Networks (BANs), banks, accountants and solicitors to bring the informal investment market to full operation. It is a resource for the whole industry and operates as a national conduit through which any company seeking investment can be put in touch with investors.

The SBS is also supporting the Business Angels Network Association (BANA), an industry-wide trade association that aims to represent the industry and, more importantly, to spread and develop good practice.

Early growth funding

A new programme of early growth funding is being developed in order to encourage risk funding of start-ups and growth firms. The aim is to facilitate the availability of small amounts of risk capital for innovative and knowledge-intensive businesses, as well as for smaller manufacturers needing fresh investment to pursue new opportunities. The SBS will target businesses seeking to raise up to £50,000 and aims to help 1,000 businesses over the next three years.

Investment readiness

To complement its supply-side interventions and to ensure that SMEs are in a better position to obtain and use equity finance, the SBS is addressing the issue of the 'investment readiness' of smaller, growth businesses. A consultation exercise has been undertaken, the results of which are being used to help draw up bidding guidance for a series of pilot projects involving both the public and private sectors. The SBS aims to build on existing investment readiness activities in order to identify those that are most effective.

1.4

Finance for Technology-based Small Firms (TBSFs)

Jonathan Reuvid

There are special problems for the owners of technology-based small firms (TBSFs) in raising finance for development and expansion, which are inherent in their key characteristics:

- initially, their products have little or no track record, are largely untested in markets and are sometimes subject to high rates of obsolescence;
- in their early stages, they lack tangible assets which would provide collateral;
- their value is derived from scientific knowledge and intellectual property and is linked primarily to longer-term growth potential.

In its report *Financing of Technology-based Small Firms* (February 2001), the Bank of England considers whether these characteristics disadvantage TBSFs particularly in comparison to other SMEs at the start-up stage in terms of the availability and cost of debt and equity finance.

Defining the TBSF and its financing needs

As long ago as 1987, the Department of Trade and Industry adopted a sectoral classification of 'high-technology' industries in the United

Kingdom.[1] This classification was reviewed and further extended in conjunction with the Organisation for Economic Cooperation and Development (OECD) and now includes the communications, IT, computing, biotechnology, electronics, medical/life science and aerospace industries. SMEs or new ventures in all of these display the three key characteristics listed above.

Firms located in different high-technology industries do not develop uniformly. Three main types of TBSF may be distinguished:

- where the product is subject to high front-end development costs (eg the biotechnology industry);
- where market entry and product development occur over an extended period of time, involving heavy research and development (R&D) expenditure and complex consultancy arrangements (eg medical and life sciences);
- where front-end development costs are lower and lead times from product to market launch are shorter (eg the IT and computer software industries).[2]

Within this spectrum of different types of TBSF, financing requirements and the nature and sources of finance through a firm's life cycle will vary considerably.

In general, there are four main stages: seed, start-up, early growth and sustained expansion. The difficulties in accessing the finance required are likely to change as the firm progresses through these stages.

In its first report on the subject (1996), the Bank of England considered these issues and reached the following conclusions:

- in common with SMEs generally, TBSFs depend heavily on internal funds at the seed stage (including the proprietor's own resources);
- seed and early-stage costs are likely to be higher for TBSFs than for SMEs because of the more complex product development process;
- equity risk capital is the main source for start-up and early-stage financing requirements, having regard to the perceived higher risks and longer development times applicable;

---

1 Butchart, R.L. (1987): 'A United Kingdom definition of high-technology industries', *Economic Trends, 400*.

2 Moore, B. (1994): 'Financial constraints to the growth and development of small high-technology firms', in Hughes, A. and Storey, D.J. (eds): *Finance and the small firm*, Routledge, London.

- TBSFs may require second and third round funding before clear profitability is established;
- as TBSFs grow, their financing needs become more similar to other SMEs, and bank debt becomes a more important source of external finance;
- in common with most SMEs, the rate at which a TBSF progresses will depend not only on its access to appropriate finance but also to such interrelated factors as the type of product, the type of market, the firm's growth objectives and the capacity of the firm's management.

The fall-out from these conclusions is a broad implication that the staged development process entails additional risks in funding TBSFs compared with SMEs in general. The financing of the innovation and development cycle of TBSFs from the initial product concept, through prototype development, initial production and, finally, product sales demands a series of cash injections. Failure to finance adequately any part of the cycle may cause the firm to fail and this, in turn, will add to the risks of any single finance provider. The biotechnology industry provides a good example, where the gestation period up to sustainable profitability may be as long as 10–15 years, which is well beyond the investment horizons of banks and most venture capitalists rooted in their 3–5 year exit strategies.

Alternative sources of finance for TBSFs

This analysis suggests that there may be a further dimension to the longstanding debate about the 'equity gap', which dates back to the original *Report of the Committee on Finance and Industry* (1931), chaired by Hugh Pattison Macmillan.

Perhaps small firms in high-tech industries experience 'gaps' in the provision of finance. There have been numerous reports and surveys on the topic of the general availability of finance for small firms, but inquiries as to whether there are supply-side or demand-side constraints that dominate in the financing of TBSFs have been inconclusive. The most recent relevant findings are from the ESRC Centre for Business Research (2000) survey, which concluded that finance was not a major constraint for high-tech firms in the sample. The survey showed that the success rate in obtaining finance was similar for SMEs in high-tech sectors as for SMEs in conventional sectors (in manufacturing 94.7 per cent against 89.3 per cent; in services 83.8 per cent against 90.4 per cent). However, the survey did not include any start-up firms and thus the picture is incomplete.

On the one hand, there is a strong feeling that although the United Kingdom has many high-tech high-growth businesses, it suffers a lack of investor interest and this supply-side constraint has been addressed in part by the public funding initiatives described in Chapter 1.3. On the other hand, a number of venture capitalists and 'business angels' maintain strongly that there is a demand-side shortage of 'investment-ready' companies, not in the sense of an absence of growth potential but as a reflection of owners' inability to prepare persuasive business plans and projections. Clearly, there is also a 'fashion' element in financing TBSFs with a marked downturn in sentiment during the period since March 2000 following the bursting of the IT dot.com bubble and disenchantment with the telecommunications sector focused on the overvaluation of 3G mobile telephony licences at auction.

Nevertheless, there is consensus among investment professionals that equity is more appropriate than debt for financing TBSF start-ups. Although the banks do provide finance to TBSFs, often through specialist units, a lack of collateral and market presence generally are deterrents to the provision of debt finance rather than equity for small high-tech start-ups. Given the substantial fixed costs, such as underwriting and advisory fees, public equity flotations are not a suitable route for raising relatively small amounts of capital. Moreover, for many small firms their lack of size and trading record preclude them from meeting the listing criteria of public exchanges. Therefore, the venture capital industry, the networks of informal business angels and the government initiatives now channelled through the Small Business Service (described in Chapter 1.3) are the main potential sources of private equity finance to TBSFs.

Research was commissioned by the British Venture Capital Association (BVCA) and carried out in 2000 by the London Business School to explore the relationship between investment rates of return (IRRs) and risk indicators, particularly in respect of early-stage funds over three-, five- and ten-year horizons. The research confirmed that, over long periods of time, returns on both early-stage and high-technology UK funds have fallen short of targets related to risk, while returns on later-stage and management buy-out (MBO) funds have generally exceeded such targets. There is evidence also that over the ten-year period to 1998 UK early-stage funds significantly underperformed equivalent funds in the United States and continental Europe. However, it seems that over the last six or seven years of the 1990s early-stage UK funds outperformed UK funds specialising in later-stage finance. The influence of the present economic slowdown, even if the United Kingdom avoids the worse effects of the global downturn, may cause the more recent trend to reverse.

As noted in Chapter 1.2, the formal venture capital industry is focused on larger and later-stage deals with a marked concentration on MBOs/MBIs (management buy-ins). It is estimated that there are currently some 18,000 actual and potential business angels in the United Kingdom, investing around £500 million annually, which makes the business angel market of equal importance to the formal venture capital industry as a potential source of finance for start-ups. There is a belief that business angels could fill gaps in the provision of small-scale equity to SMEs in general and to TBSFs in particular, either working alone or in partnership with formal venture capitalists.

Perhaps the most significant potential source of equity finance in high-tech sectors such as pharmaceuticals and software may be corporate venturing. This trend is reinforced by the growing desire of larger companies to broaden their access to new technologies; conversely, TBSFs may also benefit from not only a new source of risk capital but also new management expertise and access to the larger company's production, marketing and distribution resources. At present, corporate venturing is carried out by only a relatively small proportion of UK companies, although in the period leading up to the March 2000 watershed there was an increased level of activity as more companies established venture capital units to invest in Internet or technology spin-offs.

Conclusion

Although the accumulated evidence of the Bank of England 2001 report suggests that some, but by no means all, TBSFs in the United Kingdom encounter difficulties in accessing finance at the seed, start-up and early stages, it is not clear that these difficulties are significantly greater than for SMEs generally. The most likely explanation for the financing difficulties experienced is the actual or perceived risk–reward relationship.

There was a substantial shift in quoted equity market investors in favour of high-tech stocks between early 1998 and early 2000, which encouraged venture capitalists to invest heavily in TBSF start-ups in the expectation of high IRRs on flotation. The severe market correction post-March 2000 bears out the warnings of those who maintained that the generation of such large amounts of finance could not be sustained for companies without backgrounds of historical profit records. However, looking to the future, the capitalisations achieved by many young high-tech companies may well lead to higher realised IRRs for some early-stage capital funds over the longer term. In time, this may correct the imbalance of venture capital financing between early- and later-stage deals towards TBSFs, particularly if returns on MBOs/MBIs fade.

Acknowledgments to the Domestic Finance Division of the Bank of England for access to their February 2001 report 'Financing of Technology-based Small Firms', from which most of the material for this chapter was sourced.

1.5

Modern Company Law for a Competitive Economy – Final Report from the Company Law Review Steering Group

Keith Baxter
Royal & SunAlliance ProFin

The Company Law Review Steering Group, set up by the Department of Trade and Industry in 1998, recently presented its final report to the Secretary of State. The report contains a blueprint for comprehensive reform and modernisation of company law in a wide range of areas. The following is a brief summary of the report's principal recommendations.

Small and private companies

- The rules on a company's internal administrative procedures should be simplified so that private companies:
  (a) need not hold AGMs, lay accounts in general meeting nor appoint auditors annually unless they expressly choose to do so;

(b) are no longer obliged to appoint a company secretary;
(c) have access to a new, simpler model constitution to replace the existing memorandum and articles of association designed especially for small private companies.

- Simplification of formal decision-making procedures by:
  (a) codifying and extending the existing common law 'unanimous consent rule' by stating expressly in statute that any decision which the company has power to make may be taken without observing any of the formalities of the Companies Act or the company's constitution where the members unanimously agree;
  (b) making it easier for private companies to take decisions by written resolution without the need for a shareholder meeting.
- Encouraging mediation and arbitration as alternatives to litigation, in particular by creating an arbitration scheme aimed specifically at dealing with shareholder disputes.
- Reducing the burden of financial reporting and audit and improving the usefulness of small company accounts by:
  (a) simplifying the format and content requirements for the accounts of small companies, but removing the ability of small companies to file 'abbreviated accounts' which are currently considered to be rather uninformative;
  (b) increasing the threshold below which companies are exempt from the requirement to have their accounts audited;
  (c) extending the small company accounting regime so that companies which meet any two of the following criteria are classed as 'small': turnover of no more than £4.8 million (currently £2.8 million); balance sheet total of no more than £2.4 million (currently £1.4 million); no more than 50 employees (as now);
  (d) reducing the time limit for private companies to file accounts from the present ten months to seven months after their financial year end.
- Simplifying the capital maintenance regime for all private companies with, in particular, repeal of the present rules on financial assistance in connection with share acquisitions. In the context of private companies, and particularly where a group of companies is undertaking an internal reorganisation, the financial assistance rules are considered too complex and result in excess costs being incurred.

Directors

- The basic duties of directors should be clearly set out in the Companies Act rather than relying on common law.
- The current rules in the Companies Act on directors' conflicts of interest should be updated and clarified.
- Directors' contracts of employment should be limited to a period of three years on first appointment and one year for reappointments, unless shareholders approve a longer period.
- There should be improved disclosure requirements in relation to a director's training, qualifications and other relevant information.

Shareholders

- The law should be reformed to make it easier for investors who hold shares in nominee accounts to exercise shareholders' rights and communicate directly with the company.
- There should be more transparency about the role of institutional investors. In particular, companies should disclose in their annual report their major relationships with financial institutions. Institutional investors who manage funds on behalf of others should disclose how they have voted their shares, and the voting process on key company resolutions should be audited.
- Quoted companies should be required to circulate members' resolutions free of charge with the AGM papers where the resolution has the requisite level of support and is received by a specified deadline.

Company reporting and audit

- Most public companies and large private companies should be required to publish an operating and financial review (OFR) as part of the annual report; this would provide a review of the business, its performance, plans and prospects, and other information which the directors regard as necessary to give a full understanding of the business (eg relationships with employees, suppliers and customers). Quoted companies should make their annual report and accounts available on a website within four months of the year end; they should then be required to wait at least 15 days before finalising the AGM papers for circulation in order to allow sufficient time for shareholders to table resolutions for debate at the AGM.

- All public companies should be required to lay the accounts in general meeting and file them at Companies House within six months of their year end.
- The auditors' duty of care should not be extended by statute beyond that which develops through the courts.
- Directors and employees should have wider statutory duties to assist the auditors. Auditors should be entitled to limit their liability to the company and to third parties, but within appropriate limits to be set by the Secretary of State.

Institutional arrangements

- A Company Law and Reporting Commission should be established to keep company law continually under review, prepare an annual report on the state of company law and corporate governance, and on any need for reform and issue guidance and advice on proposed secondary legislation.
- A Standards Board would be set up to make detailed rules on accounting and reporting; make disclosure rules in areas such as information to be provided to shareholders; make rules on matters such as the conduct of AGMs; and publish guidance on other issues within its remit.
- A Private Companies Committee would also be established to examine the impact of company law and reporting requirements on private companies, with the Company Law and Reporting Commission and the Standards Board being required to take account of its advice.

Conclusion

As can be seen from this brief summary, the report is extremely wide ranging and if its recommendations are taken forward it will have significant implications for companies and their directors and officers.

The requirement that directors must be properly qualified for the board places a significant onus on the chairman in forming the board and creates significant potential for future liability. On the one hand, there are the objective measures of suitability such as academic and professional qualifications, while on the other, there are more subjective measures such as the suitability of a director's previous business experience. The task is to reconcile these objective and subjective measures into a judgement that can stand the test of law. It is probable that few chairmen would feel totally confident in doing so, recognising that most business appointments bring with them an element of risk arising from the human dimension that falls under that most uncomfortable risk category labelled 'intangible'.

When things go wrong, disappointed shareholders and their legal advisers may be more than ready to adduce that a lack of positive performance on the part of a director necessarily arises from unsuitable qualification, and therein lies the danger of an otherwise apparently benign proper qualification requirement.

Before the last General Election, the Government made a manifesto commitment to increase company accountability and transparency. The new OFR has been proposed as one way of increasing accountability by requiring directors to produce a narrative that sets out a structured account of how the company is generating shareholder value. Up until now, companies have been required to do no more than produce a set of historic accounts with limited interpretation of the future prospects of the company. The OFR is intended to change this. The extent to which it will be in the interests of a company, possibly in competition with larger businesses, to disclose its key business drivers is one possible issue. Stakeholders in the business will certainly benefit from having a better understanding of the company's affairs than has been available up until now from a review of audited accounts. So far so good, but it may not be in the interests of the company to make such a public disclosure in what are, after all, competitive markets. Certainly, competitor analysis will be easier than ever before, but this is in the interests of the competitors themselves and not the company. Perhaps language can be used in the OFR that protects the confidentiality of key business initiatives, but if this happens, shareholders will be no better informed than they are now and the purpose of the law will have been frustrated. This means that directors will have to manage the potential conflict between the confidential interests of the business and the duty to complete a proper OFR. A high level of judgement is going to be necessary in order to achieve this, tempered by the knowledge that it is a criminal offence for a director or officer of a company to knowingly or recklessly provide misleading, false or deceptive information.

The broad direction of the Company Law Review Steering Group's final report is an extension of directors' duties. Directors' duties will continue to be solely to shareholders, but there is increasing emphasis on the importance of maintaining good relationships with those who have a legitimate interest in the company's activities. The proposed code of directors' duties states that directors should have regard to relationships with their employees, customers, suppliers, communities and the environment. The extent to which directors are seen to be successful in doing so will probably determine the shape of future rules. In effect, companies are increasingly being required to serve a social function beyond the generation of shareholder value, and to ignore this aspect at this point in history would no doubt prove a big mistake. Companies must increasingly meet the social expectations of the wider society within which they operate or expect to face 'big government' policies and red tape at some future date.

There is no doubt that business is expected to be increasingly accountable. The proposed Companies Commission would serve to keep company law under constant review and would be constituted from business leaders, investors and professional advisers. The Commission's role would potentially include giving guidance on the OFR, but in its widest context, the Commission would be expected to report annually to the Government on proposed changes in business legislation. The broad intention of the Commission would be to reduce the amount of legislation that business faces and, if this can be achieved, then most people would view it as a positive development, provided that there is no sacrifice of broader or deeper business or social interest in the process.

It remains to be seen whether the proposals of the Company Law Review Steering Group will become law either in whole or part, but the proposals represent an imaginative reforming vision which it is hoped will increase the attractiveness of the United Kingdom as a place in which to do business.

Part Two

Debt Finance

2.1

Structured Finance

John Bagley
NMB-Heller

Introduction

Traditionally, corporate finance was the domain of a company's bankers, who would lend money for growth by way of overdraft facilities and loans, on the strength of the balance sheet – historic information based on the company's net worth. Now, growing businesses can take advantage of 'structured business finance', which is based on the value of a company's assets and is a more flexible source of finance than bank loans and overdrafts. Structured business finance is based on the principles of invoice discounting, taking the idea one stage further by financing other assets.

Invoice discounting is a source of business finance which advances cash against the value of sales invoices and which allows the business to run its own sales ledger and payment collection. Invoice discounting itself developed from 'factoring', the form of invoice finance that involves handing sales ledger administration over to the finance provider – and paying an administration fee for this service.

Structured business finance follows the route taken by asset-based finance in the United States and tends, in the UK, to be offered by those finance providers not owned by the high street banks. The product is driven more by asset valuation than by balance sheet valuation and, as such, is highly attractive to ambitious, expanding businesses. In general, structured business finance is used by medium to large SMEs (up to around £60–70 million turnover), which require a more flexible funding package than can be provided by mainstream banks.

Strategic structured finance

Increasingly, we are now finding that structured business finance provides an ideal solution for management buy-outs and buy-ins (MBOs and MBIs) and other financial restructurings. The more traditional use of structured business finance has tended to be for businesses that are highly seasonal – such as those which depend on the Christmas trade. Generally it is true to say that structured business finance is far more flexible than the bank overdraft, and levels of finance available are usually higher. This is because there is no monetary limit set on borrowing levels, as they are linked to assets such as stock and sales which are constantly moving. The finance provided, therefore, is matched to the assets available, not to pre-set limits. When structured business finance is provided by a company independent of the high street banks, it will generally tend to replace traditional bank overdrafts and loans.

In its present form, structured business finance has been in existence for the past two or three years and is becoming extremely popular. Although figures are not yet kept separately for this form of asset-based finance, statistics from the Factors and Discounters Association show a healthy growth in overall business volumes within the asset-based finance industry – over the last ten years a seven-fold growth from £7 billion in 1987 to nearly £50 billion in 1997. The greatest area of growth, in our experience, is in arranging MBOs and MBIs. Here, the level of flexibility which structured business finance provides is highly attractive to the corporate finance team involved in arranging the overall deal. Structured business finance can provide a source of finance for the buy-in/buy-out which enables the new management to retain 100 per cent equity in the business (rather than hand over a proportion to a venture capitalist) – an option which comes very high on the list of priorities of the new owners. The key to structured finance is the funding of invoices followed by the funding of stock. An agreed percentage is made available against both of these assets, normally up to 85 per cent against invoices and 30–50 per cent against stock. Interest costs can be less than those charged by a bank for an equivalent facility; however, they will depend on the complexity of the deal and there are administration fees. It is unlikely that the managers will be asked to provide guarantees.

Case studies

A couple of examples of structured business finance facilities for an MBO and MBI recently arranged by NMB-Heller illustrate how structured business finance works in practice, and how it can provide solutions to meet needs speedily and effectively.

Frith's Flexible Packaging Limited

The first shows how this structured finance approach was used for an MBI in David Watson's purchase of packaging specialist, Frith's Flexible Packaging Limited. Here NMB-Heller teamed with its associate company, ING Lease, to provide sufficient cash for the buy-in. David Watson worked with a corporate finance consultant, first to identify the best business to acquire, and then to source funding. Because this acquisition was intended as the first of several, a major objective was to avoid the need to raise venture capital, holding it in reserve for larger future deals. To achieve this they needed to find an asset-rich business for sale, where 100 per cent asset-backed funding could be raised, and found Friths to be the ideal choice. When it came to sourcing the funding, ING Lease was prepared to go to 100 per cent funding of the plant and equipment on its appreciation of the strength of the business plan and the competence of the incoming MBI leader. NMB-Heller was selected to provide working capital by way of a term loan and invoice finance, because NMB and ING Lease could work together to produce a fast track service, providing a turnkey funding solution that avoided the need for the client to cede equity to a third party. There was an 'agreement in principle' within 48 hours and the whole deal was completed from start to finish within three months.

Eurotec Automotive

The second example shows how Eurotec Automotive, a wholesale distributor of vehicle parts based in Wakefield, was acquired in a management buy-out jointly undertaken by the company's management team and its major customer from French parent, the CFAO Group. The business has an increasing turnover of £8 million, which has grown over recent years from £1 million under the leadership of managing director, Ron Branton. Integral to the deal was the asset-based working capital solution put in place by NMB-Heller which has supported the buy-out team and allowed it to retain complete equity control over the business. The management team can now call upon a flexible funding package that includes working capital advanced against debtors and stock, a working capital term loan and trade finance to facilitate the import of goods on letters of credit.

Crucial to the success of the deal was the ability to meet the tight timeframe set by the company's original owners for the completion of the deal. The NMB-Heller support package was implemented within a six-week period from start to finish, and enabled the management team to successfully complete the deal on time. A rival buyer from within the trade had intended to absorb the business into its own organisation, which would have resulted in redundancies for Eurotec employees. However, the NMB-Heller deal has now secured the long-term future of the business.

Summary

The ideal profile of a company that will benefit from structured business finance is one that is growing or undergoing a period of change, with experienced and forward-looking management, where the net worth of the company is relatively low compared with its turnover, but the company has good debtors and a fairly large element of finished stock on its balance sheet. Structured business finance is built upon the lender's knowledge of, and confidence in, a particular business. Timescales will, therefore, have to take into account the familiarisation process. Before any decision to invest in a company can be made, the lender needs to understand the business and the management plans and evaluate the size and strength of the assets – the invoices, stock and other assets to be funded. Normally, however, this process should not take more than three to four weeks.

2.2
Asset-based Finance

Forward Trust

How to pay for today's assets with tomorrow's money

Funding the cost of growth need not be a headache. A recent Bank of England report highlighted concerns that many British businesses still fund the fixed assets they need for growth from overdrafts or even cash flow. But short or medium-term borrowing to fund long-term investment can seriously affect businesses' corporate profitability. Equally, to use the company's own capital resources for such purchases can prove short sighted. Capital safely invested against a rainy day that produces a solid return is far more useful to the company than money spent on an asset that will depreciate. Spending these funds on an asset, even though it may be key to the company's future, reduces the company's working capital which could be better used in many ways – perhaps buying raw materials, improving wages or paying suppliers.

Using a bank loan or, even worse, an overdraft to fund asset purchases can be problematic. Interest rates can be unpredictable when what your business needs is stability in order to plan ahead to compete. Furthermore, does it make sense to have a loan secured on an asset that will depreciate as time goes by?

In spite of this, almost two thirds of the capital investment in plant, machinery, vehicles, ships and aircraft is funded either through cash flow, bank loans or the capital of the company.

But the balance is changing. Increasingly, businesses are looking towards asset finance houses to fund capital equipment. The asset finance idea is well over 60 years old and some finance houses have been providing both practical advice and capital for development for many years. Already some £21 billion of assets are financed this way and the trend, given the tax advantages and the release of capital built into the systems on offer, is increasing.

Basically, there are two ways to acquire assets this way: leasing and hire purchase. The difference is as simple as the names suggest. With leasing you have the use, but not the ownership of the asset, and with hire purchase, you have the use and the option of ownership at the end of the term.

The system that is most advantageous for your business will depend on a number of factors. Every business has its own special needs and problems, so it is wisest to spend some time discussing your own circumstances with an asset finance expert, in order to compare options. All surveys demonstrate that, since tax is tax and interest rates are interest rates, the key factor in the choice of finance house is almost always its ability to add value to the financial package, combined with financial stability.

Nowadays, leasing companies tend to be part of one of the major banking and financial services groups, and have consequently become enormously sophisticated, providing advice on a wide range of subjects, from the tax implications of your decision to the maintenance contracts you may need for your particular kind of asset. You also need to look for what added value they can bring, for example:

- Do they understand your market and the assets you require?
- Do they know how your business operates?
- Do they know what customers you have and what assets you own already?
- Is ownership necessary or will hiring fulfil your purpose?
- Will the asset be coming from Britain or abroad?
- Do you have to pay a deposit?

The questions may seem endless, but there is a practical purpose behind them. The finance company should be aiming to produce a tailored plan for your business that takes into account three key factors:

- What income will be generated by the asset?
- What is its anticipated working life?
- What will its value be at the end of the term?

Simply put, the plan they produce should always match the repayments you have to make to the income that the asset will provide for your business.

So the agreement you enter into, whether it is a lease or hire purchase, can be tailored to suit your business. Today, some top finance houses have built up a track record of specialised experience in particular industries, bringing a particular understanding of the problems and opportunities facing your industry. This means that they can frequently point you to the best supplier for the asset you need, help you to specify the equipment that will suit your business best and can actually suggest ways of working that may not have occurred to you. Some companies in your market may even be able to improve or develop new products or services for you. In addition, if you choose to lease, the financial muscle of these finance companies often means that they have considerable buying power, helping you to minimise costs.

Of course, because financial engineering is their core skill, you should also consider the ingenuity of the finance house. Competition is such that lessors must always seek to provide a financial package that makes the most of every opportunity to cover work in your favour. As well as making the most of your own position, they should also optimise the way you pay interest. For example, you may imagine that two per cent over bank rate is the same, whoever the supplier; but some companies calculate the interest you pay quarterly. So, even though you may have repaid quite a considerable sum by the end of the quarter, the interest you are paying is still being calculated on the amount owing at the start of the period. Ideally, of course, your interest should be calculated on a day-to-day basis.

The finance period is also important. An experienced finance house will understand your business and, recognising that some assets have a longer life-span than others, will advise you what the best timing should be; usually anything from three to seven years. They should also recognise that this period may well need to involve the time taken to set up the equipment – a printing press for example – before it can begin to produce an income. If this is the case, the company you choose should be prepared to look at low initial repayments, rising to the full scale when the machine is operating at peak efficiency. They should also understand the need for seasonal payment for assets such as coaches or food processing equipment for a particular crop, and cars, a subject that interests managers in most companies, are a matter of much consideration; how many miles, what type of miles, what kind of servicing? These are the kind of details that any business should consider before pursuing a relationship with a finance house. But all financing, whether hire purchase or a lease, will offer your company similar, broad benefits, as well as the particular advantages offered by individual companies.

First, it allows companies to plan ahead and provide considerable reassurance for the financial director.

Second, a choice of repayment methods, including fixed rates, means that you can budget more accurately because all your costs are pre-determined, not simply in terms of the repayments you make, but, with contract hire, in terms of the costs of running the asset itself. If, for example, you have a vehicle that the finance company has arranged to be kept in good order, you can be sure it will be properly maintained and that you will have the vital use of that asset for your business. The maintenance package may be arranged through the finance house or even through the manufacturer of the asset itself. Cars, for example, would be covered by the finance company, but heavy manufacturing machinery could well be the subject of an agreement made between the finance house and the manufacturer, to keep the asset in good running order for you. Once again, the finance house should tailor the most suitable package for your company.

Third, your financing costs can be fixed. At the start of the agreement, you agree with the finance house the period of the agreement, the repayments that are necessary, and the rates you will have to pay.

Fourth, and possibly most reassuringly, this route is increasingly proving to be the best way to use a company's resources. Because it frees up your cash flow as well as your capital, asset finance can actually help your company grow. It is becoming an important part of the overall strategic plan for a great many companies; and, as its effectiveness is proved, it is increasingly being built into a company's strategy, rather than simply being used on an *ad hoc* basis. It puts your own money to work, doing what it should do: supporting your business.

You can also benefit from considerable tax advantages when using both leasing and hire purchase. Before outlining the major benefits of these, it is sensible to consider the basic question: do you need to own the asset eventually or do you simply need to have the use of it for a certain period of time?

Though the finance house will usually help you decide the answer to this question and will provide useful pointers, it is worth outlining the advantages of the two main routes.

Hire purchase

Hire purchase is a system whereby you pay a specified amount of money over a pre-determined period. At the end of the agreement, you pay the option to purchase fee that can be arranged to suit your business' financial situation. If ownership is really important to your company, this is the way to go.

The particular tax advantages it offers are that, although the asset does not belong to you until the end of the term, you can claim a tax deduction on all the interest paid against your profit and loss account. The other advantage is that you can claim the capital allowance, so a percentage of the cost of the asset can be offset against the tax you have to pay.

In addition, if your business is VATable, you can claim all the VAT paid on the asset as if you had bought it outright. The only exception to this rule is in the case of cars, which are regarded by the Inland Revenue as a separate case.

In all these three cases, the tax rights of ownership belong to your company, although the asset is actually owned by the finance house. This is called 'deemed belonging'.

As you are treated as the owner as far as tax and accounting are concerned, you can also claim depreciation in your books. As far as the Inland Revenue is concerned, there is no difference between an asset that is yours under a hire purchase agreement and one that you own outright. It is dealt with in just the same way as any other fixed asset.

Leasing

There are two forms of leasing: Finance Leasing and Operating Leasing. The decision to go the leasing route is also a matter for discussion with the finance house and your business advisers. You might, for example, prefer to lease if you cannot claim your capital allowance due to lack of profits. If this is the case, you can benefit from the tax allowances that the finance house can claim, as they will pass them on to you in the form of lower repayments. Or perhaps the way that you look at a discounted cash flow in your business might make it more financially viable to lease; and, of course, it is possible for a lease to be off balance sheet. There are many reasons you might consider.

Finance leases

Finance leasing is on balance sheet, and operating leasing is off balance sheet, and there are strict rules governing which of the two you can have. A finance lease is simply described as one where all the risks and rewards are transferred to the lessee. If you have benefited from all the tax benefits during the contract and, when the asset is sold by the finance house at the end of the lease, you receive some of the sale proceeds, then you have effectively received the benefits of the asset. Under a finance lease, the sale of the asset is carried out by the lessee, operating as the agent of the finance company. The money from the sale goes to the finance house, but they return up to 95 per cent of it to the client. So the client never actually owns the asset, rather it is seen as being loaned to the client and so should be shown on your balance sheet.

The other benefits are that the rental interest can be variable. Again, this is part of the risk and reward factor. If the bank rate falls, you will benefit; if it rises, you will have to pay more. That is a risk calculation you alone can make.

With a finance leasing agreement you don't pay VAT on the capital cost. But VAT is charged on the rental and you can recover the VAT paid. The leasing rental is classified as a revenue expense.

At the moment, finance leasing volumes are falling off, as companies look to other, less complex forms of leasing and because recent legislation has removed some of the tax advantages they once enjoyed.

Operating leases

An operating lease, with or without maintenance, appears off your balance sheet because most of the rewards and all the risks lie with the finance house.

The way it works is simple. The finance house will discuss the asset you need in just the same detail as with any other contract. In this instance, they will be seeking to find the exact use that you will put the asset to so that they can calculate what its value will be at the end of the term. This is called the residual risk. The finance house is using its experience to determine the value of the asset when the contract is over. The reason is that the repayments you make will be based on the difference between the purchase price and the amount they believe that they can sell the asset for when you have finished with it.

Suppose that you are buying a vehicle – say an HGV and trailer. The finance house will want to know all about your business, the loads you carry, journey times and distances, the qualifications of those driving, where the vehicle will be stored and how it will be maintained. With this knowledge they will decide its value in seven years' time, the period you have decided that you want the use of the vehicle for. You will make regular payments on the pre-determined value of the asset for this period – not the whole life. As a result you will pay a lower rental. Another consideration will be the maintenance of the vehicle to ensure it is to the standard required to achieve its predicted value at the end of your agreement, although this will form part of your contractual negotiations, as maintenance is one of the added value services many finance houses offer as part of their packaging.

You will also benefit from the fact that the finance house, because it actually owns the asset and has taken the risk of forecasting its value, will be able to claim the capital allowance on it and so will be able to charge a lower rental than might otherwise be the case. For hauliers who are non-tax-payers, this reduction can be particularly useful. Your company can also charge the cost of the rental against its corporation tax and, of course, your financial director will be delighted that the payments will remain predictable and that there is no question of any risk in estimating the re-sale value at the end of the term.

The only variation to these general rules applies to cars. Because they are regarded by the Treasury as part perk and part company necessity, they are assessed differently. As a result, you cannot deduct the rental costs against your corporation tax unless the car itself cost less than £12,000. In the case of cars, it is always sensible to discuss the exact use of your fleet with an experienced finance house as they can advise on the most tax efficient route, the timing involved and the maintenance package that will suit you best. Contract hire is also one of the best ways to remove a lot of the problems of maintaining your car fleet from the shoulders of your fleet manager.

The popularity of this method of asset financing is growing rapidly, partly because of its simplicity and the increasing trend to outsourcing, and partly because the alternative route of finance leasing has become less attractive as the tax benefits have been reduced by successive governments.

In fact, so popular has contract hire become that some of the largest deals in the past few years have been on this basis. Planes and boats and trains, the big ticket assets, are very frequently financed in this way and clients have seen enormous benefits.

Case study

ScotRail

In a recent transaction with ScotRail, the client was able to afford to lease 40 trains when they had only expected to be able to lease 38. This was due partly to the construction of the financing and partly to the sheer financial muscle of Forward Trust Rail being a member of HSBC.

'Our buying power and strength in the marketplace enabled us to use the economies of scale in our negotiations with the rolling stock manufacturers,' said Peter Aldridge of Forward Trust Rail.

This particular transaction began with detailed discussions between Forward Trust Rail and ScotRail itself. If a financier is to provide the best results for the client, a detailed picture of every part of the customer's objectives needs to be established. Only when this is complete can a realistic proposal be made. The timing, specification and structure of the bid between Forward Trust and ScotRail were all ironed out prior to discussions with potential manufacturers. ScotRail specifically requested that the financiers give their best price in the tender response rather than getting involved in long, drawn-out haggling at a later date.

Time was of the essence throughout the transaction and was exacerbated by the fact that, as a result of a franchise commitment, ScotRail needed to have the rolling stock in service by March 2000. At the appointment of Forward Trust Rail, the two parties set about creating a detailed specification for the trains which was given to three manufacturers for tender.

'We had negotiated some 95 per cent of the contents of the lease with ScotRail before we even spoke to the manufacturer,' said Peter. At the same time, Forward Trust Rail negotiated both a spares and maintenance agreement with the manufacturers. Two of the 50 engineers who work for Forward Trust Rail were employed at this stage, as their expertise was vital. Forward Trust aims to work in partnership with its customers, providing a portfolio of services and knowledge in addition to finance.

The lease agreement does not require ScotRail to make payments while the trains are being built. However, Forward Trust Rail has already started paying the manufacturers in stages, with the largest payments made on delivery of the rolling stock. To protect and support the interests of both parties during the building process, four engineers from Forward Trust are working with ScotRail.

The finance house should always aim to make the purchase and use of the assets required to run your business as simple and as painless as possible. To do this:

- They need to have access to considerable financial strength because you want to be sure that they will continue to back you throughout the whole term of the contact.
- They should be independent. By not being tied to any one manufacturer, they will be able to shop around on your behalf and make the best buys for you.
- They should be able to offer you the benefits of buying in bulk that will serve to lower your costs.
- They should have the depth of expertise to be able to offer you more than just money.
- They should understand your business and the market you operate in. This will allow them not only to tell you where the best place to buy tyres can be found, but to advise you on market trends that might affect the way you run your own business.

As in so many financial markets today, it is the added value that counts; the service that goes with the cash should be the most important factor in your decision about which finance house to choose and which system will suit you best.

All reasonable care has been taken in the preparation of this article, but it is intended only to be a general guide. You should check the position of your own company, with regard to financing assets in this way, with a professional financial adviser; the treatment of leases, for example, can vary depending on an individual auditor's interpretation. You should also make certain that there have not been any fundamental changes in accounting, taxation or legal requirements.

Extract from Bank of England 'Finance for Small Firms – An Eighth Report' (March 2001)

The Finance and Leasing Association (FLA) is the major UK representative organisation for the asset-based finance industry, accounting for approximately 90% of the sector. In February 2001 the association had 95 full members and 71 associate members, drawn from high street banks' subsidiaries, merchant banks, building societies, leading finance houses, leasing companies and the finance sections of manufacturing and retail companies. Business finance excluding big-ticket items (defined as a finance facility of greater than or equal to £20 million for a single project) has grown consistently, to around 19.1 billion in 1999.

SMEs account for a significant proportion of FLA business. Firms with a turnover of less than £5 million accounted for 58% of new business in 1999. Furthermore, nearly £7 billion (30% of new business) went to firms with an annual turnover of less than £1 million. The FLA believes that asset finance provides the products that allow SMEs to grow, right through the size spectrum – from leasing a single computer to using asset finance in the run-up to flotation. The FLA is currently campaigning for the removal of the exclusion of leased assets from enhanced fiscal depreciation for SME. Owner-users of plant and equipment, who satisfy the conditions on corporate size, can generally claim a first-year allowance of 40%, but if they lease the assets, the lessor can claim 25% writing-down allowances.

2.3

Finance for Foreign Trade

Jonathan Reuvid

There are a variety of different methods of settlement in international trade, the choice of which is a key factor in the selection of appropriate finance. Before sourcing from abroad or engaging in export markets, it is important at the outset to understand how the differences between international and domestic trade can affect the importer or exporter.

In international trading, the business environment may be very different from domestic market conditions in the following respects:

- lead times may be much longer;
- transit times in the carriage of goods and documents are almost certainly longer;
- different time zones, working week cycles, holiday periods and languages may impact communications;
- political risk, customs and excise routines and local laws and business practices may cause problems to the payment mechanism or delays in the settlement of insurance or other claims.

It will also be relevant whether the foreign trade takes the form of single infrequent transactions or a continuing flow of transactions. The key consideration is to minimise any funding gap generated by the company's foreign trading activity to a level that can be accommodated comfortably within the company's financing arrangements.

Methods of settlement

The following methods of settlement are all in current use and present differing degrees of risk for either buyer or seller.

Advance payment

The payment for goods in full before they are received, possibly when the order is placed, is the optimum method for the exporter, although some form of retention until the goods are received and checked is normal. The exporter's cash flow is positive and its position is secure.

However, the importer's cash flow and risk positions are the reverse and complete confidence in the exporter's ability to perform is a prerequisite. Where appropriate, independent inspection of goods before release of payment is an obvious precaution. Asking the seller for a performance guarantee and a provision for compensation in case of non-performance and insuring against political risks are actions that can be taken in mitigation of the risk.

Open account

Under open account conditions, the exporter despatches both the goods and documents directly to the importer. The importer receives the goods and in due course remits payment to the exporter according to the terms agreed between the parties. In terms of risk, this procedure is at the other extreme to advance payment and will only be acceptable to the exporter if the importer is of high standing and can be judged creditworthy after full enquiries.

Risk mitigation can include provisions for assured remedy or compensation in the event that proceeds are not remitted on time, credit risk and political risk insurance.

Documentary collections

The normal alternative to open account, where an exporter wishes to secure payment from lesser-known importers, is to make use of the banking system to obtain payment or acceptance of a bill of exchange. Documentary collection procedures, subscribed to by almost all banks in the commercial world and national Chambers of Commerce, are covered by the International Chamber of Commerce (ICC) Uniform Rules for Collection, which came into force in January 1996.

Under these procedures, an exporter normally hands the shipping and other appropriate documents to its bank, after shipping the goods, with instructions that they be transmitted to the buyer's bank and be released against payment by the importer or against acceptance of drafts drawn on the importer. All instructions must be full, clear and precise. Before shipment, the exporter should ensure that the importer possesses an import licence which is valid for a period sufficient for the goods to be cleared at their destination, allowing for any potential delay. The exporter should also confirm that current exchange control authorisation has been granted to the importer, where applicable, enabling payment to be made immediately or at maturity of the usance drafts, in the currency of collection and as instructed.

There are two main categories of documentary collections: documents against acceptance and documents against payment.

Documents against acceptance (D/A)

In this case, the exporter hands the drafts and accompanying documents to its bank with instructions for the documents' release to the importer in exchange for payment at maturity. The drafts would be drawn at an agreed date for the payment of the bill of exchange.

Unless the documents include documents of title (eg full sets of bills of lading), the position of the exporter is little better than an open account situation. If documents of title are included, control of the goods can be retained by the bank until such time as the drafts have been accepted by the importer, after which control is lost. The risk of non-payment after acceptance can be mitigated in one of two ways:

- with the prior approval of the buyer, by asking the collecting bank to add its 'per aval' endorsement to the acceptance. (This will give the seller the guarantee of payment at maturity and assist the seller's financing, as described below.)
- if the buyer is of sufficient financial standing, by obtaining credit insurance (typically at between 80 per cent and 85 per cent of the value of the collection).

Documents against payment (D/P)

The difference from the D/A situation is that the relevant documents are released to the importer against payment. Assuming that full sets of documents of title are included in the collection, control of the goods is retained until payment is obtained and the seller is in a comparatively secure situation.

There is still the risk, as under D/A, that the goods are not taken up by the buyer, which can be mitigated by asking the collecting bank to store and insure them with a view to returning them to the seller (unless they are perishable) or to finding another buyer, perhaps at auction.

Documentary credits

There are five main types of documentary credit of which the usage is varied.

Revocable credits

Revocable credits where the buyer's commitment can be withdrawn are rarely used and best avoided.

Irrevocable credits – unconfirmed

The buyer is committed to pay and the seller has the undertaking of the issuing bank, but not the confirmation of a local bank. The risk to the seller lies in the standing of the issuing bank and in the country risk. The seller may mitigate the risk by demanding that the confirmation of an acceptable bank be added to the credit.

Irrevocable credits – confirmed

Under these arrangements the seller is assured of payment and the buyer, through the banking system which gives evidence that the goods have been shipped, is assured of receiving shipping documents. However, absolute clarity is essential in the terms of the credit and the specific documentation. The credit should be scrutinised as soon as it is received and any necessary clarification or amendments sought immediately.

Revolving credits

Documentary credits are reinstated automatically if they are stated as being 'revolving' according to written terms and conditions. They usually take one of two forms: those that revolve automatically and those that revolve periodically.

A credit that revolves automatically is reinstated after each 'revolution' until the maximum amount or the number of revolutions stated are reached. A final expiry date will be stated and care must be taken to ensure that outstanding documents are presented within the limits specified. A credit revolving periodically would be reinstated after each stipulated period of time had elapsed, again with a fixed expiry date and for the same amount or number of revolutions. For each kind of revolving credit, the credit would state whether the amounts are cumulative or non-cumulative, stipulating whether any unutilised balance from any one revolution may be carried forward to the next.

Transferable credits

In addition, each of the above four forms of credit can be expressed as being 'transferable', and can be transferred only if expressly designated as transferable by the issuing bank. Under the ICC's Uniform Customs and Practice for Documentary Credits, which came into force in January 1994, a bank requested to effect a transfer will not be obliged to do so; therefore, the beneficiary to a transferable credit can request, but not demand, that the credit be transferred. A transferable credit can be transferred once only, and only on the same terms, ie CIF (Cost Insurance Freight), FOB (Free on Board) or other as the original credit. The only permissible changes are to the amount of the credit, the unit price of the goods, the expiry date, the last date for presentation of documents and the shipping period – any or all of which may be reduced or curtailed.

Finance alternatives

In relation to the four main methods of settlement, there are a series of different finance alternatives.

Bank overdraft

In its traditional form, the bank overdraft is a potentially useful and very flexible form of trade finance for both exporters and importers alike. It suffers only from the fact that it is payable on demand and is not necessarily related to the receivables of the operation.

In cases where a manufacturer or trader agrees with its buyer to accept a documentary credit but cannot finance the manufacture or purchase of the goods covered by the documentary credit, a bank may be persuaded to provide the necessary pre-shipment finance in the form of a short-term bridging loan or overdraft facility to cover the period in question. The arrangements may provide for the bank to have control over the goods as soon as they are manufactured or bought, until such time as they are shipped and the proceeds received from the incoming letter of credit.

Bill finance

Finance can be obtained in the form of an advance, with recourse to the drawer, in respect of bills of exchange sent through the banking system on either D/A or D/P documentary collection. Progress is traceable through the banking system and the advance is liquidated on receipt of proceeds from the collecting bank.

Red clause documentary credits

Originating in the Australian wool trade and sometimes used in commodity trades where the beneficiary needs to accumulate a given quantity of stock to make shipment, red clause documentary credits authorise the confirming or nominated bank to make advances to the beneficiary to enable it to buy the produce locally in order to make shipment. Typically, such advances are made against presentation of the beneficiary's simple receipt, possibly accompanied by an invoice. The extent of the permissible advance would be specified in the red clause, having been pre-negotiated between buyer and seller, and could vary commonly from 50 per cent to almost the full value of the credit.

Green clause documentary credits

A development of the red clause credit, the green clause credit authorises the confirming or nominated bank to make advances to the beneficiary but more tangible evidence of the existence of the goods is required. For example, an advance may be made to the beneficiary against presentation of a simple receipt accompanied by warehouse warrants or receipts for the stated produce, in a recognised independent warehouse in the name of the bank. Thus the existence of the goods, their packing and quality is verifiable by inspection. As in the case of a red clause credit, the balance of the value of the goods due is claimed by the beneficiary on presentation of the documents stipulated in the credit.

Forfaiting

Forfaiting is defined as the purchase, without recourse to any previous holder, of debt instruments due to mature at a future date, which arise from the provision of goods and services. Most forfaiting transactions tend to relate to commodity trade and the sale of capital goods.

The debt instruments forfaited are usually bills of exchange or promissory notes which must be accepted by a multinational company of unquestionable status or guaranteed by the addition of a 'per aval' endorsement by a bank or government organisation acceptable to the forfaiter. The practice of forfaiting is applied most commonly to documentary collections (D/A) in respect of large-value transactions. However, small-value forfaiting transactions, eg tens of thousands of US dollars or pounds sterling, are not uncommon.

Export factoring

Available from specialist international factoring companies, many of which are owned by banks, export factoring allows the exporter to hand copies of all its invoices drawn on overseas buyers to the factoring company which purchases the debts, often without recourse. Responsibility for credit control, debt collection and foreign exchange risk may be taken on by the factoring company under a variety of schemes offered.

Equipment leasing

Generally confined to high-value capital goods such as ships, aircraft and sometimes machinery, equipment leasing enables the overseas buyer to acquire a capital asset without having to engage in foreign trade procedures. The leasing company would intervene, purchase the equipment from the manufacturer and lease it to the overseas buyer. As with any form of leasing, the buyer would have to satisfy the leasing company that it generates a sufficient cash flow to cover leasing payments.

Stock finance for importers

Finally, traders importing goods and stocking them for eventual resale on the domestic market may require finance. Banks or specialist trade financiers can provide finance against existing stock, through factoring or invoice financing as described above. Alternatively, they could open an import documentary credit on behalf of the trader, keep control over the stock and collect the receivables from the trader's customers.

Currency fluctuation

Any account of trade finance alternatives is incomplete without reference to currency fluctuations and the complex topic of currency management. Foreign trade in any currency other than the trader's own gives rise to the possibility that the rate of exchange of the 'foreign' currency may fluctuate against the trader's own currency, resulting in either an unexpected loss or realisable profit.

This concern persuades many exporters and importers to insist on trading in their own currency only, which very often results in less advantageous prices than trade in the counterpart's currency or a neutral currency, typically the US dollar, the Swiss franc or nowadays the euro. The currency exposure may be redressed by 'hedging' – the purchase or sale of a currency matching the trade contract in amount, currency and in value date.

For a more detailed account of foreign trade finance and documentation, consult: Curmi, G. (2001): International Trade Finance and Documentation, in Reuvid, J. (ed): A Handbook of World Trade, Kogan Page, London.

2.4
Legal Issues for Failing Companies and Corporate Rescue

Carrick Lindsay
Lee Crowder

Inevitably there will be a variety of matters requiring attention at the end of a company's existence. These can broadly be divided into three categories:

- Can the financial position be turned around?
- What are the formal insolvency procedures available?
- What are the director's personal liabilities or other actions arising from the failure?

Turnaround

The most important step for the management of any business to take when they are experiencing difficulties is to identify, and if possible quantify, the extent of their problem. Signs of financial difficulty are very plain, but are often overlooked by management: falling profits, falling asset values, excessive borrowing and even boardroom tension. However, there is one phenomenon that makes a corporate rescue plan a priority for management: cash, or more particularly, the lack of it. Without steady cash flow, a company is unable to pay its staff or creditors, to meet the interest obligations on its borrowings, or to provide working capital for any corporate activity. Difficulties with cash flow are the surest sign of difficulties ahead.

There are no specific legal issues exclusively associated with a company turnaround. The objective is to make the best of a difficult position, but the directors must be aware of the potential for personal liability if the turnaround is unsuccessful. The various turnaround strategies that can be adopted include:

Negotiating with existing lenders

This may entail trying to renegotiate the terms of existing debt financing, as well as attempting to obtain further finance. Although the principal lender is likely to be reluctant to commit any new money to the business, it may agree to co-operate with the restructuring of the existing financing and afford the business some breathing space. The possibilities include rescheduling capital repayments under the loans, so that only interest is paid in the short term; extending the period of repayment, thereby reducing the size of the monthly commitment; or converting some of the debt into equity.

Raising new equity

This can be done either by way of a rights issue, or by placing shares with a new or existing shareholder such as a financial institution. If this option is proposed, the directors must not mislead the potential investors as to the company's financial position (see Directors' Personal Position).

Disposal of assets

Often, the only realistic prospect of raising much needed cash is to sell assets. The disposals have to be quick and this usually comes at a cost (ie the price which the assets will attract). Alternatively, the only buyer may be someone connected with the company. The directors will have to ensure that any such sale does not give rise to a claim against them personally.

Introducing new management

It may be appropriate to consider replacing part of the management of the business. This can give a new perspective to the handling of the existing crisis and/or can indicate to lenders or investors that the business is prepared to adopt a radical programme to deal with the problem. In addition, if a suitably experienced replacement is engaged they can bring to the business essential skills to deal with the existing difficulty. However, the company must handle such a change carefully and try to avoid any further claims against the business (eg for unfair or wrongful dismissal).

Informal agreement with creditors

The company may also try and reach some informal agreement with its creditors that they will provide the company with time to make payment (often from the anticipated proceeds from a particular contract). The dangers here are that such agreements are not binding on the creditors and can be ignored by the creditor if he loses patience. Similarly, if any one creditor does not agree, that individual can undo all the hard work in persuading the majority to agree. If that individual creditor is then 'paid off', the company may have inadvertently entered into a preference (see Directors' Personal Position).

In general, a combination of these strategies will be tried by the management of a company in crisis, with varying degrees of success. If none of these strategies are suitable or have not had the effect of turning around the company's fortunes, it will be necessary for the management to consider a formal insolvency procedure.

Insolvency procedures

Definition of insolvency

Perhaps surprisingly, there is no strict definition of 'insolvency' within the Insolvency Act 1986 (IA). However, Section 123(1) IA 1986 gives a definition of an 'inability to pay debts'. A company is said to be unable to pay its debts if:

(a) a creditor serves a demand (see below) and the company neglects to pay the sum or to secure or compound for it to the reasonable satisfaction of the creditor; or
(b) execution or other process issued on a judgement is returned unsatisfied in whole or in part; or

(c) it is proved to the satisfaction of the court that the company is unable to pay its debts as they fall due (known as the 'cash flow' test).

A company is also deemed unable to pay its debts (Section 123(2) IA) if it is proved to the court that the value of the company's assets is less than the amount of its liabilities (known as the 'balance sheet' test). It should be noted that being deemed unable to pay debts by reason of failure of the balance sheet test is a rebuttable presumption – a subsidiary company with a negative balance sheet, supported by parent company loans, may well be able to pay its trade creditors without difficulty.

Statutory demand

A statutory demand is a written demand (in the prescribed form) served by a creditor on a debtor. Before winding-up proceedings are issued against a company, the creditor should either serve a statutory demand or have first issued execution on a judgement that has been returned unsatisfied in whole or in part. The demand sets out the sums claimed as outstanding and puts the debtor on notice that after 21 days from service, the creditor will be able to treat the debtor as unable to pay his debts and, as such, will be able to issue winding-up proceedings against it. The debtor company has 21 days from the service of the statutory demand to comply. Receipt of a statutory demand should signal to the directors the onset of insolvency (in the unlikely event that they were not previously aware of difficulty).

Liquidations (winding-up)

A company may be wound up voluntarily or compulsorily. Usually, a company is only wound up if it is insolvent. When a company is wound up, a Liquidator is appointed to take control of the company's assets. The Liquidator's role is to maximise the realisation from the company's assets and to distribute the realisations to the creditors. In the unlikely event that there is a surplus after payment of costs and the creditors in full (together with statutory interest), he will make a return of any balance to the shareholders.

The effect of liquidation is to terminate a director's duties and powers to the company and its creditors. The Insolvency Act imposes various additional duties on the director to provide information, documentation and general assistance to the 'office holder' (ie in a liquidation, the Liquidator) in the exercise of the office holder's duties.

Company Voluntary Arrangement (CVA)

An insolvent company can make an 'arrangement' with its creditors to avoid liquidation. The company will make a proposal to an insolvency practitioner (the nominee) who reports to the court and summons a meeting of creditors. If 75 per cent in value of the creditors agree, the arrangement is binding on all those creditors who had notice of the meeting and were entitled to vote. At the meeting, a Supervisor is appointed to oversee the arrangement (usually the nominee, although creditors may appoint an alternative insolvency practitioner). The return on a CVA is likely to be better than in cases of winding-up and allows the debtor company to keep trading in most cases. It is important for the proposals to be realistic and achievable by the company in adverse conditions. There is no purpose in promising creditors the earth, only for the arrangement to fail after three or four years.

Administration

Introduced under IA 1986, the purpose of an Administration Order is to rescue a weak or insolvent company by allowing it to continue trading or to provide it an opportunity to realise its assets more advantageously than could be achieved by a winding-up. An Administration Order may be obtained by the company, all the directors, or even the creditors making an application to court and demonstrating that one of the statutory purposes for which an Administration Order may be granted can be achieved. If an Administration Order is made, a moratorium is put into place during which time the company cannot be wound up nor can any creditor (including a landlord) take steps to enforce any security or repossess goods. The moratorium allows the Administrator time to effect the necessary arrangements to either allow the company to dispose of its business and/or assets, or to continue trading under a CVA. Following the making of the Administration Order, the Administrator must, within three months, put proposals to the creditors of the company as to how he proposes to deal with the business during the period for which the

Administration Order is in force. These must be approved by the creditors in a meeting organised by the Administrator. If an Administrator sells the whole or most of the assets of the company, liquidation usually follows. It should be noted that Administration Orders are not granted whimsically or as a matter of course and must be for the purpose of:

(i) the survival of the company, and the whole or any part of its undertaking, as a going concern; or
(ii) the approval of a voluntary arrangement; or
(iii) a more advantageous realisation of the company's assets than would be effected on a winding-up.

Administrative Receivership

This is not a procedure (not to be confused with an Administration Order) created by statute but has its roots in common law. It is based on a contractual relationship between a company and the holder of any debenture (containing a specific type of charge known as a 'floating' charge) over the company's assets. On appointment, the Administrative Receiver takes control of all the company's assets and, depending on the circumstances, may run the company as a going concern and/or attempt to sell its business and assets. The Receiver's primary function is to make sufficient realisations to enable a payment in whole or in part to be made to his appointer, the debenture holder. Usually, the debenture holder is a bank or other financial institution. Under the Government White Paper *A Second Chance*, it is proposed that Administrative Receiverships will cease to be a major insolvency procedure.

LPA Receivership

A Receiver may alternatively be appointed by the holder of a fixed charge (normally a mortgage) over specific property belonging to either an individual or a company. This is distinct from the appointment of an Administrative Receiver as detailed above, where he is appointed over all of the assets of the company in receivership. The person appointed under that fixed charge is correctly known as an 'ordinary receiver'. Since an Ordinary Receiver is appointed under the provisions of the Law of Property Act 1925 (LPA), he/she is often commonly known as an LPA Receiver. The LPA Receiver's powers are very limited by comparison to the powers of an Administrative Receiver.

Directors' personal position and other possible actions

Directors are faced with difficult issues in deciding the most appropriate course of action to take. Taking appropriate professional advice is a prudent first step.

Generally speaking, a director's duties at common law and under the Companies Acts are to act in the best interests of the company, the shareholders and the creditors (in that order) and generally to act with reasonable care and skill. However, when a business is facing financial difficulties, the emphasis changes and they must act in the best interests of the creditors first. The Insolvency Act 1986 exposes directors to potential liabilities if they fail to take every step to minimise creditors' losses.

The temptation for directors is to walk away from the company while they still can, in the hope that their potential liability will then cease. Resignation, however, is usually not appropriate – it is not normally considered to be taking every step to minimise creditors' losses. The directors will generally have to stay on board and work on a strategy (whether turnaround or one of the formal procedures described above) that safeguards the creditors' position. Resignation is more likely to be appropriate for the director who is being excluded from the management of the company by the other director(s). He/she may well not have sufficient information to enable him to make informed decisions, but will still be equally potentially exposed to personal liability as the other directors.

The directors must decide whether there is a genuine prospect that the business can survive, or whether it is inevitable that some formal insolvency procedure will follow. It is vital that the business' management obtain early advice from their professional advisers to assist them in making this decision.

The personal liabilities to which the directors may become exposed or the other specific legal actions that may arise in circumstances of financial difficulty include:

Wrongful trading

Section 214 IA 1986 allows a Liquidator of an insolvent company to apply to the court for an order declaring that any director (whether past or present) who carried on the business at a time when they knew or ought to have concluded that there was no reasonable prospect that the company would avoid going into insolvent liquidation, is to make a personal contribution to the assets of the company. The court will not make such an order if it is satisfied that after the director 'knew' insolvency was inevitable he/she took every step with a view to minimising the potential loss to the creditors of the company, as he/she ought to have taken. Proving that appropriate professional advice was taken at an early stage will help demonstrate to a court that all such steps were taken.

Fraudulent trading

Section 213 IA 1986 allows a Liquidator of a company to apply to the court for an order declaring that any person (not just directors) knowingly carried on the business with the intent to defraud the company's creditors or the creditors of any other person, or for any other fraudulent purpose. If the court makes such a declaration, it will then make that person liable to make personal contributions to the assets of the company. Section 458 of the Companies Act (CA) 1986 also makes such activity a criminal offence (although this is not limited to circumstances of insolvency). The insolvency legislation also provides an 'office holder' (usually an insolvency practitioner) with a number of powers to adjust transactions entered into by the company in the period leading up to the insolvency.

Transfers at undervalue

Section 238 IA 1986 allows the office holder to apply to court to set aside any transaction entered into at an undervalue made during the relevant period. In brief, if the company makes a gift, or other transaction for which it does not receive any payment, or the payment in money or money's worth is significantly less than the consideration provided by the company in either case at any time in the two years (if the transaction is to any person 'connected' to the company, six months if the parties are not 'connected') before the 'onset of insolvency' or in the period between the onset of insolvency and the making of an order in a formal insolvency procedure, the transaction may be set aside.

Preferences

Section 239 IA 1986 allows the office holder to apply to court to set aside any transaction entered into made during the relevant period that prefers any person. If the company does anything, or allows anything to be done, as regards one (or more) of its creditors or a surety or guarantor which has the effect of putting that person into a position which, in the event of the company going into insolvent liquidation, will be better than the position that person would have been in if that transaction had not been entered into, and the company was influenced in doing so by a desire to prefer that person, then that transaction can be set aside. In the case of a preference to a 'connected' person the intention to prefer is presumed.

The relevant time period is again two years before the onset of insolvency (if the transaction is to any person 'connected' to the company) or otherwise during the six months before the onset of insolvency.

The classic example of a preference is the payment of a creditor who has the benefit of a personal guarantee from the directors. The directors prefer that creditor so as to avoid personal liability under the guarantee.

Transaction defrauding creditors

Section 423 IA 1986 allows any 'victim' (which includes the office holder or individual creditors) of a transaction at undervalue to apply to the court to restore the position to that which would have prevailed if the transaction had not been entered into and to protect the interests of the victims of the transaction. A transaction at an undervalue includes a gift, transaction for no payment, or for payment the value of which in money or money's worth is significantly less than the consideration provided by the company. The applicant must satisfy the court that the purpose of the transaction was to put the asset(s) beyond the reach of the person who is making the claim or otherwise prejudicing the interests of such a person. It should be noted that unlike preferences and transfers at undervalue (as described above), there is no 'relevant time' during which such a transaction must have occurred. Accordingly, the applicant may be someone who was not a creditor of the company at the time that the transaction was made.

Matters affecting public limited companies

Section 142 CA 1985 (which only applies to public limited companies) requires any public limited company whose net assets fall to half of its share capital to call a shareholders' meeting to consider what to do. Failure to do so is an offence.

In addition, quoted companies must avoid creating a false market in their securities. Section 47(1) of the Financial Services Act makes it an offence to induce a person to acquire or dispose of investments by intentionally or recklessly making misleading, false or deceptive statements, promises or forecasts, or dishonestly concealing material facts. Section 47(2) makes it an offence to carry out any act or engage in any course of conduct that creates a false or misleading impression about the market in an investment if the intention is to create that impression and so induce someone to buy or sell that investment. There is the obvious temptation for a director to talk up a company in order to sell shares held by him or his family, perhaps so as to avoid the total loss that the director may suspect is on the way.

2.5

A Glossary of Debt

Christopher Gasson
Bertoli Mitchell

Asset Cover is the ratio of net assets to total debt – ie total assets minus current liabilities/debt. It is used by banks to judge the security of their lending. The level of asset cover that a bank will feel comfortable with will depend on the nature of the assets: cash might be counted at 100 per cent, property at 80 per cent, stock and debtors at 50 per cent.

Bills of Exchange are instruments used in trade finance, typically used to provide finance between the time goods are delivered and payment is made. They are in the form of a promise to pay a fixed amount on a specified date (typically three months after issue). Most importantly they are tradable, enabling the vendor to realise the debt in cash by selling it on (usually to an accepting house). The price agreed will be discounted to reflect the prevailing interest rate.

Bonds are interest bearing securities which can be traded in the money markets. They are usually the cheapest source of debt for large companies. They consist of a coupon and a principal. The coupon represents the annual interest rate payable on the principal. The principal represents the face value of the bond which can be redeemed at maturity. They trade in the financial markets at a price which reflects the prevailing interest rate and expectations of the future interest rate. This process is described under **yield**, below. They are usually unsecured, but the borrower is required to have a **credit rating**. BBB- or Baa3 are considered the lowest investment grade rating. Money can still be raised in the high yield bond (or junk bond) market on lower ratings, but a higher interest rate is required. There will usually be covenants to ensure that the company does not subsequently take out higher ranking loans. The minimum amount that a company can raise in a bond is probably £50m. This is because the market prefers liquid (ie large) bond issues.

The bond market is a public market – ownership of bonds has to be registered and they are taxed at source. This has led to the growth in the Eurobond market. Eurobonds are bonds issued outside the domestic jurisdiction of the residency of the issuer. They are payable free of withholding tax and they can be bought and sold anonymously. These tax advantages have made them a very popular means of raising debt among large corporations.

There are a number of different types of bond and Eurobond:

- *Commercial Paper*: bonds with a maturity of under one year. They offer no coupon. Instead they are usually sold at a discount to the redemption value which corresponds to the prevailing interest rate. They are used primarily by the largest, most credit-worthy institutions.
- *Medium Term Notes*: bonds with a maturity of between one and five years.
- *Floating Rate Notes*: bonds that pay interest pegged at a certain number of basis points (hundredths of a percentage point) above LIBOR.
- *Paid in kind*: bonds that issue more bonds instead of paying cash interest.
- *With Warrants*: bonds that give the right to acquire ordinary shares in the issuer after a certain period.
- *Zero-coupon bonds*: bonds that pay no interest. They are issued at a discount to their face value relating to the expected interest rate to maturity.

Charges represent security that a bank has in making a loan. They can be fixed or floating. A fixed charge is one that refers to a specific asset, e.g. a building or plant. In the event of default the lender can take control of the asset and sell it to cover the value of the loan. A floating charge refers to all the assets of a business over which there is no fixed charge. It therefore ranks below a fixed charge in a liquidation (see **Ranking** below).

Committed facilities are agreements between banks and borrowers to provide funds up to a specific amount, at a specific interest rate (usually a fixed amount above LIBOR) for a specific period of time. Term debt (see Chapter 2.1) is generally in the form of a committed facility. Unlike uncommitted facilities such as overdrafts, they cannot be removed on demand by the lender. They do however usually entail covenants which, if broken, can mean that the debt has to be repaid on demand.

Convertibles are debt instruments that can be converted into equity in certain circumstances. They include convertible bonds, which give the bearer the right to convert the bonds into shares at a pre-defined ratio after a specified date. Another example is convertible loan stock, which is often used by venture capitalists to dilute the management equity should they fail to perform (see ratchets, Chapter 3.3).

Covenants are conditions imposed on loans and bonds to protect lenders against default. They stipulate things such as:

- a minimum level of asset cover;
- a maximum level of gearing;
- a minimum level of interest cover;
- that no prior ranking debt is subsequently arranged;
- that specified assets cannot be sold without the consent of the lender;
- that the lender has the right to review the loan in the event of the business being taken over or control otherwise changing hands;
- that the lender has the right to call in the loan in the event of the borrower defaulting on other loans.

Whether or not a company accepts the covenants proposed to it by its bank will depend on the strength of its negotiating position. The very largest publicly quoted companies can usually avoid most covenants, but smaller unquoted companies may find themselves having to agree to very restrictive covenants simply because there is less competition for their business.

Credit Rating is the means by which the public debt markets assess the credit worthiness of an issuer of debt. There are two main rating agencies, Moody's and Standard & Poors. The rating systems they use are slightly different:

Investment Grade

Moody's	**Standard & Poors**	**Interpretation**
Aaa	AAA	Highest quality
Aa1, Aa2, Aa3	AA+, AA, AA-	High quality
A1, A2, A3	A+, A, A-	Strong payment capacity
Baa1, Baa2, Baa3	BBB+, BBB, BBB-	Adequate payment capacity

Speculative-Grade Ratings

Moody's	**Standard & Poors**	**Interpretation**
Ba1, Ba2, Ba3	BB+, BB, BB-	Likely to fulfil obligations, on-going uncertainty
B1, B2, B3	B+, B, B-	High-risk obligations
Caa	CCC+, CCC, CCC-	Current vulnerability to default, or in default
Ca, D	C, D	In bankruptcy or default, or other shortcoming.

The lower the credit rating the greater the **yield** required to entice investors to buy the bonds. Speculative grade-rated bonds are often referred to as high yield or junk bonds. Such issuers usually require **credit wrapping** to get their bonds away. The market's attitude to different credit ratings is dependent on the prevailing attitude to risk. A high yield bond might trade at 300 basis points above LIBOR in a stable market, but in a highly risk averse market this spread might increase to 800 basis points. Sometimes it becomes effectively impossible to raise finance at all in the bond market without a triple or double A credit rating. The process of achieving a rating takes at least three months.

Credit Wrapping is a technique by which a bond issued by a company with a poor credit rating can be shored up with the assistance of an institution with a strong credit rating. It involves the institution (usually a large insurer with a triple A credit rating) agreeing to underwrite a proportion of the amount payable in the event of default in exchange for a premium. In many cases it is the only way in which poorly rated companies can issue bonds.

Debt to Equity Ratio is a measure of the gearing of a business. It is calculated as long-term debt (usually including preference shares) divided by the shareholder funds. It is an important indicator for banks: they are extremely reluctant to lend money to businesses that are highly geared (see Chapter 3.3 on internal equity).

Discounting is a means of raising money against the value of unpaid invoices. A discounter will purchase invoices (bills) at a discount to their face value, hoping to make a profit on redemption. **Factoring** is the more common form of invoice finance in use today.

Debentures are secured long term. The security usually comes in the form of a floating charge over the assets of the business. This gives the holder of the debenture the right to appoint an administrative receiver in the event of default, giving it enormous powers over the business (see Chapters 1.5 and 2.4). The advantage of debentures for borrowers is that they generally pay a lower rate of interest than an overdraft, and they are **committed facilities**.

Eurobonds: see **bonds**.

Factoring is a means of raising working capital against trade debtors (see Chapter 2.2). There are two sorts. *With service factoring* involves assuming the credit risk for collecting debts, but only advancing the money as it becomes payable. *With service plus finance factoring* involves paying a percentage of the value of the invoice as soon as the goods are delivered.

Forfaiting is a form of invoice **discounting** used by exporters.

Gearing: see **debt to equity ratio**.

Hire Purchase is a means of structuring the purchase of capital assets such that ownership of the asset only changes hands once a certain number of instalments towards the final consideration have been made (see Chapter 2.2).

Interest cover is one of the most important ratios a bank will look at in determining whether to advance a loan. It looks at the number of times a company would be able to pay interest out of its earnings before interest and tax. It indicates at a very basic level whether or not a business will be able to service its debts. For this reason, it is more important than analysing the value of the security (ie asset cover) in reaching decisions about loans. The level of earnings at which most banks will start to get uncomfortable will be between two and three times interest.

Leasing is a means of hiring fixed assets. It is covered in detail in Chapter 2.2.

Letter of credit is a means of trade finance involving an importer's bank (the issuing bank) writing to a bank in the exporter's country (the negotiating bank) authorising the payment of a specified sum to the exporter on presentation of the shipping documents.

Loan stock is a tradable debt instrument that can either be secured or unsecured. Secured loan stock is a **debenture**. Unsecured loan stock is very similar to **preference shares** but it ranks above preference shares on liquidation. Loan stock is used in structuring venture capital deals and in situations in which loans to large companies are syndicated among a number of banks.

Mezzanine finance is a generic term for financial instruments that have the characteristics of both debt and equity. It may be secured or unsecured, and it may or may not involve a degree of participation in the up-side of the sale of the business. It usually comes in the form of variations on **preference shares** or **loan stock.** It is usually provided by mezzanine finance specialists to back management buy-outs and buy-ins.

Mortgages are loans secured against fixed assets, usually property.

Off balance sheet finance is finance that can be raised without declaring it on the balance sheet. Typically it would involve moving an asset into a separate company which then raises money against it and returns the cash to the original owner of the asset. Until Financial Reporting Standard 5 was introduced, there was no reason why such transactions should be disclosed at all in the company accounts, and it was a very attractive means for quoted companies to raise money without alarming their shareholders. Since FRS 5, companies have been required to divulge related party transactions and it is no longer so attractive.

Overdrafts are uncommitted facilities that exist to meet seasonal working capital needs. Although interest rates are higher, they are cheaper than using a term loan for the same purpose because interest is calculated on the basis of the account at the end of each day rather than the maximum amount borrowed.

Preference shares are equity instruments that behave like debt instruments. They pay interest at a fixed rate rather than dividends. Like debt, they do not participate in any increase in the value of the business, but unlike debt they are unsecured, and therefore vulnerable should the value of the business decrease. On liquidation, preference shares are ranked below loan stock and debentures, but above ordinary shares. Often they can be converted into ordinary shares if interest payments are not met. They do not usually have voting powers.

They can be structured in various different ways:

- *Convertible preference shares*: these can be exchanged for ordinary shares under certain conditions or after a certain date. Convertible preference shares are often used by venture capitalists to structure ratchets. They enable the investor to dilute the management's equity if certain targets are not achieved.

- *Cumulative preference shares*: where interest payments are rolled into the principal, to be paid off on redemption. They are used by venture capitalists to ensure that a business is not over burdened by interest payments while it is not generating excess cash. Usually the accumulated interest is paid on exit.
- *Redeemable preference shares*: which can be exchanged for their value in cash on or after a specified date or event.

Ranking refers to the order in which holders of a company's securities are paid out in the event of liquidation. The order is as follows:

- Preferred creditors (ie PAYE, NIC, VAT and wages and salaries up to a maximum of £800)
- Holders of fixed charges over the assets (i.e. mortgagees)
- Holders of floating charges over the assets (i.e. debenture holders)
- Senior creditors such as trade creditors and other unsecured debt
- Subordinated creditors such as holders of unsecured loan stock
- Holders of preference shares
- Ordinary shareholders.

A lender will always want to ensure that there are more claimants ranked beneath it than above it. The debt to equity ratio can be seen as a measure of where a lender will be in the queue: a low debt to equity ratio means that there are plenty of equity participants at the back of the queue to absorb any risks, and therefore gives banks comfort. A high debt to equity ratio means that the bank's loans will be more exposed in the event of liquidation.

Receivership refers to the appointment of a licensed insolvency practitioner to realise the value of the assets to repay the value of the outstanding debts after a company has defaulted.

Revolving Facilities are debt instruments that combine the flexibility of an overdraft with the commitment of term debt. They are negotiated for a specific credit limit for a specific period, during which time they can be drawn down or repaid. As **committed facilities** they usually involve **covenants**. Interest is payable on the whole facility whether or not it is drawn, although there will usually be one interest rate for the drawn part of the facility, and another, slightly lower, interest rate for the undrawn part of the facility.

Securitisation is traditionally defined as the replacement of bank borrowing by bond issues, but in recent years it has a more specific meaning. It is the issuance of bonds against the security of receivables. It involves transferring legal title to an income stream to a separate company, which then issues a bond back by that income stream. Should the income stream be more than enough to cover the interest payments on the bonds, then the excess is returned to the original company; should the income stream be insufficient, then the bond holders have the right to sell-on the income stream. Usually the bond holders will be protected against default by **credit wrapping**. Securitisation has been one of the growth areas of finance in the late 1990s. It is used by leasing companies and mortgage lenders as well as pop stars (securitising their royalties) and utilities.

Syndication is used where one bank is either reluctant or unable to provide the full amount to be borrowed itself. It is usually required only for the largest loans, unless there is undue risk involved.

Yield refers to the income (expressed in terms of per cent per annum) from a bond, taking into account both the interest receivable and the discount from the redemption value at which the bond is purchased. For example a ten-year 8 per cent bond due for redemption in five years' time may be trading at £90. The actual income expressed in percentage terms will be different from 8 per cent for two reasons. First, because the coupon pays interest as 8 per cent of £100 rather than 8 per cent of £90, and, second, because when the bond is eventually redeemed the holder of it will receive £100 rather than the £90 it costs on the current market. Taking both of these factors into account involves some quite complex mathematics because, strictly speaking, the value of the discount should not be amortised evenly across the remaining life of the bond. Bond analysts use 'yield curves' to calculate the yield to maturity. When the price of bonds falls, the yields rise and vice versa.

Part Three

Private Equity

3.1
Trends in Private Equity

Michael Joseph
Lloyds TSB Development Capital

New sources of money

Over the past decade there has been increasing acceptance of private equity as an asset class for fund managers. Although UK fund managers have yet to commit as much as US fund managers to private equity (private equity is 0.5 per cent of asset allocation in the UK versus 2 per cent in the US), this recognition has created enormous growth in the sector. It has been driven primarily by the very strong returns made by private equity investors, particularly as a result of seeing private equity funds buying cheap as the economy came out of the last recession, then make fabulous returns on flotation or trade sale at the top of the market. There is now £41billion worth of investment under management in the private equity sector (according to the British Venture Capital Association).

This growth has a number of implications:

1. There has been a tremendous swing towards managing money for other people, as opposed to own-balance sheet finance. The difference between own-balance sheet funds and managed funds is that managed funds have to be returned to their owners at some stage. If a portfolio has to be liquidated according to a fixed timetable, then those managing the investment will naturally want to pursue opportunities which offer short-term gains rather than long-term gains, and gains which can be easily realised.

2. Funds are getting bigger. The natural response to this is to look for bigger opportunities. The result has been that competition for the largest buy-outs is very tight.
3. Funds are looking to Europe for opportunities. As the UK private equity market has become more competitive, the European market has begun to look very attractive.

The result of these three trends is that the sources of capital available to you if you are running a small to medium-sized enterprise (ie up to £30m value) have probably declined.

Furthermore, within the SME sector the trend has been towards management buy-outs and buy-ins, because there is a perception that the returns are great and the risks are small. It is also easier to engineer an exit from a buy-out within a short timescale. The result is that most of the venture capital funds available have been going towards restructuring ownership rather than enabling entrepreneurs to grow their businesses.

Less money is invested in development or expansion in the UK than in the US. This has meant that the willingness of quality management to go into start-ups and developing the potential of SMEs is very much less than it is on the other side of the Atlantic. The British venture capitalist is not a venture capitalist in the true sense of the word.

While the big funds in the UK market have been concentrating on big deals and looking to Europe, this has not necessarily been a total success for all concerned.

The unanswered question about the current European environment is whether the deals that have been done will generate liquidity within the time frame of the funds. It is still doubtful whether funds devoted to France and Germany are making an adequate return on capital now, ten years or more after the market was first opened up. If there are any winners they will be in the big ticket deals.

The downturn in 2001 will have a knock-on effect on the private equity sector. In times of financial turmoil, people launching new funds will find it harder to make their targets. It should be remembered that historically a downturn has been a very good time to invest in private equity. The three to five year time horizon means that one is buying at the bottom of the cycle and selling at the top.

The tax environment is now very much more favourable to venture capital investment, both at the institutional level and the individual level, than it was ten years ago. This alone may be enough to ensure that private equity prospers in difficult times.

It is unlikely that fund managers will reduce the assets allocated to private equity because of short-term conditions in the public markets. There is now an awareness of entrepreneurialism. Most people now want to work for themselves. There is no longer any security in a big company. There is a wide appreciation of the benefits of equity ownership. It has been a quiet entrepreneurial revolution. It is not going to turn back.

Case study

Lloyds TSB Development Capital (LDC) and SMEs

Lloyds Development Capital's view of the market is different from many of its competitors. It has concentrated on the UK and on the SME market within the UK. It has no intention of raising outside funds, so it can take a slightly longer-term view of its investments than it would have to if it were operating a closed end fund.

As part of its strategy of supporting SMEs, it has been diversifying its activity outside London. It now has offices in Nottingham, Reading, Leeds and Birmingham, as well as the capital.

Over the last few years, LDC has become one of the largest and most active venture capitalists in the UK (it is the leading investor in the mid-market sector). It has invested in over 350 businesses in its 20-year history, recently investing £105 million in 25 deals in 2000 and £115million in 27 transactions in 2001.

Typical of the type of deal it gets involved in is Encon.

The Encon story

In 1987, LDC led an equity syndicate of five members which invested £2 million of risk capital in the Encon Group. Encon, a private company, was then a distributor of insulation materials with a small number of depots in the UK and a contracting/installation subsidiary.

Encon's trading track record, pre the equity investment, was as follows:

£ million

y/e 31August	*1985*	*1986*	*1987*
Sales	1.5	4.0	12.2
PBT	0.06	0.2	0.37

The equity funding of £2 million, along with £5 million of overdraft and loan funding provided by Bank of Scotland, enabled Encon to purchase the assets of two moribund insulation manufacturing plants in Scotland. The plants were acquired for a knock-down price of £850,000 (the full replacement costs of the assets would have been many millions) and the balance of the total £7 million of funding was used to cover:

(i) re-start of the plants, including additional engineering capital expenditure;
(ii) working capital to cover the planned growth of stock and debtors for the expansion in group trading activities.

The equity investors obtained an equity stake of 22.5% in the Encon Group.

The next three years (1988–90) were years of real achievement. The manufacturing businesses produced quality products and won market share in a tough sector. The Group also made a number of acquisitions with the assistance of additional bank funding. The largest of these helped to double the size of its distribution business to 20 depots. Encon's first overseas depot was also opened in France.

The business then grew rapidly:

£ million

y/e 31 August	*1988*	*1989*	*1990*
Sales	19.0	31.0	60.0
PBT	0.232	2.0	2.7

The benefits from rationalisation of the cost base following the acquisitions were still to come through. The business looked to be on track to achieve a full stock exchange listing in line with the aspirations of Encon's senior management and the investing institutions.

By 31 August 1990, Bank of Scotland had increased its support to £12 million (split equally between overdraft and term loan) secured primarily by good book debts of £17 million.

To strengthen the balance sheet, the equity investors 'followed' their initial stake with a second stage capital injection of £3 million in December 1990, which was used to reduce some of the bank debt. The investors increased their equity stake to 32.5% in the process.

The trading year 1990–91 proved to be the most difficult one in the Group's relatively short history. The UK economy weakened, moving from 'slowdown' status to an ever deepening and seemingly endless recession. The building construction sector suffered enormously. Housing starts fell rapidly, new commercial builds halted and, not surprisingly, the price of building materials fell.

Encon fought hard to maintain its market share, but with prices falling and bad debts increasing it soon became impossible to make sufficient earnings to cover fixed overheads. A programme of rationalisation was begun during the trading year, but this involved closure costs of circa £1 million. In the year end 31 August 1991 the following trading result ensued:

Sales £71.0million
Loss (£3.1million)

The compounding effect of very high interest rates on a highly geared business dependent on the construction sector during an economic recession was graphically illustrated in that result.

LDC, as lead investor, maintained its belief that Encon, by now a sizeable player in its market, still had considerable unrealised potential. With hindsight, Encon's management had made some strategic errors during the previous growth phase. But the team were intelligent, receptive, hardworking and motivated to restore company performance – though it was recognised that any turnaround would take two to three years.

A series of meetings took place between management/investors/Bank of Scotland and it became clear that Encon required a further capital injection to see it through the recession.

The Bank of Scotland exposure had, by now, increased to £13 million (split equally between overdraft and term loan) but Encon's debtor book had fallen to £16 million, and the Bank's cover was reducing.

LDC succeeded in arranging third-round funding of £3.5 million from the syndicate (although at this stage one investor dropped out). The total equity from the investors increased to £8.5 million, and their equity stake rose to 85%. It was also acknowledged that Encon was unlikely to be in a position to pay any dividends for at least another two years.

Bank of Scotland agreed to suspend its scheduled loan capital repayments and also agreed to reduce its interest rate to a fixed charge of 5% for one year to assist cash flow.

As a condition of the new equity funding, the investors appointed a new non-executive Chairman with turnaround experience to assist the management team.

The trading year 1991–92 was another year of mixed fortunes. The programme of rationalisation continued and exceptional costs that year from redundancies and closures totalled £1.8 million. Bad debt write-offs rose to £1 million as numerous customers 'went under'.

In terms of the bottom line, the year ended 31 August 1992 was the nadir in Encon's history:

Sales	£67.0million
Operating Profit	(£1.1million)
Exceptionals	(£1.8million)
Bank Interest	(£1.9million)
Trading Loss for Year	(£4.8million)

The reliance on Bank funding had increased to circa £15 million (£8 million on overdraft, £7 million on term loan). This was secured by debtors £12 million, stock £4 million, freehold £1 million, plant and machinery £6 million. On a forced sale basis, it was unlikely that Bank of Scotland would have fully recovered their lending and any shareholder value had gone completely.

Despite the trading results, the fundamental operations of the business were sound and improving all the time. Working capital was under firm control, stocks had been reduced, credit control tightened and the product sales mix improved. The simple things were all being done well and it was possible to envisage a picture where rising sales and improved margins – as the UK moved out of recession – would restore profit to the bottom line.

LDC and two of the remaining four co-investors agreed upon a capital restructuring, and the management and Bank of Scotland were involved at every stage in the negotiations. The bank debt reduced by £5 million, and the balance sheet picture improved. The investors injected a further £2.5 million of equity and retained a 60% equity stake. Bank of Scotland agreed to convert £2.5 million of debt to preference share capital, and also obtained a 15% equity stake.

Management were incentivised by seeing their equity stake increase from 15% to 25%.

Between 1993 and 1997, Encon continued its recovery and the results speak for themselves:

£ million

y/e 31 August	*1993*	*1994*	*1995*	*1996*	*1997*
Sales	60.0	60.0	69.0	74.0	78.0
PBT	(1.4)	0.4	2.3	3.6	4.2

No magic wand was involved – simply a combination of hard graft, innovation, and determination from a totally focused and dedicated management team. For their part, the investors and Bank of Scotland had kept their nerve in strengthening the Group's capital base. As the economy in the UK improved, Encon's board was able to focus more on future strategies rather than on fire fighting, which had been a feature for so long in the past.

Towards the end of 1996, the shareholders discussed the possibility of seeking an exit, probably by way of a trade sale. At this stage the company's auditors, KPMG, were also brought into play through their corporate finance specialists and they indicated that Encon might be valued somewhere between £30 million to £40 million. A discreet selling process was then begun.

In November 1997, the shareholders sold out their stakes to another institutional investor. Encon was valued at £35 million – not a bad result compared to the situation in 1992! The result was a good one for all classes of shareholder:

- The management team made a substantial capital gain.
- Those investing institutions which kept faith with the Group recovered all the cost of their investment plus a substantial capital gain.
- Bank of Scotland recovered all their debt, preference shares, and made a substantial capital gain.

At one stage, it had looked as if everyone might be a loser. By working together and understanding each other's needs, the pain was shared by all the interested parties during Encon's most difficult trading period. Ultimately, all the shareholders enjoyed the satisfaction and reward of a successful turnaround which had depended upon all round co-operation.

3.2
Shaping Up for the Market

Mike Stevens
KPMG Corporate Finance

While the economic environment will greatly influence the total value and number of transactions in the market at any given time, smaller transactions suffer less from the impact of the cycle and have a habit of continuing to happen. It is a fact of life that private companies are overcome by events (generally filed under death, divorce or debt – the infamous '3Ds' beloved of estate agents) and have to be sold come what may.

Businesses need to get into shape regardless of whether the market is up or down and there are a number of considerations to think about if you have the luxury of planning your sale.

Focus on strengths

In the capital markets it is easier to value a company that can be pigeonholed – and in the capital markets no one wants difficulty. Even relatively small companies often find that they have developed a number of differing strands to the business, which makes it difficult to categorise them.

Many public companies are currently selling off non-core parts of their businesses at a loss. These 'less sexy' elements have had the effect of analysts down-rating the business as a whole and significantly reducing value. For example, Tomkins plc recently sold Smith &

Wesson Corp at a loss of over £100 million and increased its overall value.

Put yourself in the position of a prospective purchaser and think what would catch their eye about this business. Is it the breadth of your customer base? Perhaps your expertise in a certain area? If you are in a service industry, is it your people?

Make sure that everyone knows what the company does. Make sure that it is good at that one thing and take care not to get distracted by dabbling in areas of peripheral interest.

Gain critical mass

There is no doubt that scale is king. Without the right critical mass you will not attract the attention of buyers who themselves have access to funds to pay for your business. Your size could hinder your organic growth if customers regard you as too small to handle their contracts. You are unlikely to retain good staff if you are unable to offer the same career opportunities as larger competitors.

While you need to be achieving organic growth, an acquisition or alliance is more likely to make the difference that you require in profit multiples. The reduction in overheads and other savings that you can shake out of the balance sheet, plus the increased volume of sales, will help to progress your profits up the scale from £100,000 to your first £1 million and onwards to £10 million. Each step up the scale will add to the multiples used to value the business.

Thus, you must start thinking about possible acquisitions, or, alternatively, build up alliances with companies that you might subsequently acquire. Look at gaining greater geographic reach by aligning yourself with a similar business in a different location. Another option is to hook up with a company offering something slightly different but drawing on the same customer base. Avoid at all costs an alliance with a business that has a very different offering to your own or with companies either up- or downstream from you in the process, for these rarely work.

Geographic or sector coverage

This ties in very closely with focus – you need to know what sector you are in and achieve good coverage. Concentrate on building sector coverage – companies that have made it to number one or two in their chosen market are far more attractive than those that are number three or less.

Alternatively, you can achieve good geographic coverage with a degree of monopoly wherever you are. Because the world is getting smaller, geographic growth flows more easily and quickly than in the past. Few companies achieve world coverage, but concentrating on a single geographic market can have dire consequences as companies with exclusively US markets have recently discovered to their cost.

Intellectual property and barriers to entry

How do you protect and distinguish what you have got? Barriers to entry take all forms and you have to be clear what they are. There are plenty of obvious physical barriers in terms of the location you are delivering products from, but there are many others in terms of comfort levels. Quite often, services or products are prescribed by professionals outside or beyond the buyer, and that becomes a barrier. Approved supplier lists where purchases are only made from parties known to a group is another. The slow decision-making and tendering processes of certain parts of the public sector create a barrier to trade. How do you protect your intellectual property – is this another barrier? Have you got anything special to offer?

People and incentives

Your employees will always have a view of where they stand in comparison to their contemporaries in the market. Managing their expectations can be hard work as life becomes more sophisticated. Delivering tangible benefits generally has a much better long-term effect than pure monetary rewards. As a rule of thumb, it is not usually the salary that keeps people in their jobs but seemingly niggling things that drive them into the arms of competitors. Is their working environment comfortable? How family-friendly is your company? Attracting and retaining good people is a vital ingredient in the process of shaping up for the market, whether in attaining mass or having the appropriate skills base to boost your market position.

Sale planning

The external perceptions of the company need to be looked at. You need to have something to say to the outside world that differentiates you – and this can be done by employing a good public relations adviser to make sure that you are on the map. Nowadays, the vast majority of businesses seeking to go to market have reasonable websites, but it is surprising how few have made a name for themselves through press coverage of their activities. The smaller the community in which you operate, the more important this becomes. It is too easy to assume knowledge out in the wider world when none actually exists. You should be constantly on the lookout for opportunities to raise the profile of your company.

As part of your strategic considerations, you might want to consider whether flotation is a serious option. There are times when having a listing can make a difference; the market or the sector might expect it of you or you might need to offer marketable securities to attract other companies or joint venture partners. Today, however, with almost limitless private equity funding readily available, investment requirements can usually be fulfilled without the need to float.

Often, there is a need to think about a change of leadership or management. The person who has the wherewithal to get the business up and running may not be the best qualified to manage the growth phase taking the company to the next stage in its development. There should be a structured evolution within the management team to allow the business to expand and grow – and personal development and training are crucial for this. Clearly, the owner wishing to sell up and retire must first become superfluous to the company.

Flexible focus

The world is changing so rapidly that you must continually review what you are doing and how you are doing it – and thus change to meet market demands. This is not at complete odds with making sure that you stay focused on your business. You need to be flexible enough to review what is happening around you and keep your options open to opportunities as they arise. If you look around at companies that have achieved their goals, this is perhaps the crux to their success.

3.3

Raising Venture Capital – A Working Guide for Entrepreneurs

Nick Jones
Tenon Corporate Transactions

Many ambitious entrepreneurs seek venture capital to fuel the rapid development of their businesses. The good news is that the amount of funds raised for venture capital investment is growing at a rapid rate. In 2000, external institutions and private individuals committed £8,995 million to UK managed private equity funds for future investment. This constituted an increase of 55 per cent on the 1999 figure of £5,813 million. This substantial increase was principally due to increased commitments from overseas insurance companies.

In 2000, £1,885 million was invested in 341 companies. The distribution of this investment is shown in Table 3.3.1.

This guide focuses on advice to entrepreneurs seeking funding for early-stage or expansion projects, which received 75 per cent of the funds invested in 2000. The comments do not apply to start-up ventures, which are generally difficult to fund.

With the end of the Internet investment bubble in the first quarter of 2001 and the continuing volatility in the TMT (technology, media and telecommunications) sector, the investment criteria of venture capital companies has changed substantially. They are now focused

Table 3.3.1 Distribution of investment, 2000

Financing stage	Number of companies			% of companies			Amount invested (£ million)			% of amount invested		
	2000	1999	1998	2000	1999	1998	2000	1999	1998	2000	1999	1998
Start-up	153	101	115	13	9	10	175	128	111	3	2	3
Other early stage	256	159	126	22	14	11	528	219	177	8	4	5
Total early stage	409	260	241	35	23	21	703	347	288	11	6	8
Expansion	498	481	484	42	43	43	2,012	980	688	32	16	18
Secondary purchase	44	51	72	4	5	6	99	137	131	1	2	4
Refinancing bank debt	6	7	5	–	1	–	11	39	3	–	1	–
Total expansion	548	539	561	46	49	50	2,122	1,156	822	33	19	22
MBO	190	255	218	16	23	20	3,297	4,282	2,129	52	69	56
MBI	35	55	102	3	5	9	249	384	536	4	6	14
Total MBO/MBI	225	310	320	19	28	29	3,546	4,666	2,665	56	75	70
Total	1,182	1,109	1,122	100	100	100	6,371	6,169	3,775	100	100	100

Source: BVCA report on investment activity 2000

on businesses with revenues, profits and cash flow following a period where these attributes were not deemed essential to receiving funding. It is therefore critically important to gain early input from an experienced adviser on the merits of your proposals and the venture capital investors most likely to respond positively to your proposals.

In the film *Clockwise*, John Cleese said, 'Lord I can cope with the despair, but it's the hope which I can't cope with'. It is far better to obtain some clear advice on the prospects of success at the outset of your efforts to raise venture capital finance than to work very hard in vain for months. Your response to this could be to point to many successful entrepreneurs who raised equity finance for their businesses against the odds and today enjoy the fruits of their labour based on fulfilment of their dreams. The well-known golf professional Gary Player responded to the comment that he was lucky by saying that the more he practised the luckier he got. Success in raising the finance you need to succeed in your business will be created in great part by your determination to succeed. That said, it is always useful to weigh up the odds at the outset through discussion with experienced advisers and then use their experience to the maximum to improve the probability of success.

What sort of businesses are venture capital companies attracted to? This is an important question to which it is difficult to give a specific answer. A few general guidelines are set out below:

- established, with track record and a proven business model;
- good management team;
- profitable;
- good visibility of future revenue;
- excellent growth prospects;
- credible exit potential;
- limited exposure to changes in external factors such as markets, customers or suppliers.

Thus, what are the key points to remember in raising equity finance?

- getting started;
- creating the business plan and the investment proposal;
- dealing with investors;
- the small print.

Getting started

First of all, you must define what you want to achieve as proprietor of the business through raising the finance and implementing the business plan with the involvement of your investment partner. You need to confirm that the changes resulting from the investment process are acceptable in view of the potential gains from successfully building your business and realising your goodwill through a trade sale or flotation at a future date.

Carry out some initial research by attending seminars and other relevant events that deal with the topic. Speak to other entrepreneurs who have 'been there and got the T-shirt'. Gather documentation on the subject and draft a brief summary of your proposals.

Through this initial research, identify advisers who can add value to the investment process. Contact these advisers, send them your summary and interview them to confirm how they can help you. Subject to your conclusions on adding value, appoint your financial adviser based on clearly agreed terms of engagement including fees.

If possible, organise the management of your business so that account is taken of your time commitment to the fundraising process. You will be spinning many plates during this period and the business needs to perform to plan to avoid problems in dealing with due diligence. Communicate your plans with key managers and consider providing them with share options so that they are fully committed to the future of the business.

Creating the business plan and investment proposal

As the entrepreneur you must own the business plan. You should work closely with your advisers to finalise the plan. This document is crucial in the fundraising process. It must provide a transparent understanding of the business and create the basis for a positive dialogue with potential investors. Key contents include:

- a punchy executive summary that can be detached from the main plan and presented as a summary of the plan;
- an analysis of the market supported by accredited research together with explanation of your competitive advantage, your main competitors, your marketing plans and your marketing channels;
- a definition of the customers you currently deal with together with

those you have targeted in implementing the plan and achieving your sales targets;
- an explanation of your operations and the way in which they will support the growth of the business;
- a description of the management team, including CVs;
- comprehensive financials.

The plan should be concise. Careful editing will make it more appealing to the investor who sees too many unappetising plans. Presentation of the plan is crucial.

The plan should also include a clear analysis of the finance required, the source of this finance including bank, asset finance and equity, and the use of it in implementing the plan.

With your advisers you should define the offer to the investor. Venture capital companies use a number of basic benchmarks for evaluating returns on their investments. By applying these to the finalised business plan you can define the offer which is likely to interest the investor. You should also take account of debt finance which can be raised in parallel with the equity to finance the plan. By raising debt finance you can reduce the equity exchanged for the investment provided by the venture capital company. The equity you retain as a result of raising debt finance will become increasingly valuable as the business plan is successfully implemented and the prospect of a trade sale or flotation becomes more likely.

Dealing with investors

The British Venture Capital Association has 130 venture capital companies as members. Each of these companies has different investment criteria and appetite for investment. They are bombarded with business plans and they tend to look in detail at only about 15 per cent of those they receive. Your financial adviser should know which investors to approach and have relationships with investment directors in those selected companies. As a result, you should get to meet the investors.

You should be well prepared for the initial meeting with the investors. A clear presentation of the business proposition by key members of the management team is crucial. As a result of this meeting you should expect further detailed questions and some indication of a draft term sheet setting out the structure of the investment and the matters that need to be dealt with to finalise the term sheet. It is important to get a clear response from this initial meeting, be it positive or negative. Focus on the positive responses. Do not get involved with half-baked responses from investors, as these go nowhere.

Aim to get at least three positive responses. Keep the initiative with each of these by setting a timetable for the process. Your objective is to obtain a final term sheet from each investor. Negotiating with investors to secure the best deal at this stage is crucial. The conclusion of this stage is the decision on which investor gets exclusivity to finalise. A short exclusivity period of six weeks is realistic to allow the investor to conduct due diligence and deal with the legal documentation. You should keep the other investors warm during this exclusivity period.

Small print

Ensure that you have an experienced lawyer on board at an early stage. The amount of legal documentation needed will surprise you. Protecting your interests in entering into this sort of arrangement is very important. It is also important to keep the initiative in dealing with the documentation so that you meet the timetable agreed and drive the process during the exclusivity period.

Your corporate finance adviser should take centre stage in the final stages of the process. He needs to be a good negotiator to deal with the inevitable 'wobbles' that will occur in finalising the agreements.

The legal framework created as a result of the agreement with the investor will change your business behaviour substantially. You will have:

- non-executive directors;
- a service agreement;
- a new set of rules on your behaviour as a shareholder;
- rigorous financial targets to meet.

You will also have the opportunity to realise your business plans.

Summary

The comments above provide a short summary of the path to raising equity finance from venture capital companies. Each investment will have unique features which will need to be handled in the right way to achieve a successful conclusion.

3.4
Legal Due Diligence Issues

Gregory T Emms
Lee Crowder

On almost any type of acquisition, whether of assets or shares or whether by way of trade purchase, buy-in or buy-out, legal due diligence is essential, to a greater or lesser extent. The extent of the legal due diligence will depend on the circumstances. On a management buy-out (MBO), management might feel less inclined to spend money investigating matters with which they are familiar, although the institution(s) funding them may not be so relaxed. On the other hand, in a trade purchase or a management buy-in (MBI), the purchaser should consider investigating everything for which it will or may be taking responsibility. Entering into a transaction with eyes wide open and being aware of the issues (after any consequent renegotiation of the price) will almost certainly be a better outcome than a possible warranty or indemnity claim after the event.

Areas of investigation may include:

Contracts

The assignability or otherwise of contracts of the vendor or target company should be considered. In general, such issues are less problematic on share sales since the contracts will usually be in the name of the target company and the purchaser will need merely to understand the provisions of those contracts without the need to transfer them. More problematic are asset sales, where contracts will need to be transferred. Typically, many smaller-value contracts will simply be assumed without any formal agreement on the part of the other party to the contract, although this mechanism should not be relied upon, and a formal assignment of the agreement should be obtained, where the contract is of significance – for example, a finance contract relating to an important asset used by the target business. Sometimes, even in a share sale, consent or approval of another party to the contract will be required by virtue of change of control provisions. An example would be a contract with the Ministry of Defence or other government department. Generally, in the absence of any prohibition on the transfer of contracts, the benefit of a contract may be freely transferred whereas the transfer of the burden of a contract requires the agreement of the person who has the benefit of it (a novation).

Consents

Due diligence may reveal that external consents of one sort or another may be required in relation to particular types of business. Examples include licensed premises, transport businesses and newspapers.

Employees

Employees are a major area of concern. Clearly, the purchaser will need to be satisfied with the costs associated with employees and the terms of their employment. Many employers will have employees of a similar grade on standard form contracts or statements of terms and conditions of employment to ensure compliance with the Employment Rights Act 1996. Many, however, do not and a purchaser may wish to ensure that such issues are dealt with prior to completion. In relation to more senior or key employees, an analysis of the individual terms of employment is advisable. Obligations on termination of employment are important – purchasers will wish to see that such employees are restricted from competing with the target on termination and that such purported restrictions are in fact likely to be enforceable (as they are frequently overly ambitious in their scope and duration, thereby rendering them potentially unenforceable).

On a share sale, the employee's position is not usually affected. An employer will not usually change. Note, however, that a purchaser may wish to bring the new or incoming employees into line with its own pay and conditions structure post-deal and this can create its own problems.

In relation to an asset sale, where there is a purchase of an identifiable business or economic entity the business transfer will almost certainly give rise to an automatic transfer of the employment of the employees to the purchaser under the Transfer of Undertaking (Protection of Employment) Regulations 1981 (TUPE). Regulation 10 of TUPE obliges the vendor of the business to provide information and consult with employee representatives prior to the transfer. The purchaser is to provide information to the vendor of any 'measures' which it envisages taking in relation to the transferred employees, or if there are none, to provide assurance to that effect. 'Measures' would include alterations to pay and other remuneration levels, redundancies etc. The obligation under TUPE is not limited to employees of the vendor – employees of the purchaser who are affected are also to be consulted. Strictly speaking, where there are no 'measures' envisaged, the obligation to consult is reduced to an obligation merely to inform. In commercial terms, many employers find the prospect of discussing with employee representatives a proposed sale of the business totally unacceptable. There is often the need to maintain commercial confidentiality. Consultation with employee representatives means listening to representations made by them and taking account of them, although there is no obligation to agree or give effect to the representations. Failure to comply with notification and consultation provisions can lead to a 'protective' award of up to 13 weeks' pay being made by an employment tribunal, although the level of the award will depend upon the consequence of the failure to consult for the relevant employee(s). The obligation to consult may not apply where there are special circumstances rendering it impossible, for practical reasons, to consult (eg on a sale by an administrator or receiver), however a simple desire to keep the transaction confidential by the party would not usually be accepted as a special circumstance. Any liability arising from a failure to consult is likely to transfer from the vendor employer to the purchaser employer under TUPE along with other rights and obligations of employment, so the purchaser should be satisfied that the consultation has been undertaken.

Pensions

Pensions can frequently be the cause of great angst in share and business sales. This is particularly the case with employers having a large number of employees in their scheme. On a share sale, or particularly where there is a stand-alone company, pension issues will usually be limited to establishing what the actual and contingent liabilities of the employer are in relation to the pension scheme. Where a company or business is being extracted from a group, issues are more complicated – including calculation of transfer values etc.

Final salary or defined benefit schemes (now becoming far less common) are more problematic than money purchase or defined contribution schemes, since the employee entitlement in relation to a defined contribution scheme will simply be to his individual account within the fund. By contrast, in a defined benefit scheme, an employee will be entitled to a fraction of his final salary irrespective of the amount of contributions made and performance of the fund. The employer will be required (in relation to a final salary scheme) to ensure that the contributions it makes are sufficient to meet the fund's anticipated liabilities. The minimum funding requirement introduced by the Pensions Act 1995 has created a requirement for a valuation of the fund every three years on a prescribed basis. The effect of this is that many funds previously regarded as being well funded have now been required to obtain further funding by way of increased contribution rates from the employer.

In relation to money purchase schemes, the due diligence issues relate principally to an evaluation of relevant documents, satisfaction with the tax status of the scheme and whether contributions have been made by the employer as required. Similar considerations also apply in relation to final salary-type schemes.

On a sale of assets, employee rights under an occupational pension scheme (ie a pension scheme of either final salary- or money purchase-type whereby the trustees of the fund are nominated by the company and investment decisions made by those trustees (with advice), as compared to a group personal plan – usually an off-the-shelf policy purchased from an insurance company where the individual members have a discretion to direct the nature of their investment – are exempt from TUPE. The purchaser employer is not obliged either to make contributions or to assume liability for accrued benefits pre-completion. By contrast, obligations relating to a scheme that is not an occupational scheme, such as a group personal pension plan or an individual pension plan, are assumed under TUPE (eg the liability to make deductions from employees' salaries or to make contributions on the employees' behalf). However, notwithstanding that a purchaser does not acquire the liability under TUPE, he may be required by the terms of the asset purchase agreement to provide continuance of benefits to employees and, indeed, in most cases would be well advised to do so, so as to maintain employee goodwill.

A recent development has been the requirement of employers of more than five individuals to offer stakeholder pensions. These are government-designed schemes designed to provide low-charge and low-cost pension provision for employees who previously had not felt able to afford to make pension contributions. An employer's obligation in relation to stakeholder pensions is to facilitate pension provision and not, at the present time, to make contributions on the employee's behalf. During the due diligence process, compliance with stakeholder pension obligations should be checked. In many cases, the purchaser may wish to replicate or assume the arrangements carried on by the vendor. Clearly, in a share purchase, such arrangements will come by virtue of acquiring the legal entity. It will be necessary to establish whether or not there are any relevant employees and whether or not any exemption applies. It is thought likely that the current minimum employee number of five will be reduced in the future.

Merger control

Merger control issues should be considered on larger-value transactions. The responsibility for merger control will fall either within the ambit of UK or European Union (EU) authorities. EU merger control provisions are unlikely to apply other than to the larger transactions. A transaction should not seriously fail to be considered in the context of European law unless the aggregate community turnover of the 'concentration' (ie the combined business) exceeds €100 million. It is worth noting, however, that a 'concentration' includes a joint venture arrangement. The joint venture between two subsidiaries of two separate larger groups of companies could cause the aggregate turnover of both companies to be taken into account.

In the UK, merger control issues arise only if world-wide assets of the business being acquired exceed £70 million or the purchaser and the target are, prior to the transaction, in competition with each other and their combined UK market share exceeds 75 per cent of the total. In the UK, once these thresholds are crossed, the Office of Fair Trading has the power to investigate the transaction and to refer the transaction to the Competition Commission (formerly the Monopolies and Mergers Commission).

The Competition Commission or European Commission has the power to order various remedies including break-up, sales or restrictions on voting powers. However, it is possible to apply for prior clearance.

City Code (Blue Book)

The purchaser or the target may be subject to the City Code on Takeovers and Mergers. The Code applies to companies listed on the Official List as well as the Alternative Investment Market (AIM) and OFEX or companies previously listed at any time during the past ten years. A company is also subject to the Code if it has filed a prospectus offering its own shares at Companies House within the last ten years. Many unlisted public limited companies (plcs) treat themselves as being bound by the Code, particularly if contemplating a listing on the public markets. One of the key provisions of the Code is the requirement that any shareholder or concert party which acquires or offers to acquire shares which will cause it to hold in excess of 30 per cent of the equity capital of the company, is required to make an offer for the whole of the company, unless the offer is 'whitewashed' (ie the other members agree that they do not require such an offer to be made to them). A company with less than 12 members may contract out of the Code if the panel agrees.

Anti-competitive practices

A purchaser should be wary of arrangements or practices carried on by the target that may breach domestic UK or European competition laws. Similar considerations apply to both asset and share purchases. If the same business is to be carried on by the same individuals post-completion, it is likely that the same practices as were followed under the vendor's regime will continue. Following the introduction of the Competition Act 1998, UK and EU competition laws are very similar.

European law applies in relation to arrangements that may affect trade between member states whereas UK law applies to arrangements that may affect trade within the United Kingdom. Note that both regimes catch informal arrangements and understandings as well as formal written agreements. Arrangements that are problematic are arrangements that prevent, restrict or distort competition. There are two categories of agreement or arrangement, namely:

- horizontal: arrangements or agreements between different parties operating at the same level in the market, ie those that are ostensibly in competition with each other. Such arrangements include agreements about pricing, carve-ups of territory and agreements not to compete with one another.
- vertical: agreements or arrangements between different parties operating at different levels in the market place, eg manufacturer and retailer. Such arrangements include restrictions on sale prices, and where and to whom goods may be sold.

A block exemption may apply – perhaps the best known is the block exemption allowing exclusive distributorships in the motor trade. However, if there is a suspicion by the purchaser that there are anti-competitive agreements or arrangements in place, individual exemptions should be obtained from the relevant authorities. If no exemption has been obtained, there is the risk of a significant fine being imposed. Also highly significant from the purchaser's perspective is an understanding of the extent to which the profitability of the business or company being purchased depends upon anti-competitive practices, which may not continue.

Before the Competition Act 1998 came into force, a different regime applied under the Restrictive Trade Practices Act 1976. This was a registration-based system whereby restrictive agreements were required to be registered with the Office of Fair Trading. Proof of the registration of any such agreements should be sought. Unregistered restrictions will be void.

Prohibitions imposed by both European and UK domestic law on the abuse of a dominant market position are more likely to be of relevance only in larger transactions or in relation to a business where the market is small. For this purpose, 'dominant' means the ability of a business or company to act independently of market forces, and is generally presumed if a business controls over 50 per cent of a particular market. Prohibition on abuse would apply to such practices as excessive pricing, refusal to deal with specified customers or groups of customers, or the imposition of onerous terms such as an obligation to buy further goods and/or services as a condition of the original sale. The acquisition by a purchaser of a competitor may have the effect of creating a combined entity that has a dominant market position. In addition, there is the possibility of the target having previously abused its dominant market position. The penalties include fines, in the case of Europe-wide markets, of up to 10 per cent of world-wide turnover of the group of companies in question.

Property issues

On sale of a limited company, the purchaser should be aware that a transfer of the shares of the target might fall within the definition of an assignment of the lease of the target's premises. Accordingly, landlord's consent may be required, even if there is no change of tenant.

Obtaining landlord's consent can be frustrating and time-consuming – the landlord and his lawyers have little incentive to comply with the timescale set by the vendor and purchaser. Sometimes such problems can lead to a 'view' being taken on obtaining the consent before completion. Sometimes an informal indication of the availability of the consent will be given, and the legal mechanics of the consent will follow later. Obviously much depends on the importance of the property to the business or company being acquired and an analysis of the ramifications, in practical terms, if consent is ultimately not given.

The effect of the Landlord and Tenant (Covenants) Act 1995 (which operates in certain cases to reverse the previous rather draconian position where an original tenant was always liable under a lease irrespective of subsequent assignments) means that landlords are more careful about assignment clauses and to whom they allow an assignment to be made, since they will no longer have the covenant of the original tenant to rely upon. Note that this only applies to post-1996 leases: a target which was a former tenant of an older lease may be contingently liable for premises no longer occupied if the current tenant defaults. A landlord may not unreasonably withhold consent, although this does not apply where a lease contains an absolute prohibition on assignment.

The purchaser should also be alert to the possibility of a tenant being exposed to claims from a landlord under the current lease – for example, repairing and/or decorating obligations.

Environmental issues

Concerns about environmental law fall broadly into two categories – namely, liability in relation to past breaches by the target or its predecessors and current practices.

Past breaches

Past breaches usually relate to contamination of land. Other breaches such as the release of chemicals into the atmosphere are naturally going to be much more difficult to prove. However, where a target company has in the past breached environmental laws its poor past track record may make it an unsympathetic target for prosecutors despite the new ownership. A minor infraction could result in a heavy penalty.

In relation to land, the Environment Act 1985 can make an occupier of land liable for clean-up costs, even if the current occupier was not the polluter. The responsibility for the remediation of contaminated land is primarily that of the polluter, but if the polluter cannot be found (eg if committed by a now-defunct company) environmental authorities can impose clean-up costs on the current owner of the land or even a tenant or other occupier. The degree of due diligence to be undertaken in relation to land depends upon the nature of the site. Greenfield sites are less likely to be contaminated than the site of a former chemical works. The nature of the business carried on on the site is also relevant. A relatively inexpensive 'desktop' survey can be helpful and will provide information about prior use of the site, groundwater levels and extraction points etc. One such desktop survey commissioned by a client of the author included the provision of photographs taken by the Luftwaffe (presumably with a view to bombing the site in question!). If there are doubts, expensive physical inspections may be necessary. This will usually involve drilling sample boreholes and making an analysis of the soil. Boreholes may need to be drilled through concrete floor plates, causing disruption and leaving open the issue of who is to be responsible for rectification of damage caused by drilling. Physical examinations can have a detrimental effect on the timing of a transaction.

Current practices

The purchaser needs to be comfortable that the target is complying with all relevant laws. If the business is carried on a 'prescribed process' without a licence, a regulatory authority could close the business down. There could also be costs associated with effecting compliance. Other current practice compliance issues include dealing with waste management and the possible need for a waste management licence. Even if a waste management licence is not required, the producer of the waste will need to ensure that the person who disposes of the waste has appropriate licences and facilities. In addition, there are obligations in relation to the recycling of waste packaging material and consents required for the discharge of certain trade effluents into public sewers.

Group companies and prior transactions

Where assets have been previously transferred at an undervalue, in the context of the insolvency of the transferring company, a court may be asked to make an order to reverse the transaction. Clearly, this would be a disaster for the purchaser of a company or assets from a company which made such a purchase. This is particularly the case in relation to a transaction between companies within the same group, or between persons otherwise 'connected', since the time period after the transaction in question during which reversal may be effected is extended to two years (otherwise six months). Furthermore, there is a case law to the effect that a disposal at an undervalue to a company within the same group, where the disposer has insufficient distributable reserves, constitutes an unlawful return of capital, which may make it susceptible to reversal. Accordingly, a purchaser should be wary of acquiring assets which are the subject of any such disposal.

Summary

Legal due diligence usually plays second fiddle to financial and accounting due diligence, for the simple reason that if the financial questions are not satisfied, a transaction will not proceed. Legal due diligence is usually undertaken by the purchaser's lawyers, sometimes by the provision of a written report. Whether such a report is required depends upon the nature and value of the transaction and the issues arising. Where a deal is funded by venture capitalists or banks, they may insist on a legal due diligence report, addressed to them, being prepared. The principle source of information for legal due diligence will naturally be the target company or business and its documents as well as its directors and managers. In addition, there are various external sources of information such as registries, local authorities etc.

What is a potential purchaser to do with the results of his due diligence investigation? Part of the benefit of the process is to satisfy the purchaser that he is in fact acquiring what he hopes to acquire, and that the benefit of the acquisition will be as anticipated. If defects are revealed, these may be dealt with either by the seller giving a specific warranty in relation to the defect identified or, in more serious cases, an indemnity (which does not required the claimant to demonstrate that loss has been suffered as a consequence of the breach). In more serious cases, a warranty or indemnity may be backed up by part of the sale proceeds being deposited in a separate escrow account, subject to release when the contingency or the issue in question has been satisfactorily dealt with. Such arrangements are frequently linked to mechanisms as regards the price. Clearly, if a defect is identified as being extremely serious, this may lead to a significant price reduction or indeed the deal not going ahead at all. In almost all cases, a reduction in price or a price reduction/adjustment mechanism will be preferable to a claim being made after the transaction has been completed.

Part Four

Public Equity

4.1

Flotation

Guy Peters
Old Mutual Securities

Part 1: The public equity market

The public equity markets offer significant access to risk capital. The amounts invested have been very large, with over £12.2 billion raised in new issues (ie flotations) on the London Stock Exchange in 2000 and over £6.7 billion in the 11-month period to 30 November 2001. It is also arguably the cheapest source of external equity funding, largely because of the reduction in an investor's risk, due to there being a market in the shares. If public equity investors believe that the risk/return profile of an investment is no longer attractive to them they can seek to exit from that investment through the stock market. This is not usually an option for private equity investors and, as their investments are less liquid (ie tradable), they will require a larger share of the company relative to their investment to compensate for the risk of illiquidity.

There are, however, various drawbacks to being 'quoted'. Shareholders of public companies have an expectation of continuous growth in value and this puts management under greater pressure than would generally be the case in private companies. There are also increased regulatory and reporting requirements. For owner managers, flotation will lead to some loss of control, initially to outside shareholders and potentially to a predatory bid. Risks associated with flotation are considered more fully in Part 4.

The decision whether to float or not will be driven largely by financial considerations. The principal consideration will normally be whether the cost of quoted equity is appropriate relative to alternative sources of funding. If debt funding is available then this may be attractive, but before making the decision to take it, the additional risk of debt funding to existing equity shareholders should be considered. If debt funding is not available then sources of equity funding should be considered (i.e. flotation, venture capital, development capital, etc).

Reasons for flotation that are not purely to do with funding the company at the time of flotation, include:

- providing an exit or partial exit for existing shareholders;
- providing quoted shares within incentive schemes for employees;
- improving the company's profile with customers, suppliers, landlords, etc;
- having the additional resource of quoted shares in negotiating acquisitions; and
- raising further equity at some later date from the public equity market.

Part 2: Suitability for flotation

There are a number of technical requirements a company has to meet to qualify for admission to public markets. In addition to those there is the equally important requirement that the company must be attractive to potential investors.

The principal technical requirements and the general profiles of the Official List (the main market of the London Stock Exchange), AIM (the second market of the London Stock Exchange) and NASDAQ Europe (a Brussels-based market affiliated to NASDAQ in the USA) are as follows:

Technical requirements of the London Stock Exchange and NASDAQ Europe

	Official List	AIM	NASDAQ Europe
Minimum proportion of shares in 'public' hands	25 per cent	no minimum	20 per cent
Minimum financial track record	3 years*	no minimum	no minimum (but need €1m PBT)
Minimum track record of management within the business	'appropriate expertise'	no minimum	no minimum
Last audit	within 6 months	no requirement	within 6 months (135 days, in some cases)
Minimum total asset value at flotation	no minimum	no minimum	no minimum
Minimum capital and reserves at flotation	no minimum	no minimum	€10 million
Minimum aggregate share value at flotation	£700,000	no minimum	no minimum
Number of companies on the market**	2,270	612	50
Aggregate value of market**	£4,097 billion	£11.126 billion	€8.7 billion
Number of flotations in 2000 calendar year	135	198	9
Funds raised on flotations in 2000 calendar year	£10.836 billion	£1.395 billion	€468 million
Aggregate value of flotations in 2000 calendar year	£53.35 billion	£5.419 billion	€2.675 billion

* There are certain limited circumstances where an applicant to the Official List will not need to meet these requirements.

** Derived from the most recently published information for each market.

The criteria of investors are somewhat different. They are seeking a sufficient return to balance the risk of the equity investment. There is no such thing as a typical flotation candidate, but core traits that investors will be looking for are:

- a business with a defined, realistic strategy which will achieve increased returns for both existing and new equity shareholders;
- a capable management team to implement and control that strategy; and
- a historic demonstration of the quality of the business and management – most likely demonstrated through historic financial growth.

Investors will prefer to see a track record for both the flotation candidate and its management. If investors are being asked to pay a high price for shares because of an expectation of substantial growth over the next few years, it helps credibility if the company has demonstrated substantial growth over the previous few years. Similarly, if growth is largely to come from acquisition, then investors will consider whether the management team has a proven record of making successful acquisitions. In both these scenarios, history lends credibility to the likelihood of future outcomes and in doing so potentially reduces the risk in the eyes of the investor.

Most companies going to the market are valued at below £100million (in terms of market capitalisation) at the time of flotation and the principal institutional investors will therefore be the 'small company' funds. Small company funds are generalists in the main – ie not limited to any particular sector specialisation. They are able to invest in a wide range of potential flotation candidates provided they believe that the growth prospects of their investment are suitable to meet their particular risk/reward requirements.

There are, at any one time, certain business sectors that are viewed by investors as being able to provide excess returns and are consequently more popular with investors. Caution should be exercised, however, as investment fashion can be a double-edged sword. The dot.com flotation boom of late 1999 and early 2000 clearly illustrated that even professional investors can get carried away by market euphoria. Many of those companies that did float subsequently underwent huge internal and market trauma and for every successful float there were many more companies that failed to get away, frequently having incurred significant costs along the way. The lessons for all revolved around the dangers of early stage companies and/or inadequately thought-out business plans. Consequently it is likely to be some time before investors flock to invest in any companies without substantial existing businesses and demonstrable track records.

Although there is a vast amount of money invested in public equity markets, it must be remembered that the supply of cash is not infinite and investors will always search out the best returns. The laws of supply and demand apply and it is easier to market the flotation of a company if it is in a sector that is popular with investors than if it is in a sector which is in the doldrums.

All this is not to say that companies with a complex or difficult to understand product, or diversified range of business do not make successful flotations, but it may be harder to achieve, and that fact may ultimately be reflected in the valuation.

What investors tend to like least is uncertainty, particularly post the dot.com boom and bust referred to above. With certainty of return and certainty of risk, an accurate assessment can be made of what the appropriate price would be to deliver the investors' required return. Unfortunately, we do not live in an environment where certainty is stock in trade. The art of investment is based on uncertainty. However, the lesson here is to deliver to the investor as much certainty as possible in preparing a company for flotation. A period of 'grooming' prior to flotation is very wise. The grooming period may vary between three months and two years, dependent on the circumstances of the company. Typical areas that might require attention in a growth company prior to flotation would be:

- strengthening the management team, which may be a reflection of the growth of the business or to reduce dependence on key personnel;
- prioritisation of business growth;
- improvement in financial controls and reporting – often in a fast growing company this vital aspect lags behind the growth in the company; and
- identification of knowledge gaps and sourcing of appropriate non-executive directors to fill these.

It is best to present an investment opportunity in a focused business to potential investors. The more focused a company is about what it is seeking to achieve and how it plans to achieve it, the simpler it is for the investor to assess the potential likelihood of success and hence the risk and return. Typically, institutional investors will mitigate the risk of any particular investment going wrong by way of holding a portfolio of stocks. There is, therefore, arguably no reason for any one company to diversify its risk by investing in unrelated areas and it should instead focus on core activities. Although there is a converse argument to this, the low stock market rating of companies which have heavily diversified and are described as 'conglomerates' reflects the investment community's view of which is correct.

Additionally, the simpler and more focused the opportunity that the company represents, the easier it is to get that across to potential investors. In considering the amount of time that an institution will have to consider a potential flotation candidate, one must look at how many other flotation candidates an institution may be reviewing, as well as the number of already quoted companies that they are looking after in their portfolio; their time is limited. Typically, the marketing of a flotation candidate to institutions will comprise of a short analytical document, which will give the stockbroker's view of the company's business case; the prospectus, which is a legal document that forms the basis of the investment; and a number of meetings with institutional investors which typically last about 45 minutes to an hour. The marketing of a flotation candidate is considered more fully in Part 6.

Part 3: The flotation timetable

Within reason, the more time there is to organise a flotation the better. Management involvement in the flotation process can be planned and spread over a reasonable period, creating more opportunity to continue the smooth day-to-day running of the business. This, it is hoped, then avoids the necessary distraction of the flotation process damaging the business.

A reasonable period over which a flotation process could be drawn would be six months, as demonstrated by the bar chart overleaf. However, ideally, a company will have sought advice earlier than that as to the best way to groom itself for the flotation process and make it as attractive as possible to potential investors. A company seriously considering flotation should seek to interview a number of potential financial advisers and/or stockbrokers to identify those that the management or existing shareholders wish to work with towards the

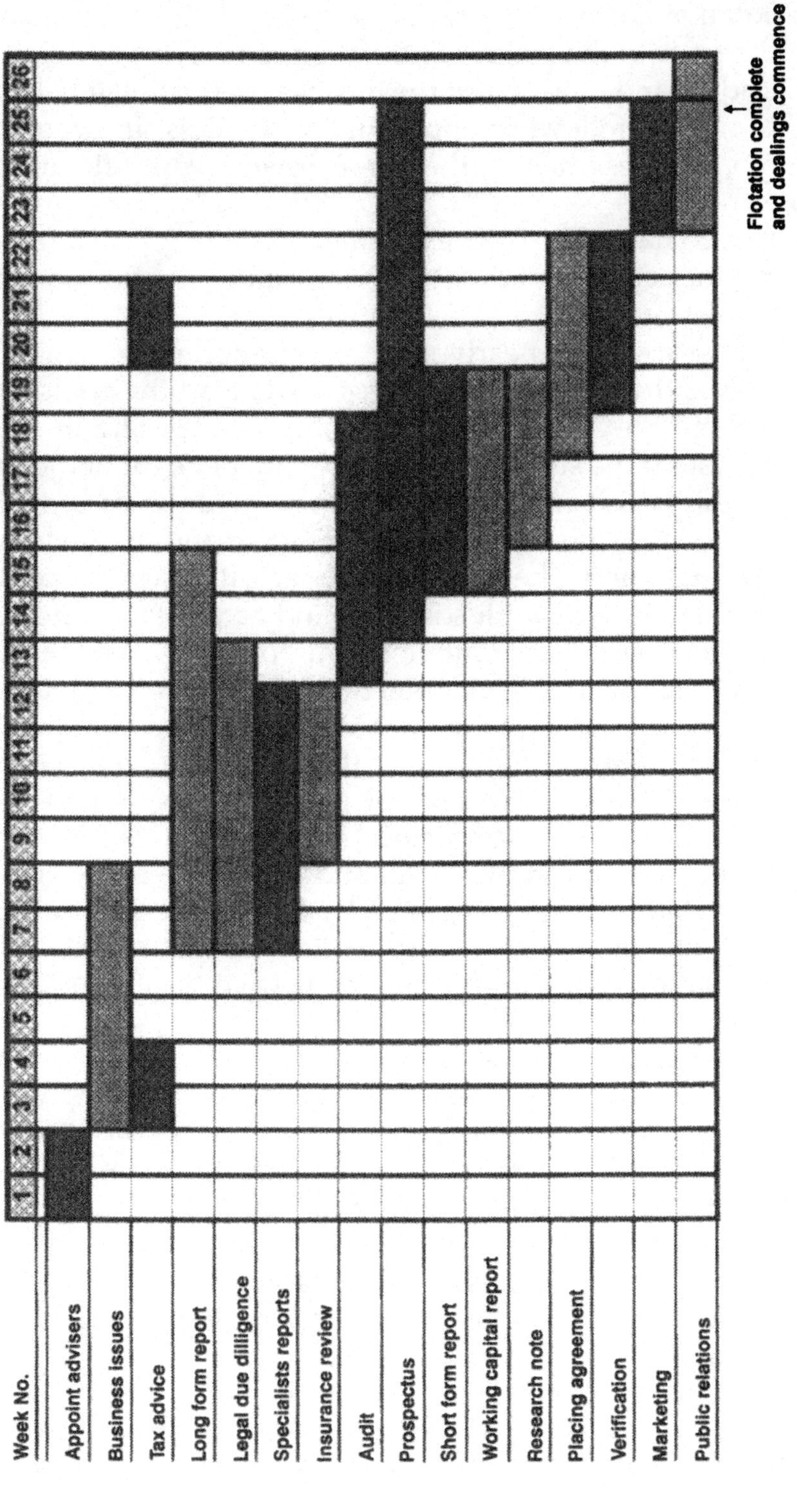
Week No.
1 2 3 4 5 6 7 8 9 10 11 12 13 14 15 16 17 18 19 20 21 22 23 24 25 26
Appoint advisers
Business issues
Tax advice
Long form report
Legal due dilligence
Specialists reports
Insurance review
Audit
Prospectus
Short form report
Working capital report
Research note
Placing agreement
Verification
Marketing
Public relations
Flotation complete
and dealings commence

goal of flotation. Such a 'beauty parade' might be held as early as 12 to 18 months prior to the proposed flotation date. The adviser(s) would seek to understand more about the business of the flotation candidate over the months following appointment, to assist in grooming the company's business before the more intensive pre-flotation work begins.

The above chart shows an example of a flotation timetable of 26 weeks and the activities at each stage are explained briefly below.

Appoint advisers. At this early stage it is important to decide which firm will be the financial adviser, as it will lead the advisory team. This will most likely be the first appointment specifically related to the flotation. If the stockbroker is to be independent of the financial adviser, this is also an appointment to be made at an early stage in order to assess value, stockmarket sentiment and the likelihood of a successful flotation. The financial adviser will assess the company's existing relationships with solicitors and accountants and advise if there is a necessity to appoint new firms for the flotation; as flotation is a new stage in the development of a company, it may be that current advisers' strengths are not in areas required for flotation.

Business issues. During this period, the financial adviser will seek to attain a clear understanding of the business of the flotation candidate. This then allows early identification of business areas that require attention prior to flotation and thereby maximises the time available to address them. The appointment of appropriate non-executive directors will also be driven to some extent by this. The appointments are most often made from the end of the overall timetable.

Tax advice. There are a number of areas where tax advice may be necessary or advisable. These may relate to the company or the position of existing shareholders. They may be the resolution of historic tax issues or may relate to the structuring of the company pre-flotation for tax efficiencies in the future. Where the advice relates to the company, it is most likely to be the accountants to the company who will provide this. Where issues relate to existing shareholders these may be dealt with by a separate adviser to the shareholder(s).

Long form report. 'Long form report' is the name given to the document which most completely describes the business of the flotation candidate. This document is prepared by the accountants to the flotation. The document will provide a considerable level of detail on all aspects of the business and will be the foundation for much of the rest of the preparation. As well as considering the prospects of the business, the long form report will also highlight areas of weakness that will require rectifying as much as possible and which potentially will be reported in the flotation prospectus. The financial adviser and/or stockbroker will review this report carefully and may, as a consequence, require further work to be undertaken on certain areas of the business. This report will be produced by the reporting accountants to the flotation which may be a separate firm to the company's accountants.

Legal due diligence. In a similar way to the investigation in the long form report, the solicitors will be instructed to examine the legal aspects of the business. This will range from checking that all required information has been properly registered with the Registrar of Companies to a critique of the company's terms of trade. The financial adviser and stockbroker will, again, review this report carefully and may require further work to be undertaken in certain areas.

Specialist reports. If the activities of the company are such that a specialist could provide an insight to risk or return by providing a report, then such a specialist may be engaged (eg a property report where property is an integral part of the business or a minerals report for a mining company). Depending on the stockmarket that the flotation is to be on, a specialist report may be a requirement in certain circumstances.

Insurance review. This is another part of the due diligence process and seeks to confirm that the company has an appropriate level of insurance cover to provide for all aspects of its business.

Audit. This may not be a requirement for every flotation but a recent audit is preferable, regardless of whether it is a specific stock market requirement. This will be undertaken by the accountants to the company. Whether this falls within the timetable will depend on the company's accounting period end.

Prospectus. This is the legal document which is published and on which investors will rely to make their investment decisions. Consequently, it is a legal requirement that the prospectus presents the business of the flotation candidate in a balanced way, covering both the potential returns and the risks associated with them. The preparation of the prospectus is co-ordinated by the financial adviser but will require input from almost all of the advisory team. The prospectus should be complete prior to the marketing commencing, in order that a 'pathfinder' prospectus can be produced. This is a version of the final prospectus which omits the price of the issue and information that is calculated from that.

Short form report. This is not an abbreviated version of the long form report as may be implied by the title. Instead, it is a summary of the financial history of the company over the most recent years and this is included in the prospectus. Preparation of this report is the responsibility of the reporting accountants to the flotation.

Working capital report. The working capital is considered as part of the flotation process in order to assess whether the company will have sufficient funds to sustain it for a reasonable period, typically 12 to 24 months, once floated. The document concerning working capital typically takes the form of a board paper, compiled by the company under the guidance of the reporting accountants to the flotation and with the input of the financial adviser and stockbroker.

Research note. An analyst from the stockbroker will undertake a review of the company and publish a background research note in advance of marketing commencing. The purpose of this is to provide potential investors with information from an analytical perspective at an early stage in order to aid their assessment of the risk and reward potential from the flotation candidate.

Placing agreement. This is the legal document prepared by the solicitors engaged by the financial adviser and/or stockbroker (the solicitors to the issue) which sets out the mechanism under which the company engages the financial adviser and/or stockbroker to place shares with investors to raise money for the company and/or for existing shareholders. This will typically require the management and vendors to enter into warranties (covering commercial issues associated with the business as well as title over securities and other such mechanical issues) and an indemnity. If the financial adviser or stockbroker is guaranteeing to buy shares it cannot find investors for, then this 'underwriting' arrangement will be included in the placing agreement.

Verification. It is a requirement of law that the information provided to investors is accurate and not misleading and the directors of the company are personally liable if this is not the case. Consequently, all information that is published will require verification. The principal verification exercise will revolve around the prospectus but, in addition, the marketing material, press releases and other published material will also require verification.

Marketing. Marketing will typically be in the form of a number of meetings with potential investors, which will be arranged by the stockbroker. The potential investors will usually have seen the research note and possibly the pathfinder prospectus prior to the meeting. During a meeting the company will make a presentation on its business, typically followed by a question and answer session.

Public relations (PR). Towards the end of the flotation timetable, coverage in the press of the flotation should prove useful. Often, just prior to marketing commencing, the PR adviser will seek to place an article in the business section of a major Sunday newspaper and the additional recognition that that might bring will assist the stockbroker when setting up meetings with potential investors. From that time on, a positive newsflow will assist in marketing to potential investors, pre- or post-flotation. An additional benefit may be to raise the company's profile with customers or suppliers.

Flotations can be achieved in less than 26 weeks but there are risks to the company. The intensive involvement of key management in the flotation process may cause the business to suffer; the cost to the company may increase and, if there is something untoward identified in due diligence, it may not be possible to deal with it within such a short timetable. All these topics are examined further in Part 4.

Part 4: Risks of flotation

At all stages, the primary risk to a flotation is the state of the stock market and investor sentiment towards the sector that a company is seeking to join. If the stock market as a whole, or if the sector specifically, is weak then this may cause downward pressure on the price at which the flotation can be achieved, or halt the flotation altogether.

Pulling out of a flotation is very much the last resort. However, market conditions do change over time, sometimes quickly and sometimes slowly. Given that the flotation exercise can be a protracted one, it must be accepted as a commercial risk that there is potential for such a change to take effect at some time in that process. The important factor here is an on-going dialogue between the existing shareholders and management of the flotation candidate and the stockbrokers to the float. From the perspective of the existing shareholders and management, they will wish to know on a regular basis what the chance of a successful flotation is in order that they can plan the company's future. It is no good for the stockbroker to be appointed at the beginning of the process, only to be brought in at the end to market the shares if, during the flotation process, had the stockbroker been asked, it would have said that the flotation was no longer a realistic alternative. In that scenario, significant costs would have been incurred which might not have been incurred had there been an on-going dialogue with the stockbroker. However, if a flotation is to be halted at all, it is best that this happens prior to any marketing or any press coverage of the potential flotation. This way the company can seek to float at a later time and not be seen by potential investors as having failed earlier.

Another area that may halt a flotation, regardless of the state of the market, is 'due diligence'. It is in the company's best interests and, therefore, the interests of both existing shareholders and management, for the advisers to be fully conversant with both the prospects and the risks, comprised within the business. This will allow them to formulate a realistic and balanced marketing strategy prior to seeking new investors at flotation, and, additionally, investors will be comforted by the knowledge that the company has been examined in detail.

In order to attain a position where the company's advisers are in possession of the relevant facts to assess the prospects and risks, there must be a considerable due diligence exercise undertaken as described in Part 3. It may be that, at this stage, something is discovered which makes the company inappropriate for flotation in the short term and the problem needs to be addressed prior to a delayed flotation date. This delay may mean that the company misses out on the opportunity it was seeking to access by attaining the flotation. The likelihood of this happening can be lessened by working with the company's advisers from an early stage and informing them that flotation is a real prospect in the view of management and existing shareholders. Advice can then be given with a possible flotation in mind.

A less documented risk of flotation is the detrimental effect it may have on the business. This may occur where either management's attention is distracted by the flotation process away from the running of the business, or management see flotation as an end in itself and relax their efforts following flotation because of this. Either way, the business may suffer or slow down as a function of management's 'eye being off the ball'. The first year as a quoted company is arguably the most important year. It is the year in which the company has to prove that it can sustain its historic growth, prove that the prospects against which it persuaded new investors to invest are there, or the acquisitions that it said were available are delivered. If a company does not perform to expectations in its first year and falls out of favour with investors then it may take some time to regain credibility in the eyes of the investors. It is important not to promise too much about the company's prospects in the future or to play down the risks attached to such prospects, and therefore not to be greedy in pricing an issue thus leaving little for new investors to benefit from in the future. Instead, it is vital to be realistic in order to establish the company as having a credible perception with investors, with the goal of establishing a profitable relationship in the future for all investors, new and old. After all, it should be remembered that a key advantage of a flotation is the future use of quoted equity to make acquisitions and to raise money.

A further risk, which may well befall a company with a disappointing performance in their early years, is the risk of the company itself being taken over. As a quoted company, there is an increased requirement to publish information about results, trading, prospects, etc. and therefore competitors will be more easily aware of the performance of a quoted company over that of an unquoted company. How widely the equity of a company is owned will also affect the risk of a take-over. If, for example, management have retained more than half of the equity, a bid is unlikely, but if the equity is widely spread, a hostile approach may become reality.

The final risk covered here again relates to the requirements on a quoted company to publish more information and more often than an unquoted company. This might lead to competitors taking commercial advantage of that position without resorting to make a take-over.

What happens then if the flotation has to be halted? Depending on the other factors influencing a company, there are a number of alternative routes open to the company if a flotation is halted. There are a number of companies that have successfully floated at the second attempt, so to wait for better market conditions is a very real alternative. If the company does require equity in the shorter term, a private placing may be an option or indeed venture or development capital. If an exit for existing shareholders was one of the primary driving forces behind flotation, then the sale of the entire company may be an appropriate alternative route.

Part 5: The costs of flotation

Although the return required by investors in the public equity markets is low, relative to unquoted sources of equity, the initial costs of tapping into the quoted equity sector may exceed those of unquoted equity. The costs are largely those paid to the advisers, and the need for the advisory team is considered below.

The advisory team is used for a number of reasons:

- There are some advisers that are commercially required (eg the stockbroker will physically raise the money required), and some that are commercially preferred (eg the PR) in order to maximise any beneficial effect there may be for the company associated with becoming a quoted company.
- There are few company directors who have gone through the flotation process more than once. Consequently, it is logical to hire expertise from a source which has greater experience of such matters to co-ordinate the process. This expertise will come in the form of the firm acting as financial adviser.
- Investors require assurance that they have been given a thorough and balanced view of the company's prospects. The knowledge that there has been a comprehensive due diligence exercise performed by the advisory team will assist in providing that assurance. In this regard, an investor may also consider who was in the advisory team and review the quality of the advisers.
- Legal requirements which affect a company seeking investment from public equity sources will most typically be different and more stringent than those that applied in equity raising in the company's past. With such legal responsibility ultimately resting with the directors, good advice to avoid mistakes in this regard is plainly appropriate.

The costs associated with a flotation will depend on a number of factors, including onto which market or stock exchange flotation is sought, the complexity of the business of the flotation candidate, the need for expert reports and the time available to achieve the flotation. Additionally, there is an economy of scale relative to the amount of money to be raised as, typically, the commission associated with the fund raising will be percentage based but other fees will be set amounts. Consequently, the more money raised, the lower the aggregate costs are as a percentage of funds raised.

The costs of a flotation will vary dramatically depending on which market the company is floating, the size of any fundraising, how complex its business is, whether it operates in an area with which prospective investors are reasonably familiar or whether it is in a market or area that requires some significant explanation and how the company or group is structured. Accordingly, it is impossible to define the 'typical' flotation candidate and therefore equally impossible to define the costs associated with it. A method of cost saving often used in the flotation market is to merge the role of financial adviser with either the firm of stockbrokers, who have been acting in this dual role for some time, or accountants, some of whom have more recently marketed themselves as being able to undertake both roles. This will normally result in a lower aggregate fee for the two roles. Although the total costs as a percentage of funds raised may be high, it must be remembered that these are one-off costs and, once floated, a company will typically be able to raise additional equity at a later stage at a lower relative percentage cost. Although there is typically a lower required return to public equity investors compared with private equity investors, the cost of accessing each type of equity must be included when considering the cost of equity. For small amounts of money, the quoted equity market may not prove an economic option.

Part 6: The placement process

There are a number of ways in which a company can raise equity on flotation, the most common of which is a placing. The mechanism works by the stockbroker placing shares, either new shares issued by the company or existing shares being sold by vendor shareholders, with investors. These investors may include insurance companies, pension funds, investment trusts, unit trusts and private client stockbrokers. The rules that cover the sale of shares to such 'sophisticated' investors are easier and cheaper to comply with than a general offer to the public and allow for the exercise to be completed more speedily, all of which make the placing route an attractive option.

Although the placing will be effected on a single day, the impact day, there is a considerable build-up to that point. This starts approximately six weeks prior to the impact day with the publication of the stockbroker's research note referred to in Part 3. This will cover a range of areas and most likely include background on the business, the management team, prospects and risks, comparison with quoted companies and comment on valuation. This research note is sent out by the stockbroker to sophisticated investors who are known to be interested in flotations in order to provide background to potential investors.

In the fourth week prior to impact day the prospectus will be verified and complete, save only for information dependent on price. This document may then be made up as a 'pathfinder' prospectus. The final version of the prospectus is the document that an investor will rely on in making their investment decision and, as this will not be available until impact day (ie when the price is known and the document can be completed), this pathfinder prospectus is provided. The pathfinder prospectus will usually be sent by the stockbroker to the same potential investors who received the research note.

Three weeks from impact day the physical marketing begins. As referred to in Part 3 this will take the form of a timetable of meetings with potential investors, either one at a time or in small groups depending on the preference of the investor. There may be as many as five meetings in one day and the meetings may stretch up to impact day. At these meetings, investors will want to meet the key members of the management team who would be responsible for providing them with a return on their investment. The first part of the meeting will typically be a well-rehearsed presentation by the company's management, which is then followed by a question and answer session that allows the potential investors to ask questions arising from the research note, pathfinder or the presentation itself.

A representative of the stockbroker will attend each meeting and will follow-up after the meeting to get an indication of whether the investor wants to buy shares and, if so, how much. At this stage most declarations of interest are indicative as, with the impact day being some time away, the price is not set. Additionally, the investor will not wish to commit in case there is a change in the market or sector sentiment or indeed in case they see another investment which is preferred.

As the marketing period draws to a close, the stockbroker will seek to clarify potential investors' declarations of interest in order that a final view on price can be given to the flotation candidate. Typically, the marketing will have been done against the background of a range of valuations and, although the stockbroker will have discussed pricing with the flotation candidate from the outset of the flotation process, now is the time for fine tuning the valuation and deciding the price.

In the day prior to impact day, the placing agreement is signed and this sets out the mechanism under which the placing is to be effected. A copy of the prospectus called the 'placing proof', is sent to each of the investors participating in the placing, along with a letter detailing the price and the number of shares they have been offered. They are required to confirm their commitment orally to the stockbroker with a written commitment to follow.

On impact day the successful placing of shares and intention to join the relevant stock market is announced. The prospectus is registered with the Registrar of Companies and the application is formally made to the UK listing authority (UKLA) concerned for admission of the company. This application process will take approximately one week, even though the UKLA will have been involved at a much earlier stage. The process is not a rubber stamping exercise but it is unlikely that a company would be turned down at this stage.

Approximately one week after impact day the shares of the company will be admitted to the stock exchange and dealings commence. The company and any vendor shareholders will then receive the money from the placing as investors receive their shares.

A placing is the most frequently used method of selling equity at the time of flotation. Other mechanisms are an 'intermediaries offer', where shares are marketed to financial intermediaries who in turn allocate the shares to their own clients, or an 'offer for sale/ subscription', where shares are offered to the general public (in the way of most of the government privatisations). Both of the mechanisms can be effective in the appropriate circumstances but are not covered here as they are typically more expensive than the placing route and consequently used far less for smaller and medium-sized company flotations.

Part 7: Pricing an offer

The price at which a company is floated is determined by the advice of the stockbroker who, in turn, will assess the likely level of interest from potential investors and draw comparisons between the flotation candidate and currently quoted companies. Potential investors will also make such comparisons. This may allow them more quickly and accurately to understand the business of the flotation candidate, whilst at the same time provide a basis for valuation comparison.

Therefore, the easiest and arguably the best measure of a company is to look at the nearest quoted alternative, or the valuation of the sector into which a flotation candidate is entering.

Assuming a situation where there is a comparable quoted company with a very similar business profile to a flotation candidate, then the flotation pricing would be derived by calculating an appropriate discount or premium to the valuation of the existing quoted company based on the appropriate valuation method of the quoted company, i.e. price earnings ratio, cash flow analysis or asset-based valuation. The discount or premium will seek to reflect:

- the quality of the flotation candidate relative to the quoted comparable(s);
- the fact that the quoted company has a track record on the market already; and
- the flotation will be priced to increase by between ten and fifteen per cent when dealings commence, to encourage investors to participate.

In determining the flotation price, it is not a question of getting the highest possible price but of getting the right price. It is neither to the company's advantage to be over-priced nor to be under-priced. If it is over-priced, then it runs the risk of its share price going below the flotation price in the early stages of its stock market career and once it has done so it may prove difficult to re-establish the shares above the flotation price. If the price does not perform, the 'currency' of the company's shares is less attractive both to investors and to potential acquisition targets. If it is under-priced, then the question of there being a premium to the flotation price is not an issue. Instead the question is whether the company sold too much equity to attain the required funds and whether existing shareholders were disadvantaged either by selling too cheaply or by being diluted through an excessive issue of shares.

One perception is that stockbrokers will sell an issue as cheaply as possible in order to advantage their own investor clients. There is, however, a flaw in the logic to this argument. If a stockbroking firm establishes itself as only selling flotations cheaply, it will not attract new flotations and therefore its business in that area will dry up. The stockbrokers will typically be looking for the pricing to achieve an appropriate upward movement of the share price in the days following flotation of some 10–15 per cent. At such a premium the vendors and the company issuing new shares should be content that they have not given away too much and new investors should be content that they have had an appropriate initial profit to assist in making their participation attractive.

In terms of how a company can ensure that it gets the 'right' price, it should seek to have a clear understanding of how its stockbroker has arrived at the valuation suggested at the very outset. The company should also continue a dialogue on the stockbroker's views on valuation throughout the period of flotation preparation.

With the right price and appropriate post-flotation support by the stockbroker, and subject always to market conditions, the flotation candidate should not see their share price fall below the flotation price. It may well trade on a plateau for a period and the end of that period may be marked by the announcement of the maiden set of results. The logic is that the market is waiting to see the company's results before it adjusts the share price significantly from the flotation price.

Poor share price performance post-flotation does matter because the company will typically be floating to increase its access to further equity capital in the future, as well as the equity it raises at the time of flotation. Such future equity might be in the form of a rights issue or placing, or may be in the form of issuing quoted shares to acquire another company (the fact that they are quoted will make them considerably more attractive to a vendor than if they were unquoted and therefore not marketable). Therefore, if the share price goes up, then for the company to raise further money in the future or pay for an acquisition it will need to issue less new shares and therefore existing shareholders will suffer less dilution. If the share price stagnates or declines, the level of dilution will be greater – or worse, it may not be attractive to investors to put up more money or for vendors of acquisition targets to accept shares as consideration.

Low liquidity (ie where shares are traded infrequently) is another problem that affects some companies. Illiquid shares are particularly sensitive to relatively small share transactions and the rises and falls in share price may be pronounced. Many investors prefer to avoid such companies because of the difficulty in buying and selling shares without affecting the price. Liquidity is affected by a number of factors, including the number of shareholders, size of shareholdings and the effectiveness of the company's stockbrokers.

Illiquidity should be taken seriously by a company. An illiquid share will be an unattractive share to new investors and will therefore limit the potential use of new equity in terms of raising further money and the use of a company's shares in making acquisitions – ie if the recipients under either of those scenarios believe that to sell their shares would prove difficult, then they will not be attracted to them in the first place.

Illiquidity may arise from a tightly held shareholder list. Possibly the original founding equity holders (family or partners) perceive that to release more equity would be to lose control. It may be that they cannot be persuaded otherwise, but most often a single shareholder, or group of shareholders, can exercise control despite holding below 50 per cent, particularly if it is a widely held shareholder base. The Panel on Takeovers and Mergers have, in setting the requirements for any individual, or group of individuals acting in concert, to make a bid at above 30 per cent, indicated their opinion that effective control may be exercised at or above 30 per cent.

Part 8: Life as a quoted company

A mistake that can be made by management in seeking a flotation is to see the flotation itself as the end, whereas flotation should be just the beginning. Investors in the quoted market are looking for growth and are seeking to identify the companies that will achieve that growth. Also, the market provides some liquidity in their investments so they are able to swap from one company into another if a better opportunity is presented to them. This should therefore force management of a company to perform to the best of its abilities at all times in order to ensure that existing investors stay with the company, and indeed that the company attracts new investors. In an unquoted environment, if a company has a poor year the investors may be forced to stick with their investment as there is no option to liquidate their shareholding. In the quoted market they are able to sell out of their investment and return in a year's time, thereby creating a period of weakness in the company's share price and therefore vulnerability.

Another difference in being a quoted company is the amount of information a company is required to place in the public environment. It is required both to place more information and to provide such information more quickly than if it were a private company.

This, therefore, provides more information to competitors, customers, suppliers, etc. This may be good or bad. For example, a customer might feel more comfortable with the company being quoted and more information being available and therefore provide more business to the quoted company. Alternatively, a competitor may be able to take advantage of the information or indeed may mount a takeover bid.

Ongoing communication with investors and potential investors, once floated, is key. As has been emphasised already in this chapter, an investor is looking at two things in considering any investment: risk and return. Once they have made an investment, this does not change and they will wish to receive a flow of relevant information in order that they can update their view on both risk and return on a regular basis. It is easy to see why companies wish to trumpet their successes to investors and the press at large, which is great for investors in making their ongoing risk/return assessment as they have information readily available. However, companies often fall into the trap of having an information blackout when there is bad news. Faced with this scenario, an investor will often assume the worst in order not to get caught out. This might therefore push them into making an investment decision, ie a selling decision, which they might not have made had they been in possession of all the facts.

It must be borne in mind that an investor buying shares in a company does accept that the company's prospects, relative to the risks, offer a good investment. The investor wants the company to succeed as they will then benefit from it financially. It is certainly not in their interests to see the company fail and therefore institutional investors should be seen as an asset to a company both in times of success and distress.

It is both correct and incorrect to say that institutions take a short-term view on their investments. It is correct in that they have quarterly or half-yearly meetings at which they have to justify their performance. In this way they are interested in the short-term performance of the portfolio. However, a fund manager will not be likely to invest in a company that only has a short-term strategy. Fund managers are interested in seeing a business that has real growth prospects over a long term, has a defined strategy to optimise its prospects and has the management to execute the strategy. Fund managers are therefore vitally interested in the long-term strategies of companies.

4.2
Public Equity Markets

Jonathan Reuvid

Functions of public equity

The opportunities for SMEs to gain access to public equity markets have increased significantly since the 1970s. Although the experiences of those who have achieved listings in second-tier markets, in particular SMEs engaged in more traditional industrial sectors of the 'old economy', have not been universally felicitous, the advantages of a flotation as a source of finance for larger SMEs are sufficiently compelling to persuade some directors to embark on the 'going public' adventure.

Reason for flotation include:

- permanent capital for corporate development;
- substantial funds from a broader investor base with decreased dependence on one or several institutional investors and/or debt finance;
- quoted 'paper' which is acceptable consideration for acquisitions;
- exit route for private equity investors, including the owner-managers of the business;
- motivation of employees.

Provided that stock markets are buoyant, all of these objectives can be realised. If the market falls sharply in the period following flotation, as in the case of dot.com companies in 1999–2000, the first two objectives may have been achieved temporarily, but the last three are likely to be frustrated.

Until the 1980s, UK private companies had only two routes for raising public equity, following a consolidation of the smaller regional stock exchanges into the Stock Exchange, London at the end of the 1960s. They could seek a listing on the re-designated London Stock Exchange (LSE), which has strict entry requirements in terms of minimum market capitalisation and trading record *inter alia*. For smaller companies, the main stock market was so heavily regulated that market entry was either unattainable or inappropriate. As an alternative, SMEs could seek entry to the over-the-counter (OTC) market. The disadvantage of the latter was that it was largely unregulated and therefore unattractive to many investor groups, particularly institutional private equity investors.

In some western European countries, the absence of effective public equity markets for SMEs has been addressed by the creation of second-tier equity markets. A three-tier equity market is now a common structure, consisting of an official list, a 'junior' market or league of the official list for smaller companies with a less demanding entry and trading regime, and an unregulated OTC market.

The second-tier market enables SMEs to gain access to public equity at an earlier stage than waiting to qualify for a full listing. In addition to advancing the introduction of public equity, second-tier listing provides a vital ingredient in attracting private equity funds at an earlier stage – namely, the prospect of an exit route (other than a trade sale) within the three-to-five-year time span which venture capitalists expect and with which other private investors are generally comfortable.

UK public equity markets

The Official List

The Official List of the LSE is segmented by market capitalisation, as well as by industry sector classification, according to which data are published daily in the *Financial Times* (FT). The smallest segment is categorised as the FTSE Fledgling market (market capitalisation of less than £65 million) and the middle-size segment as the FTSE Small Cap market (market capitalisation of between £65 million and £400 million). The LSE also launched the All Small market index, which encompasses the FTSE Fledgling, Small Cap and techMARK indices. TechMARK is the 'market within a market', launched in November 1999, for some 180 companies with a technology bias already in the Official List.

TechMARK also has a less onerous listing procedure for innovative high-growth companies. The LSE introduced Chapter 25 (Innovative High-Growth Companies) into their listing rules at the beginning of 2000, which allows innovative, high-revenue growth companies to seek a listing and to join techMARK without a three-year trading record. A minimum market capitalisation at the time of listing of £50 million (based on the issue price) and a minimum value of shares sold to new investors of £20 million are required.

The contemporaneous arrival of NASDAQ Europe as a recognised investment exchange somewhat overshadowed the launch of techMARK, but the latter has flourished in spite of the collapse of some high-technology sector stocks.

Second-tier equity markets

The UK experience

Over the last 20 years, the United Kingdom has enjoyed a varied experience of second-tier markets. The Unlisted Securities Market (USM) was introduced in 1980 and was at first successful. Initially, it attracted most of the companies which had previously traded on the OTC market and a number of new entrants. However, the recession of the early 1990s caused the flow of new entrants to dry up. At the same time, the advantages of the USM were eroded by relaxation in the main market's listing rules, and the reduced liquidity of small company shares led to a decision by the LSE in 1993 to close down the USM. In the absence of a second-tier market alternative, investor and issuer pressures were exerted successfully to delay the final closure until 1996.

By this time, the LSE had conceded that the Official List alone remained insufficient as a channel to provide smaller companies with access to public equity and, in spite of the USM experience, the Alternative Investment Market (AIM) was established in its place. Subsequently, the general issue of whether UK equity markets provide an appropriate and sufficient capital base for smaller quoted companies (SQCs) was addressed by the Treasury Working Group on Small Quoted Companies under the chairmanship of Derek Riches, which reported to the Paymaster General in November 1998. The report concluded that the LSE could be more proactive in increasing the profile of SQC shares by creating a supportive market environment and helping to stimulate the launch of techMARK and recognition of the FTSE Fledgling and FTSE Small Cap market classifications.

The Alternative Investment Market (AIM)

Introduced in June 1995 as a second-tier market for small or young companies whose shares were not publicly traded, AIM grew strongly and by the end of 2000 had achieved a total market capitalisation of £14.5 billion with 524 companies listed. The 347 companies listed 12 months previously had a market capitalisation then of £12.1 billion. In fact, 2000 was a record year for raising capital in AIM, with some £3.1 billion raised – more than three times the amount raised in 1999 (£0.9 billion).

Altogether since its launch, more than £6.1 billion has been raised in AIM, while more than 70 of the companies listed have moved up to the main market.

In principle, as intended, the less onerous preconditions and operating requirements have improved smaller companies' access to public equity. Particular attractions are the absence of minimum:

- capitalisation requirement;
- asset levels;
- profit levels;
- free float of shares.

However, the attractions of AIM have been blunted for some companies as regulations have tightened both to maintain investor confidence and to encourage institutional investment. A revised set of AIM rules introduced in February 2001 now clearly prohibit AIM companies from issuing information which is misleading or materially incomplete.

Third-tier equity market

The unregulated OTC market within the United Kingdom is OFEX, an off-market trading facility launched in 1995 by J P Jenkins Limited, a market maker/agency broker. It was intended that OFEX would replace the unregulated Rule 42 market under the previous regime for companies not wishing to join AIM or the Official List. Although

OFEX is not regulated by the LSE, J P Jenkins is itself bound by Stock Exchange and Financial Services Authority (FSA) rules, and OFEX is expected to feed companies, as they qualify, into AIM or the Official List in the medium term. Since its launch, OFEX has raised £895.8 million through 586 issues and, as at the end of November 2000, 42 companies had graduated to AIM with a further upgrading to the Official List.

Pan-European equity markets

Current pan-EU markets

EASDAQ

Prior to the announcement of NASDAQ entry into Europe, the European Commission had already published *Risk Capital: A Key to Job-Creation in the European Union* (April 1998), which identified the need for a similar pan-European risk capital market to finance technology-based firms. A parallel development was the creation of EASDAQ in 1966, which is now regarded more as an exchange for high-growth mid-sized businesses rather than a market for small and medium-sized companies with a high-technology bias. Minimum listing requirements are total assets of €3.5 million and capital reserves of €2 million. Supervised by the Belgian Banking and Finance Commission and regulated by the Belgian Ministry of Finance, EASDAQ had 62 companies listed at the end of 2000 with a total market capitalisation of €23.9 billion.

Euro-NM

Euro-NM was a business and marketing alliance concept between the Amsterdam, Brussels, Frankfurt and Paris Stock Exchanges, launched in 1998 and enlarged in 1999 through the addition of the Milan Stock Exchange. Starting from May 1998, there were linked trading platforms at the Brussels Euro-NM and the Paris Nouveau Marché leading to common exchange membership. The declared objective of Euro-NM was to stimulate the listing and trading of high-technology European start-ups and growth companies. However, as a result of structural changes in equity capital markets, Euro-NM terminated its operations as of 31 December 2000.

Comparison of European second-tier markets

The average market capitalisation per company on AIM and OFEX in £million as at the end of December 2000 and of EASDAQ and Euro-NM in €million as at the end of November 2000 are compared in Figures 4.2.1 and 4.2.2 below.

Consolidation of European stock exchanges

With the acquisition of the London International Financial Futures Exchange (LIFFE) in October 2001, the Paris-based Euronext which

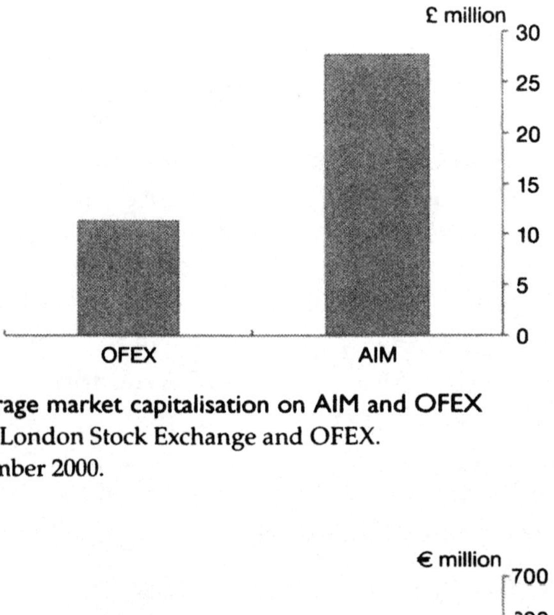

Figure 4.2.1 Average market capitalisation on AIM and OFEX
Sources: Datastream, London Stock Exchange and OFEX.
Data as at end-December 2000.

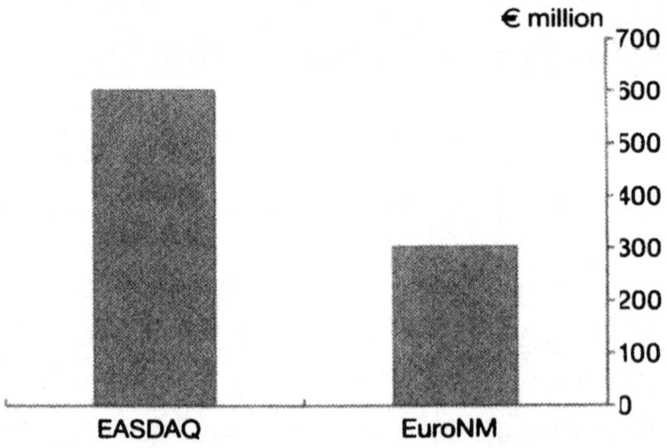

Figure 4.2.2 Average market capitalisation on EASDAQ and Euro NM
Sources: EASDAQ and Euro NM.
Data as at end-November 2000.

unites the Paris, Amsterdam and Brussels bourses has become a serious contender for the leadership of Europe's securities industry. A year ago, there were 33 regulated stock markets and 18 regulatory organisations within the European Union. Although a combined market would, in principle, offer higher capitalisation and liquidity, and thus more certain exit routes – the *raison d'etre* for last year's proposed link-up between the LSE and the Deutsche Börse – the obstacles are formidable and the London–Frankfurt project has foundered.

Having failed to merge with the Deutsche Börse in 2000 and having lost out in the contest to acquire LIFFE, the LSE is now in a seriously weakened strategic position, although it did successfully fight off the opportunistic bid by the OM Group of Sweden. The LSE is now itself a listed company and is again a potential takeover target – a factor reflected in its share price, which rebounded swiftly following the news of Euronext's victory.

The goal of an eventual single trading platform is only one step in creating European financial integration. The ultimate prize is 'global straight-through processing', which will fully automate the tasks of buying and selling any security and settling accounts worldwide. Although this further step in integration will significantly reduce the high costs of completing trades internationally, its achievement demands not only close collaboration both sides of the Atlantic between regulators and investment banks but also heavy investment to re-equip the banks to handle straight-through processing. This is hardly a propitious time to embark on such a commitment, and the move to next-day settlement in the United States, which is an essential prerequisite, has been put back from 2004 to 2005.

At present, there is more concern in the United Kingdom about the proposed Brussels prospectus directive, intended as a 'single passport' for securities to make it easier for companies to raise capital across borders within the European Union. The intention may be laudable, but the proposal involves more onerous disclosure and reporting requirements across the board and it is so far unclear how the directive, which the EU Commission claims is a broad framework only, would preserve companies' choice of listing on primary markets or on lightly regulated second-tier markets. Directors of smaller UK quoted companies fear that the costly requirements of the directive, such as mandatory annual updating of prospectuses, would sound the death knell for key second-tier markets such as AIM and the German Neuer Markt.

The author acknowledges with thanks his indebtedness to the Bank of England Domestic Finance Division for much of the material contained in this chapter and published previously in the Bank's Seventh and Eight Reports 'Finance for Small Businesses' (January 2000 and March 2001).

4.3

Taxation Aspects of Flotation

Maurice Fitzpatrick and Jay Sanghrajka
Tenon Group

The object of this chapter is to examine the principal tax implications of a flotation, concentrating for the most part on the personal tax position of the owners of the company being floated.

The first part of the chapter will act as a 'tool kit', by briefly setting out those aspects of capital gains tax (CGT) and inheritance tax (IHT) that may be relevant in terms of understanding the CGT and IHT implications of the flotation on the owners of the company. The second part of the chapter will briefly set out a number of relevant tax planning areas for further consideration. Needless to say, professional advice should always be sought regarding the impact of the flotation on the IHT and CGT positions of the shareholders of the company being floated, particularly as the flotation may well represent the largest single financial transaction in which the shareholders will ever be involved.

'Tool kit' regarding relevant tax parameters

CGT

There are three main areas to bear in mind:

- hold over relief (HOR);
- retirement relief;
- tax complications of taper relief.

Each of these is now looked at in turn, in the context of a company being floated, E Co.

Hold over relief (HOR)

Prior to the flotation of E Co it would normally have been possible for the company's shareholders to gift shares without incurring a CGT liability based on the market value of the shares at the time they were given away. This would have been achieved by the shareholder who had made the gift (the donor), and the recipient of the gift, jointly electing for HOR to apply to the gift, with the result that (broadly) the recipient inherited the CGT base cost of the donor of the gift. After flotation, the ability to make an HOR election may be lost, unless either:

- the flotation concerned is on the Alternative Investment Market (AIM) or OFEX; or
- even after flotation, the shareholder making the gift broadly owns at least 5 per cent of E Co.

Retirement relief

After the flotation of E Co, those shareholders who would previously have qualified for retirement relief (which in the current 2001–02 tax year can exempt up to £100,000 gain from CGT altogether, and can halve the rate of tax payable on up to a further £300,000 chargeable gain) may find that they are denied retirement relief on disposal after flotation, unless, as for the ongoing availability of HOR:

- the flotation concerned is on AIM or OFEX; or
- even after flotation, the shareholder concerned broadly owns at least 5 per cent of E Co.

Retirement relief is gradually being phased out and will be abolished altogether in respect of disposals after 5 April 2003.

Taper relief

Taper relief was introduced in 1998 and subsequently changed in 2000. There are two types of taper relief: standard taper relief (STR) and the more valuable business taper relief (BTR). STR will apply wherever BTR does not apply.

STR operates so as to exempt a proportion of the gain made on the disposal of a 'non-business' asset. Up to 40 per cent of such a gain can be excluded from the charge to CGT, although this 40 per cent reduction is only achieved once the asset concerned is deemed to have been held for at least 10 years at the time of disposal. This will give a maximum rate of CGT of 24 per cent. In terms of computing how long the asset has been held at time of disposal, for the purposes of computing the rate of STR, the acquisition date is taken as:

(i) the actual acquisition date if the asset was acquired after 5 April 1998; or
(ii) in the case of assets held on Budget Day 1998 (17 March 1998), 6 April 1997.
(iii) in the case of assets acquired in the period 17 March 1998 to 5 April 1998, 6 April 1998.

BTR is much more valuable to the taxpayer than STR; BTR is available on business assets. Under current legislation, under BTR 75 per cent of the gain is exempt from CGT once the asset has been held for more than four years at the time of disposal. This will give a maximum rate of CGT of 10 per cent. In the case of disposals after 5 April 2000, and purely in terms of computing how long the asset has been owned at the time of disposal for the purposes of computing the rate of BTR, the acquisition date of the asset is the later of the actual acquisition date or 6 April 1998.

In terms of shares in a company, such shares will qualify as a business asset in the hands of the shareholder for the purposes of BTR, provided certain conditions are satisfied, as follows:

(a) the company concerned must be either a trading company or the holding company of a group of trading companies. In each case the trading company concerned, or the group, must not carry on to any substantial (not defined in the legislation) extent activities carried on otherwise than in the course of a trade; and
(b) one of the following conditions must be satisfied:
    (i) the company is unlisted (companies whose shares are dealt with on AIM or OFEX are regarded as unlisted); or

(ii) the shareholder is an employee (full-time or otherwise) of the company; or
(iii) the shareholder concerned broadly owns at least 5 per cent of the company.

While a definition of substantial is not contained in the tax legislation, it is generally interpreted by the Inland Revenue as meaning more than 20 per cent of the overall activities of the company or group concerned.

The 2001 Finance Act has introduced a further situation in which an asset can be regarded as a business asset for the purposes of BTR. Specifically, employees who work for non-trading companies (such as property investment companies) can regard shares that they own in their employer company as a business asset for BTR purposes, subject to certain conditions.

Finally in connection with BTR, the Treasury announced in June 2001 that the period of ownership required to achieve the 75 per cent reduction in a chargeable gain as a result of BTR will be reduced from four years to two, following the March 2002 Budget. The precise effect of the legislation enacting any such change will need to be looked at when it is published in April 2002.

The above conditions apply in determining whether shares qualify for BTR for the period since 6 April 2000. In respect of the period prior to 6 April 2000, the conditions which had to be met in order for the shares to qualify for BTR were more onerous (see Note 1 at the foot of this chapter).

In any event, it follows from the above that some or all of the shareholders of E Co may lose BTR in respect of their post-flotation periods of ownership. Specifically, shareholders of E Co who qualified for BTR prior to flotation would cease to qualify unless:

(i) the flotation is on AIM or OFEX; or
(ii) the shareholder remains an employee (part-time or otherwise); or
(iii) the shareholder retains (broadly) at least 5 per cent of the company.

The implications, for the shareholder concerned, of losing BTR status on his shares in respect of his post-flotation period of ownership can be quite considerable. Where an asset has qualified for BTR during part of the period of ownership, and STR for the balance of the period of ownership, it is necessary to apportion the total gain and apply BTR to part of the gain and STR to the balance. In other words, the total gain is hacked out into two separate gains, with taper relief on one gain (Gain A) being computed using BTR rules, and with taper relief on the other gain (Gain B) being computed with reference to STR rules.

Gain A will represent the total gain times *y* per cent, where *y* is that part of the 'relevant period of ownership' of the asset during which the asset qualified for BTR, divided by the 'relevant period of ownership'. The 'relevant period of ownership' always commences with the later of the date of acquisition of the asset and 6 April 1998, and ends with the date of disposal of the asset.

Gain B is the total gain times *x* per cent. *x* per cent equals that part of the 'relevant period of ownership' during which the asset qualified for STR, divided by the 'relevant period of ownership'. As above, the 'relevant period of ownership' always commences with the later of the date of acquisition of the asset and 6 April 1998, and ends with the date of disposal of the asset.

If the above calculation sounds somewhat complex, it is probably because it is. An example will make the position clearer. Take the position of a shareholder of E Co who first purchased some shares in E Co in 1995. The holding was such that the shares qualified for BTR until E Co floated on 30 September 2001, after which time the shares did not qualify for BTR in the shareholder's hands but merely for STR.

The shareholder then disposes of the asset on 30 September 2007, realising a chargeable gain post-indexation relief but prior to taper relief of £950,000.

The 'relevant period of ownership' is the nine and a half years from 6 April 1998 to 30 September 2007. The period within the 'relevant period of ownership' during which the shares qualified for BTR is the three-and-a-half-year period of 6 April 1998 to 30 September 2001. The period within the 'relevant period of ownership' during which the asset qualified for STR is the six years from 1 October 2001 to 30 September 2007.

Gain A will therefore be (3.5 over 9.5) x the chargeable gain of £950,000, ie £350,000. Gain B will be (6.0 over 9.5) x £950,000, ie £600,000.

The rate of taper relief for Gain A is calculated with reference to the rules for calculating the rate of BTR as set out earlier, and with reference (for this purpose) to the entire taper relief period of ownership of the asset (notwithstanding the fact that the asset only qualifies for BTR for part of such period of ownership). At the time of disposal on 30 September 2007, this being a disposal for BTR purposes after 6 April 2000, the asset is deemed to have been owned for BTR purposes for nine and a half years (from 6 April 1998 to 30 September 2007) and thus qualifies for the 75 per cent taper relief available (under current legislation) for the disposals of assets owned (for BTR purposes) for at least four years.

The rate of taper relief applicable for Gain B is similarly calculated with reference to the entire taper relief period of ownership of the asset, again notwithstanding the fact that the asset only qualified for STR for part of the period of ownership, using the rules governing the rate of STR as set out earlier.

For this purpose, the asset (having been disposed of in circumstances where STR is applicable) was deemed to have been acquired (purely for the purposes for determining the rate of STR) on 6 April 1997 since it was an asset held prior to 17 March 1998.

As of 30 September 2007 the asset is deemed to have been held (purely for the purposes of computing the rate of STR) for ten and a half years and therefore qualifies for the full 40 per cent STR.

The overall calculation of chargeable gain is set out in Table 4.3.1.

Table 4.3.1 Chargeable gain for CGT

	Gain A £	Gain B £	Total £
Chargeable gain	350,000	600,000	950,000
Less taper relief 75%/40%	262,500	240,000	502,500
Taxable gain subject to annual exemption	87,500	360,000	447,500

The overall chargeable gain after taper relief is £447,500, which, using a CGT rate of 40 per cent, produces CGT of £179,000. By contrast, had the asset qualified for BTR for the whole of the relevant period of ownership, the chargeable gain would have been just £237,500, being £950,000 chargeable gain pre-taper relief less 75 per cent BTR, producing a CGT liability of £95,000.

Had the asset continued to qualify for BTR for the whole period of ownership after flotation, there would thus have been a potential CGT saving of £84,000 (ie £179,000 less £95,000).

IHT

Prior to flotation, the shares in a company being floated, E Co, would normally qualify for 100 per cent business property relief (BPR) for IHT purposes. In other words, they would be disregarded altogether in terms of valuing a person's estate on death. Broadly, IHT is payable on all but the first £242,000 of a person's estate on death. Again, in general IHT terms, gifts of an asset made more than seven years before death escape IHT, while gifts made within seven years of death may attract IHT on death. Gifts of assets qualifying for BPR made within seven years of death still escape IHT, provided (broadly) the asset concerned was still owned by the recipient at the time of the death of the donor and still qualified for BPR at the time of death of the donor.

After flotation, the shares in E Co will not qualify for BPR unless the flotation is on AIM or OFEX, and BPR status may be lost.

As a result of losing BPR status:

- gifts made by the shareholder shortly before flotation could be within the charge to IHT should the shareholder concerned die within seven years of making the gift; and
- shares owned by the shareholder at time of death (after flotation) will not qualify for 100 per cent BPR.

Planning issues

Clearly, every shareholder of a company being floated needs to consult his professional adviser and assess to what extent his CGT or IHT position is going to be affected by the flotation. If the flotation is on the main list of the Stock Exchange, with the result that certain tax reliefs previously enjoyed will cease to be enjoyed, then certain action may be considered prior to flotation, such as:

- gifting shares while they still qualify for eg CGT HOR;
- realising shares gains on which may qualify for CGT retirement relief.

In terms of taper relief, the earlier example makes it clear how valuable (in terms of minimising CGT) it is for the shares to qualify for CGT BTR even after flotation. Every effort should be made by the shareholder concerned to ensure that the shares continue to qualify for CGT BTR (eg in the event of a full listing on the Stock Exchange) by becoming an employee (even part-time) of E Co (if he is not already, and subject of course to commercial and tax considerations).

It is apparent from the above that floating on AIM or OFEX helps to 'lock in' a range of capital taxation reliefs for the shareholder concerned, with those reliefs being potentially extremely valuable. While the overall decision as to whether to go on AIM or OFEX on the one hand, or the main list of the Stock Exchange on the other, will largely be determined by commercial factors, the tax reliefs concerned should not be ignored in terms of making the final decision.

Note 1

For periods prior to 6 April 2000, shares in a company qualify for BTR in circumstances where:

(a) the company concerned was a trading company or the holding company of a trading group; and
(b) either
   (i) broadly, the shareholder owned at least 25 per cent of the company; or
   (ii) broadly, the shareholder owned at least 5 per cent of the company and was a full-time working employee of the company.

The pre-6 April 2000 definition of shares for BTR purposes is thus considerably more restrictive than the post-5 April 2000 definition.

Thus, prior to 6 April 2000, in order for the shares to qualify for BTR the shareholder concerned either had to have a fairly significant (ie 25 per cent plus) holding in a company, or he had to have a material (ie 5 per cent plus) holding in the company and be a full-time employee. By contrast, after 5 April 2000 any size holding in an unquoted trading company/trading group qualifies for BTR, regardless of whether the shareholder is an employee or not.

4.4

Legal Aspects of a Company Flotation

Mark Gibson
Lee Crowder

Introduction

This chapter primarily deals with the procedure and the involvement of legal advisers for a UK company seeking a listing for its shares on the official list of the London Stock Exchange plc.

It should be noted that in addition to the main list of the Stock Exchange, there are various other public markets on which a company may seek to have its shares admitted to trading.

Those markets include the Alternative Investment Market of the Stock Exchange (AIM, the successor to the Unlisted Securities Market) and OFEX. OFEX was established in 1985 to provide a share-trading platform for unlisted and unquoted securities. While OFEX is not a recognised investment exchange, its objectives are akin to those of AIM and the main market of the Stock Exchange in that it provides a market for companies to have a public method of trading their shares. The majority of the principles and the role of the company's solicitors in a flotation process will apply to each of these three markets, although naturally there are variances between the three.

The decision to seek a public listing is undoubtedly a major landmark in the development of any company. A listing will be thought likely to dramatically enhance the company's reputation and profile and may well generate substantial capital to fund the expansion of the company. One must, however, appreciate the challenging nature of a public listing and the time commitment that this involves for the directors. The marketing of a public company's securities is strictly regulated in order to afford as much protection as practicable to potential investors. The bulk of this regulation is set out in the Financial Services Authority's listing rules commonly known as 'the Yellow Book', although the colour of that book is now in fact purple! In addition to the listing rules, one must pay particular attention to the provisions of the Financial Services Act 1986 (FSA), the Financial Services and Markets Act 2000 (FSMA) and the Public Offers of Securities Regulations 1995 ('the POS Regulations').

Legal due diligence and pre-float grooming

One of the early tasks of the company's solicitors will be to undertake a thorough legal due diligence exercise into the company. This process will inevitably involve a large amount of management time as solicitors seek to establish and review the constitutional/contractual position of the company. Matters will include:

- review of the company's memorandum and articles of association;
- establishing directors and current shareholders;
- establishing employees and their contractual terms of employment including benefits, pension schemes, life assurance etc;
- details of any subsidiary, associated or other group companies;
- the company's banking relationship and any security provided to its financiers;
- intellectual property rights owned or utilised by the company and the establishment of valid licensing agreements relating to the same;
- principal trading relationships with both the company's suppliers and customers and the proper regulation of those by means of carefully drafted contractual agreements providing sufficient protection to the company;
- any litigation with which the company is involved;
- property owned or occupied by the company;
- environmental issues affecting the company and licensing requirements.

Once the company's solicitors have obtained this information, they will then produce a detailed due diligence report. Contained within the report are likely to be a series of recommendations for further 'legal grooming', for example properly documenting the company's relationship with its suppliers and customers/preparation or revision of employment contracts and quite possibly a requirement for reorganisation of the company, if part of a group, prior to flotation. It is perhaps self-evident but worth noting, however, that a company seeking to offer its shares to the public will need to have the status of a public limited company rather than a private limited company. The requirements for a public limited company include an issued share capital of no less than £50,000, which must be a least one-quarter paid up. It may therefore be necessary to re-register the private company as a public company prior to flotation. It is also usual to reorganise the company's capital structure to create sufficient share capital to ensure that any shares to be issued can be offered at a price that the market will find attractive. New long-form articles of association are generally adopted which will need to be CREST-compliant and also to ensure that shares are freely transferable and do not contain any form of transfer pre-emption rights. CREST is the paperless settlement system that provides electronic book entry transfer of registered stock.

Company prospectus/listing particulars

The principal document produced as part of the flotation process will be the prospectus or listing particulars. This is the document which is made public and is intended to provide a potential investor with sufficient information upon which to base a decision to invest. While the directors often initially view this document as a sales document, it is the document which presents the greatest risk to the directors if the content is inaccurate or misleading. The prospectus will cover the following issues:

- the persons responsible for listing particulars, namely the directors, the company and the auditors;
- the shares for which the application is being made;
- the issuer and its capital;
- the group's activities;
- the issuer's assets and liabilities, financial position and profits and losses;

- the management team;
- recent developments and prospects of the group.

The legal advisers will play an active role in the drafting and preparation of the prospectus and, in particular, the statutory and general information section dealing with the company, the terms of its memorandum and articles of association, the directors and their interests in the company, the terms of directors' service agreements and emoluments, the company's working capital, share option schemes in place or to be put in place by the company, the company's property interests, any litigation with which the company is involved, material contracts (outside the ordinary course of business) involving the company and taxation.

The persons responsible for the prospectus include the company and the directors personally. This includes a general duty of disclosure in addition to requirements in respect of the contents of the prospectus. In order to satisfy this general duty, the prospectus must contain all such information as investors and their professional advisers would reasonably require, and reasonably expect to find, for the purpose of making an informed assessment of:

(a) the assets and liabilities, financial position, profits and losses and prospects of the issue of the securities; and
(b) the rights attaching to those securities.

It is not sufficient that each statement in the prospectus document is factually accurate. Liability may also arise not only for untrue information but also for misleading information or omissions.

Potential liability areas

(a) Pursuant to Regulation 14 of the POS Regulations, the persons responsible for the prospectus may be liable to pay compensation to any person who acquires any of the securities concerned and who suffers loss in respect of those securities as a result of any untrue or misleading statement in the prospectus or the omission from it of any matter which should have been included under the general duty of disclosure referred to above.
(b) The directors of the company may also incur civil liability under the placing or underwriting agreement, details of which are set out

later in this chapter. Such agreement is likely to contain warranties, representations and indemnities from the directors of the company given to the sponsor or merchant bank acting on behalf of the company. In the event that there is a breach of any of the warranties, representations and indemnities, the sponsor or merchant bank would be entitled to claim damages from the directors on behalf of purchasers or subscribers for securities for any losses that they suffer.

(c) A director may also incur liability at common law in relation to the prospectus for deceit or negligence in its preparation.

(d) Criminal liability. Under Section 47(a) FSA it is an offence for a person i) to make a statement, promise or forecast which he knows to be misleading, false or deceptive, or ii) dishonestly to conceal any material fact, or iii) recklessly to make (dishonestly or otherwise) a statement, promise or forecast which is misleading, false or deceptive if he does so for the purpose of inducing, or is reckless as to whether it may induce, another person to enter into or offer to enter into an investment agreement. An offence pursuant to this section can be committed if a person makes a false or misleading statement 'recklessly', even though he does not realise that it is false or misleading. Case law in this area has established that a person is 'reckless' if, before doing an act, he either fails to give any thought to the possibility of there being a risk of harmful consequences or having recognised that there is a risk of harmful consequences such that an ordinary prudent individual would not feel justified in ignoring, nevertheless goes on to do it.

(e) Section 19 Theft Act 1968 makes it a criminal offence for any officer of a company to publish, with intent to deceive its members or creditors about its affairs, a written statement or account which 'to his knowledge is or may be misleading, false or deceptive in a material particular'.

(f) Section 57 FSA 1986 prohibits the issue of an 'investment advertisement' unless it has been approved or issued by 'an authorised person' under the FSA. An investment advertisement includes any form of advertisement, whether written or oral, which, broadly, either invites persons to enter into an investment agreement or contains information which is calculated to lead directly or indirectly to a person entering into an investment agreement. There are both civil and criminal sanctions for breach of Section 57 and any investment agreement entered into pursuant to an unauthorised investment advertisement will be unenforceable and any sums paid as a consequence are recoverable. Compensation may also be payable for any loss suffered.

Verification

In view of the potential liabilities set out above, it is essential that every director should believe, and should have reasonable grounds for believing, that:

(a) each item of information contained in the prospectus is not only in accordance with the facts, but is also not misleading in its context;
(b) all expressions of opinions are reasonably based and properly held;
(c) the prospectus gives all such information as is necessary to give a true and fair view of the company's business prospects and nothing has been omitted which is necessary to enable investors to make an 'informed assessment' of the company.

In order to satisfy the directors' obligations, a process called 'verification' is carried out in respect of the prospectus and any placing proofs that are issued to prospective placees prior to publication of the final form prospectus. It is therefore standard practice to prepare detailed verification notes effectively proving each and every statement in the prospectus, ideally by external authoritative sources, and explaining and justifying the basis upon which any statements of opinion are based. The purpose of these notes is to record the source of each fact and the person responsible for checking its accuracy such that a permanent record is then retained in the event of a claim under any of the provisions referred to above.

Material changes

If, between the issue of the prospectus and the commencement of dealing in the securities on any market, a director becomes aware of any significant new matter or change affecting any matter contained in the prospectus, that director must immediately inform the company and the sponsor or merchant bank with a view to considering whether it is necessary to issue a supplementary prospectus.

One of the purposes of the prospectus is to ensure that all potential investors are given equality of information relating to the company upon which to base any decision to invest. It is therefore imperative that internal systems are established such that none of the directors or senior employees gives information to a potential investor which is not contained within the prospectus or otherwise made available to all with a view to influencing that investor's decision as to whether or not to apply for shares.

Placing agreement/underwriting agreement

Another key document in the flotation process will be the placing or underwriting agreement to be entered into between the company, its directors and the merchant bank.

Under the terms of a placing agreement, the merchant bank or issuing house will agree to use its reasonable endeavours to procure subscribers for the shares at a set placing price. The company appoints the merchant bankers as agents to procure contracts for subscription of shares between investors and the company.

In the case of an underwriting agreement or, indeed, an underwritten placing, the underwriter or merchant bank will agree not only to use reasonable endeavours to find investors for the shares, but also to underwrite the investment, ie to purchase any shares which are not taken up by investors. This latter method, while clearly a more expensive option for a company seeking admission, at least guarantees the raising of the funds sought.

As mentioned above, a placing or underwriting agreement will also contain indemnities given by the directors to the merchant bank in respect of:

(a) breaches of the Yellow Book rules and any other statute or statutory regulation in relation to admission;
(b) inaccuracies in the prospectus;
(c) any liability incurred by the merchant bank in carrying out its obligations and duties under the placing or underwriting.

In addition, it is common practice for the directors and the company to provide the merchant bank with warranties that:

(a) the prospectus is accurate and not misleading;
(b) the financial information is accurate;

(c) since the date of the last audited accounts of the company there has been no material adverse change in the financial or trading prospects of the company;
(d) the company is properly insured and holds all licences necessary for the continuation of its business;
(e) there is no litigation ongoing against the company save as disclosed in the prospectus;
(f) the company's tax affairs are in order and up to date.

Orderly market

It is also common for a merchant bank or a sponsor to insist upon provisions relating to an orderly market for dealings in the shares of the company. This may be dealt with within the body of the placing or underwriting agreement or by means of a separate orderly market agreement if intended to catch shareholders who are not also directors. Effectively, the agreement places a restriction on the parties to it not to sell all or a proportion of their shares in the company for a particular period of time without the consent of the merchant bank. Its purpose is to prevent the dumping of shares and a potential collapse of the market for that company's shares within a period of 1–2 years following flotation.

Continuing obligations of directors

Once the company's shares have been admitted to dealing on a recognised investment exchange, there are then further substantial requirements placed upon the directors. While the purpose of this chapter is designed to deal with the process leading to flotation, it should be noted that these continuing obligations include:

(a) reporting requirements to the company announcements office of the London Stock Exchange of any major developments, financial condition changes or other price-sensitive information;
(b) directors' interests and those of any connected person of the director in the securities;
(c) changes to the board of the company;
(d) publication of annual and half-yearly accounts;
(e) dividends and any other distributions in relation to the shares.

Furthermore, the company becomes subject to the provisions set out in the City Code on Takeovers and Mergers in respect of any acquisition or disposal which it may undertake and/or material changes in its shareholder base. The City Code and Yellow Book primarily set out these provisions.

In addition, the company is obliged to adopt the Model Code for Share Dealing by its directors and certain of its employees. The Model Code's principal requirements are:

(a) a director must not deal in any securities of the company on considerations of a short-term nature;
(b) a director must not deal in any securities during the company's close period, namely prior to announcement of annual or half-yearly reports;
(c) a director must not deal in any security of the company while in possession of unpublished price-sensitive information.

Conclusion

To conclude, while the flotation process is undoubtedly a material step in the history of any company, it is also a time-consuming and testing period for those involved. A strict timetable will be established at the outset of the flotation process, an example of which is set out in Table 4.4.1 (overleaf), and any directors involved must take great care to obtain advice on their obligations in light of the substantive liabilities which they could incur.

Table 4.4.1 Timetable for listing

Preliminary	• Appointment of professional advisers • Company's constitution changed (if necessary) • Accountants' long-form report commissioned • First draft of prospectus compiled • Impact date booked with Bank of England (if applicable)
D –60	• Long-form report available • Drafting meetings for prospectus
D –30	• Completion EGM convened • Verification process begun • Draft prospectus submitted to Stock Exchange for its consideration
D –14	• '14-day documents' submitted to Stock Exchange include: – prospectus; – application forms to subscribe for shares; and – accountants' reports
D –3	• Completion EGM held
D –1	• Final version of verification noted approved by board • Completion board meeting held • Final version of prospectus submitted to Stock Exchange • Price of shares finalised
D (Impact Day)	• Offer for sale agreement exchanged • Stock Exchange approves prospectus • Prospectus registered at Companies House • Underwriting arrangements completed • Sub-underwriting letters sent to sub-underwriters
D + 2	• Publication and advertising
D + 3	• '48-hour documents' submitted to Stock Exchange
D + 5	• Application for listing heard by Stock Exchange
D + 6	• Application lists opened and closed
D + 7	• Basis of allotment announced
D + 12	• Letters of acceptance or rejection posted to investors
D + 13	• Admission to listing on Stock Exchange effective • Dealings in shares commence
D + 53	• Last day for splitting letters of acceptance
D + 55	• Last day for registration of letters of acceptance

4.5

Public-to-Private Transactions are Here to Stay

Charles Milner
KPMG Corporate Finance

Private equity-backed public-to-private (PTP) transactions have been on the increase in recent years. The total value of PTP transactions rose from £3 billion in 1998 to £8.9 billion in 2000, almost a 70 per cent increase. While the year 2000 total included the largest single PTP transaction yet recorded (£3.5 billion for property group MEPC), the trend is nevertheless set to continue. By value, PTP transactions in 2000 constituted some 50 per cent of total transaction value in the United Kingdom for transactions with a value of £10 million or more. Not only is this trend here to stay, but with in excess of 1,500 listed companies with a market capitalisation of less than £250 million, there are also plenty of potential targets.

Institutional shareholders have made it very clear over the last 2–3 years that, when it comes to the smaller end of the market, they are more than pleased to consider the changes of ownership represented by companies moving out of the public market place and into private ownership. It has become increasingly less efficient and less attractive to invest in smaller capitalised companies.

While the PTP market could not be described as mature, there have been an increasing number of transactions undertaken since the first of the recent wave of these transactions in 1997, when Electra Fleming bid for William Cook plc as part of its 'white knight' defence strategy against an unwelcome bid. Certain private equity houses, banks and advisers now have strong track records in handling PTP deals, this familiarity further facilitating the current strong flow of these transactions.

Candidates for PTP

As the recent KPMG survey into investment in smaller quoted companies (SQCs) has confirmed this year, 90 per cent of this group fall well below the ideal minimum market capitalisation desired by institutional investors. Fund managers increasingly find themselves under pressure to invest ever-larger sums of money in bigger, more liquid stocks. Despite the SQCs' strong performance in the market, their stocks are too illiquid – often due to shares being held by family members or one major shareholder – and do not bring the returns required to warrant fund managers researching and reporting on them. With investment prospects fairly remote and retaining a listing both relatively expensive and restrictive, more and more SQCs are contemplating de-listing. As an aside, this also accounts in part for the dramatic decline in initial public offerings (IPOs) seen in 2001, with reported activity at its the lowest level for over a decade. As an exit route for private equity investors, if the stock is not in the technology, media and telecommunications sectors the prospect of an IPO is clearly worse than it was, for example, 2–3 years ago.

For companies that are experiencing short-term trading problems but have a sound business plan, this inability to raise funds from their investor base also makes it increasingly attractive to seek private equity investment through a PTP transaction, particularly if bank lending is also close to loan facility limits. There are also a few niche companies to be found that are reverting to private ownership – whose business and/or largely entrepreneurial management style does not fit well within the public market or which perceive the market as either disinterested or consistently undervaluing their business – and which perhaps should not have gone to the market in the first place.

Key factors in a PTP transaction

A disparate shareholder base will create difficulties. One rule of thumb is that the top six shareholders should cover a good proportion of all equity votes – ideally at least 50 per cent. This means that you have relatively fewer parties to approach at the relevant stage in the process and have the opportunity to build up a strong percentage of irrevocable undertakings to accept the proposed offer.

The reasons for choosing a PTP route can be varied – a shortage of capital, management succession gaps, family shareholders seeking an exit, or perhaps the need for acquisitions are among those most commonly cited. Over and above the premiums that shareholders are likely to achieve on the market value of their holdings, presenting a coherent case for a PTP can be half the battle in allaying any possible suspicions about the proposed deal and in gaining support from shareholders, staff, analysts and the media.

In the past, bidding for public companies entailed an acceptance of limited due diligence. This contrasted with private equity investors' needs for very full due diligence prior to investing. The process is now well understood by those with experience of PTP transactions, including the manner in which proper due diligence may be completed prior to the making of an offer.

There is a belief in some quarters that the proposition of a PTP transaction is enough to motivate investor interest. This is clearly not the case – you still need to look at the business plan; make sure that you have a strong management team in its own right; and have a view on the eventual exit. These will need to be in place before a private equity house will seriously entertain a deal.

Given that a number of PTP propositions come about because a company is experiencing trading difficulties, you need to be clear that it is because the market is against you, and not that the incumbent management is the root of the problem. Private equity investors would be looking for returns on their capital and would require to be persuaded that the adverse trading can be corrected in the short to medium term.

Management buy-ins are virtually a non-starter in this sector of the market since outside management will not be deemed to have sufficient knowledge of the business to execute the PTP successfully. However, nowadays the incumbent management team is often supplemented by external managers who are perhaps well known within the industry, have the relevant contact base (or have been backed before) and therefore have a track record with the private equity investors. This creation of the team – a buy-in management buy-out or 'BIMBO' – has certainly become more common. Further, the private equity investors will usually wish to appoint one or more independent non-executive directors to the board of the company.

The price of PTP

You also need to look at the type of premium that will need to be paid in order to take a company private. The premium currently attributed to the quoted price of the equity ranges on average between some 38 and 44 per cent, although clearly worked out on a case-by-case basis depending on prevailing circumstances. The price of the shares, including any premium, together with any debt to be refinanced plus the costs of executing the PTP, will add up to the total sum to be funded.

The way in which a prospect is reviewed by a private equity institution is fundamentally exactly the same whether it is private or public; the only difference with a PTP transaction is in the process that has to be undertaken in order to complete the deal involving many technical issues, all of which must be addressed. These include obtaining access to information, due care in holding discussions with potential backers and the taking of security by the banks backing the PTP. In all cases, the takeover panel will be consulted at an early stage.

A number of additional parties will be involved in a PTP transaction who would not usually be involved in a non-PTP situation. They include communications and PR firms, share registrars and company brokers. Their activities, together with the requirements to produce certain public offer and related documentation, have an impact on the overall costs of PTP transactions. The overall level of costs involved in taking a company private can therefore accumulate and any transaction below £20 million should be reviewed in this respect (ie the proportion of costs in relation to the overall deal becomes increasingly high below this level).

Beyond 2001

With a potentially inexorable shift in funding from institutional investors to private equity houses, the prospects for companies seeking to go private by this route are constantly improving. Private equity investors are different types of owners and will want to be close to the businesses in which they invest. Those with proven track records will bring with them the experience to create better businesses for the market and for managers and employees.

One cannot ignore the current downturn in economic activity, although perhaps this time round it will not be as deep as has been the case in the past. In contrast to the recession of the early 1980s, the United Kingdom is at virtually full employment and interest rates appear to be sustainably low. Vendor price expectations will certainly need to realign but the reality is that starker economic conditions also create new opportunities. Such opportunities will be taken up by private equity investors, particularly given the significant levels of funds raised over recent years. Within these opportunities there will be PTP transactions which will remain a feature of the private equity landscape for the foreseeable future.

Part Five

Mergers and Acquisitions

5.1
Buying a Business

David Houghton
TMG Corporate Finance

Introduction

UK merger and acquisition activity totalled approximately £329 billion during 2000, consisting of 3,049 deals (source: Thompson Financial Securities Data).

Trends in deal activity generally coincide with the wider economic situation; merger and acquisition (M&A) activity levels are often subject to the availability of new external funding in both the private and public equity markets, which in turn is dependent upon economic confidence in the United Kingdom and abroad.

Recently, economic conditions in the world's largest economy, the United States, deteriorated significantly as both sales and production weakened. In response, US interest rates were cut to ease the debt burden and stimulate a recovery in equity prices.

Changes in the US economy have been reflected in a more moderate slow down in the United Kingdom and the Eurozone.

Predictions for the UK economy indicate that it will achieve a relatively soft landing, in line with the latest Treasury consensus forecast for 2001. Hence, it is hoped that activity in the UK M&A market will be only moderately affected in the short and medium term.

Motives for buying

The rationale for buying businesses usually includes one or more of the following:

- consolidation – purchase of a competitor to strengthen a company's position, by increasing their critical mass and hence their buying power;
- market protection – defensive move to prevent another competitor buying the same target;
- diversification – through the purchase of a company in a related industry, a purchaser can diversify their product range, cross-selling related products to new customers in the same market sectors;
- new markets – widening geographic coverage, through the purchase of a business located in new markets;
- synergies – a common theme running through all corporate acquisition strategies is that of synergistic benefits, ie cost savings by amalgamating overheads and stripping out any inappropriate duplication;
- market value enhancement – in the quoted company market, prices paid for businesses should result in an enhancement in the value of the newly formed group, beyond the sum of the two separate parts, ie the multiple of profits paid for the target should be less than the trading multiple of the purchaser, therefore immediately enhancing the value of the purchaser's enlarged group;
- Management buy-outs and management buy-ins (MBOs and MBIs) – existing or new management teams seeking to buy businesses and grow them under their own strategies;
- institutional purchases – financial institutions buying businesses to add to existing investments, or to back new management teams – normally with a view to selling in the medium term.

Notwithstanding the above logical reasons for purchasing a business, almost every acquisition leads to problems beyond those envisaged. Integrating different management teams with different cultures and ideals and achieving effective cross-selling and efficiencies can be a lengthy process. Getting it wrong can be disastrous and many ill-advised purchases have brought down substantial groups in the past.

Valuing a business

Owner-managed sector

There are two principal methods for valuing a private limited business. The first is based on a company's net assets and is usually applied where the profit stream has been erratic, where losses have been incurred, or where the future of the business is highly dependent on the owner-manager's personal relationships with providers of work. In these circumstances, a price for goodwill is hard to justify.

The second method is based on the expected future profit stream. This is usually applied when the company has a profitable track record and the business is of such a size that it is the company name and reputation, rather than that of its owners, which is the main reason it continues to gain new business.

Although price is critical, other considerations such as loss of business independence and the long-term interests of employees are often just as important to the vendor. Where family businesses are concerned, there may also be a number of shareholders involved who have differing requirements.

Public company sector

A quoted company's value is publicly available and is equivalent to its share price, as traded on the stock market, multiplied by the number of shares in issue, ie its market capitalisation. Shares are traded at prices that reflect the market's view of the future growth prospects of that stock. When buying a publicly quoted company, the purchaser generally pays a price which includes a premium above its quoted price, to entice the shareholders into selling.

Structuring a purchase

Deals generally involve a combination of cash, shares and deferred consideration; it is rare for a purchaser to pay the full consideration in cash at completion.

Shares in the new combined business may well be attractive to a vendor if, for example, they are ordinary shares in a quoted company and the vendor has banked or guaranteed a substantial amount of their consideration already.

Purchasers and their financiers generally prefer a structure that involves the vendor deferring a tranche of their consideration, payable at a future date. The deferral is often in the form of loan notes or redeemable preference shares, which often attract returns greater than the vendor could achieve in the external market place. The issue here is to make the vendor comfortable that their deferred consideration will be as safe as reasonably possible. This is often achieved by the vendor remaining involved in a consultancy capacity post-acquisition, for example, until their deferred consideration is realised.

Another term often used in deal structures is 'earn out'. This arrangement is often employed where the target company has considerable growth potential in the short term but needs an alliance with a larger organisation in order to achieve it, for example. The target's existing shareholders often remain with the company post-deal and hence continue to influence its growth. Consequently, a deal for their shares involving a ratchet, triggered by certain levels of future profitability, is often appropriate to both sides.

Interestingly, the introduction of taper relief for capital gains tax over the last few years, has led many vendors to prefer deferring their consideration, as the effective tax rate falls to as little as 10 per cent by April 2002. Consequently, vendors wishing to crystallise the value of their shares over the last couple of years, but not suffer higher rates of tax, have opted to defer their consideration usually into some form of fully secured instrument, to be realised at future dates.

Enfranchising the target's management

Ensuring that the management team of the target, who are often nervous about what life is going to be like post-acquisition, are fully on board and incentivised properly to take the business forward is key to any successful purchase. Without cohesive senior management teams sharing the same goals, any integration is going to be fraught.

The introduction of a suitable share option scheme is commonly used, giving individuals a feeling of personal financial participation in the future growth of the business. Numerous Inland Revenue-approved schemes exist, varying from widely recognised quoted company schemes to, say, employee benefit trusts in private limited companies and 'phantom share option schemes', which are effectively bonus arrangements with favourable tax structures.

Funding an acquisition

Owner-managed sector

The three principal sources of external acquisition finance are debt, equity and mezzanine. The right mix of funding is key to providing the foundation for success post-acquisition; appropriate gearing levels are crucial to avoid overstretching the company's finances. A strong working relationship with the funders is also required and therefore partnering with the right group of funders is also essential.

Debt

Debt finance, ie secured lending against a company's assets that attracts interest, can be structured in many different ways ranging from traditional overdraft and term facilities with a bank, to more specialised asset-based facilities and revolving credit arrangements. The level of debt facilities offered by lenders is based upon future cash flow projections and asset cover.

Equity

Equity finance does not carry any security and normally attracts dividend income, not interest. It is also longer-term, often involving no repayments of capital in the early years. However, to balance the risk of being unsecured, the reward is considerably more than that of a debt provider. Returns in the order of 30–35 per cent per year are generally sought by equity investors and hence the growth profile of the businesses post-acquisition needs to be substantial.

Equity investment, in funding purchases of businesses in the owner-managed sector, comes mainly from the venture capital (VC) market and to a much lesser extent from private individuals, ie 'business angels'. There are several hundred venture capital organisations in the United Kingdom, including subsidiary divisions of large UK and overseas banks, plus numerous independent equity houses. Venture capital funds come from a cross section of sources including the parent bank if appropriate, other financial institutions including pension funds and insurance companies, and internally generated funds. Where external funding is utilised, the funds borrowed are normally over a term of up to 10 years. Therefore, VC providers usually look to exit their investments within five years on average.

Mezzanine

Mezzanine finance has evolved during the recent past and is now offered by a number of leading banks and independent organisations. In essence, this type of finance falls between debt and equity in that it generally involves an interest-bearing investment, sometimes with a secondary charge over the business' assets, and carries a higher rate of return than debt but less than equity.

Public company funding

Public companies source their acquisition finance from debt, equity and internally generated funds. The structure of the debt element is similar to that of the owner-managed business sector, while the equity is raised via an offering of new shares on the stock market, often in the form of a rights issue to existing shareholders.

Steps to buying a business

Appoint an adviser

Buying and integrating a business is usually fraught with difficulties and frustration and is a critical time in the life of any business. The process of negotiation with the vendors, arranging new borrowing facilities, undertaking due diligence and project management of the whole process, is extremely time-consuming and should be undertaken by an external firm of professional advisers, leaving the purchaser's management team to get on with running their business.

An adviser's role is also to add significant value to the process when negotiating the pricing and structuring of a transaction. Previous experience and a lateral approach should produce a creative structure for the purchasers which hedges their risks as far as possible, while at the same time also satisfying the vendors' requirements.

Discussions with the target

Companies often approach the acquisition market with an open brief on the type of business they are looking to buy. Therefore, the role of the professional adviser in this first instance is to assist in developing a shortlist of potential acquisitions from their knowledge of the market, supplemented by extensive research. Confidential targeting of a proposed shortlist of businesses is then performed by the adviser. When a preferred target has been identified, negotiation will take place with a view to securing an agreed head of terms.

Confidentiality agreements should be secured at the outset, prior to the exchange of any sensitive information, in order to protect the parties involved.

From the purchaser's point of view, exclusivity should also be secured as soon as possible to prevent the target entering discussions with any other parties while the purchaser is concluding the deal and incurring fees.

Confirming viability of the deal

Having identified the appropriate target, the purchaser's management needs to confirm in detail the commercial strength and financial fit of the organisations. Typical questions to ask include:

- what synergies and earnings enhancements can be achieved?
- what cross-selling can be done?
- how will the market respond?
- what return on capital invested will be achieved and when?
- how will buying power be affected?
- how can facilities be integrated?

A detailed business case and plan should be prepared in support of the deal, encompassing each of the above issues and highlighting the risks.

Funding

Naturally, acquisition finance needs to be secured where appropriate, based on the business plan and detailed financial projections. Presentations to existing and other appropriate financial institutions are given in conjunction with the purchaser's advisers.

Due diligence

Appropriate due diligence is crucial to highlighting any major issues, to help protect the purchaser's position and help them gain further knowledge, including:

- Financial due diligence, focused on understanding the trading profile of the business and its asset and liability dynamics; typical areas of focus include stock pricing methods and levels of provisioning. A review of accounting policies should also be undertaken to highlight any significant differences to the purchasers and how that will impact on future results if the policies need realignment.

- Revaluations of significant balance sheet assets are often performed to confirm their carrying values or development potential.
- A review of the tax position is essential to ensure that there are no substantial liabilities not reflected in the company's accounts and that all appropriate statutory filings are up to date.
- Pensions due diligence is usually very important to ascertain whether the target company's scheme is fully funded and confirm that there are no substantial liabilities to make good any deficits. Final salary or defined benefit schemes require very careful consideration; potential future additional contributions to make good underperforming stocks and shares can be considerable. This area of concern has proved a 'deal breaker' on many occasions in the past. It is also important to understand how the target company's pension scheme will be incorporated within the purchaser's existing scheme.
- Environmental issues can often be crucial to an acquisition and a full-scale review of environmental issues is often required.
- Commercial due diligence is also normally undertaken to consider market conditions, competitor and customer profiles.
- Legal due diligence is undertaken to ensure that property matters, employee issues and all statutory matters are in order.

Overview of the sale and purchase agreement (SPA)

The sale and purchase agreement (SPA) is usually drafted by the purchaser's lawyers. It is this important document that sets out the terms of the contract.

The principal areas of the SPA will include consideration, restrictive covenants and warranties.

Consideration

The terms and nature of the consideration will be set out, identifying which shareholders receive what and when.

Restrictive covenants

If the vendors are leaving the company upon completion, or if they leave in the future, the purchaser needs to protect against the vendor setting up in competition and enticing existing employees and contacts away. The SPA should provide appropriate restrictions against this scenario.

Warranties

Purchaser protections will also be incorporated through the vendors giving warranties against the integrity of information supplied, including the company's accounts, asset and liability values, pensions, employee matters, environmental issues and property matters. The timeframe for making a warranty claim is generally 2–3 years.

Protection against any future unprovided tax liabilities are covered by a separate tax deed, which normally runs for six or seven years.

The extent of vendors' liability to warranty claims is usually limited to the amount of cash consideration paid. Whether the warranties are shared jointly and/or severally between the vendors is down to the individual circumstances of the deal.

Each purchase is completed in the hope that the SPA is filed away and never tested. However, although negotiations usually commence and complete in an amicable fashion, a purchaser needs to tread very carefully throughout the whole process of buying a business. It is not normally something most business people do very often during their careers, and it is therefore essential that proper professional advice is taken, appropriate diligence is carried out and protection, so far as is reasonably possible, is secured during and after the deal.

5.2

Thinking of Selling Your Business?

Tony Sharp
KPMG Corporate Finance

For many, the sale of a private company is the culmination of a lifetime's work. More often than not, this will be a once in a lifetime transaction – with only the one opportunity to get it right.

This chapter contains answers to the 12 most frequently asked questions put to KPMG Corporate Finance about selling a business. The role of an independent financial adviser is usually integral to responding appropriately to the questions asked.

When is a good time to sell my business?

Timing, of course, is vital.

An objective overview should be taken of your business, your industry sector and the overall economic picture, to assess if and when it is a good time to sell. Some circumstances make it easier to sell a business regardless of timing – for example, if you operate a niche market with good contacts or have an excellent customer base.

Almost without exception, a good-quality business should sell.

An independent adviser can undertake such a review for you, and if they think the timing is wrong, you will be told so. The very best of impartial advisers have built their reputation on providing realistic quality advice and not on chasing goals for short-term gain.

How much is my business worth?

There is only one way to accurately value a business – sell it! All other methods hold a degree of subjectivity, not least because they involve taking a view of the future and, logically, not everyone shares the same view.

However, to assess the value of your business, you need to consider a number of factors – track record, future potential profit trends, competitors' actions, net assets and property values. In addition, the most recent deals in the same sector give a useful indication of the price that potential buyers might pay; this information will be provided by a dedicated valuations team.

An adviser's experience of selling businesses, allied to the knowledge they have of sales across a wide range of sectors, enables them to provide you with a good indication of how much your business is worth before you make a commitment to sell.

How long does it take to sell a business?

Typically, the sales process takes 4–6 months. However, there is no given formula to predict how long it will take, and thus some businesses will sell in a matter of weeks while others will take much longer.

Once your personal objectives are clearly defined and the key business issues identified, you should be able to gain a frank assessment of the timescales involved.

Whatever the time frame, you need an adviser who will stay involved throughout, enabling you to continue running your business right up until completion, ensuring that you realise the full value of the business.

Do I need to do any preparation?

Owners are able to significantly impact the price achieved upon sale by careful planning. It is never too early for a business owner or owners to start to plan for the eventual route out of, or succession to, the business. All businesses need to consider how best to position themselves to maximise the value or benefit to the shareholders.

Apart from the obvious need to sell a business at the point in the economic cycle when company disposals are likely to be successful, owners need to ensure that the business is appropriately groomed for exit.

An adviser will assess when the business is ready to sell and provide advice on the practical steps that you may need to take in order to help maximise value.

Can I sell the business discreetly and in confidence?

Yes, in all likelihood, but confidentiality is vital; a fine balance is needed between preventing knowledge of an impending sale leaking to customers and staff and, at the same time, ensuring that they do not hear the news from a third party. Both scenarios can prove damaging to goodwill and loyalty.

Most advisers will recommend, and can help you put in place, a communications plan to pre-empt any such eventualities.

How do I find a buyer if I don't advertise?

The answer is that you don't – your adviser does through a number of sources.

Your adviser will have an in-depth knowledge of acquisition companies, and will be in regular contact with colleagues in their counterpart's offices across the country and their international networks worldwide. In addition, the major advisory firms employ dedicated research analysts to track deal activity, and they will know who is going to be interested in buying your business.

How does the sales process work?

Typically, the sales process goes through a number of stages:

- planning and preparation – preparing the business for sale, drafting an information memorandum about the business, researching potential buyers;

- marketing and negotiations – distributing the information memorandum, evaluating interest levels, receiving offers, negotiating and reaching agreement in principle;
- contracts and completion – contract drafting by lawyers, final tax restructuring, overseeing purchasers' due diligence, completion of sale.

What do I need to tell a buyer?

Great care is required in preparing an information memorandum and controlling the release of information to prospective buyers. Too little or too much information, or the wrong emphasis in the wrong place, can have adverse consequences.

During a sale, buyers are provided with sufficient commercial and financial information to enable them to determine the amount that they are prepared to bid for the business.

What about my tax position?

There is both good and not so good news. The not so good news is that the sale may result in a capital gain for tax purposes. The good news is that a relief has been introduced which operates to reduce the marginal rate of tax in respect of capital transactions. The tax rate will depend on how long you have held the shares and whether they qualify for business asset or no business asset taper relief.

With careful planning the tax charge may be deferred and/or reduced.

The deal management team will include dedicated tax specialists whose job it is to ensure that you are left with the maximum net proceeds.

What about my role, and that of my workforce, after the sale?

Your position depends very much on your own wishes and the requirements of the buyer; it is not unusual to have a handover period, but the length of time can vary enormously. If you have strong views on what you want to do, these can be incorporated into discussions at an early stage.

In common with most employers, you will probably feel responsible for your employees. However, agreeing provisions to safeguard employee interests, over and above statutory entitlements, is not always easy. One of the best ways of ensuring a satisfactory outcome for your employees is to make sure that the business goes to 'the right home'. Assessments of prospective buyers will help you achieve this.

When do I receive the proceeds from the sale?

You can receive the proceeds of the sale in a number of ways – eg cash, loan notes or shares in the buyer – which will need to be established. However, unless the deal is subject to an earn-out (ie when the price is linked to future profits), a significant proportion (if not all) of the proceeds should be handed over to you on completion of the sale.

What are the risks?

There will always be risks associated with selling your business. Perhaps the most common is committing time and expense if a deal aborts for whatever reason.

However, working with a top-quality adviser ensures an independent and honest assessment of the risks and rewards right from the start. At all times, you remain in control of the transaction and can put a hold on the deal if your situation changes during the sale process.

The principal risk is underselling your business and that is one risk that an adviser will try to ensure you do not take.

5.3

Valuation

Christopher Gasson
Bertoli Mitchell

Introduction

There is only one way to value a company accurately: sell it. All other methods involve a degree of subjectivity not least because they involve taking a view of the future – who is to say that there is a buyer in the market who shares that view?

Of course nobody wants to go as far as selling a business to get an idea of its value. That said, it has to be remembered that mathematical methods of valuation can be manipulated where necessary:

- An unscrupulous broker asked to value a business, as part of a beauty parade to select a firm to handle the sale, will calculate a value based on the highest figure they can quote without stretching their credibility.
- Financial advisers asked to value a business for tax reasons or for the purpose of valuing a minority shareholding may well calculate the lowest value they think they can justify.
- Venture capitalists investing in established companies can reach absurdly low valuations to ensure that they obtain the largest possible shareholding for the smallest possible investment.
- More acceptably high and low valuations can be bandied about during the sale of a business, as the buyer and seller attempt to massage the expectations of the other.

Making different valuations, based on different assumptions, is, in fact, essential to the sale process:

- They can tell an executive how much a business is worth to his or her company, and therefore inform the maximum amount he or she should be prepared to pay for it or, in different circumstances, the minimum amount he or she should accept to sell it.
- They can tell an executive how much other bidders at an auction might be prepared to bid for a business, enabling him or her to decide on a bid which is high enough to secure the asset, but still low enough to ensure there is a margin of profit from acquiring the business.
- They can tell an executive how his or her shareholders might view an acquisition: whether they would consider it to be a good investment or a bad investment.

However, it is the determination of the market price today that is the aim of most valuations.

In publicly quoted companies, whose shares are regularly traded on the Stock Exchange, this valuation can be calculated very simply by multiplying up the share price by the number of shares in issue.

Everyone else has to use one of the subjective methods: discounted cash flow, price ratios, or asset based. The only way they can ensure that the valuation they obtain is as close to being objective as possible is to make sure that the assumptions are as objectively sustainable as possible.

Even then, one has to accept that the valuation reached is going to be justified for a very short space of time. Just as share prices on the stock exchange change daily as assumptions about future earnings change, so should valuations calculated by mathematical methods.

It is also important to remember that markets are far from perfect. While the auction process has become more widespread, and the expansion of the private equity sector has meant that there are always financial buyers around to pick up under-valued assets, there are still a number of obstacles to the establishment of a free market in businesses:

- *Businesses are not alike and interchangeable*: some will command a premium because they are unique, others will be ignored because they do not fit in, regardless of the financial value they could deliver.

- *There are fashions in corporate strategy*: vertical and horizontal integration, globalisation and empowerment focus have all created waves of corporate activity which have rarely had a long-term effect on earnings, but have had significant short-term effects on valuation.
- *Auctions are often oligopolistic*: usually there will be only three or four serious buyers. If their ability is impaired for any reason (such as they are between chief executives, or they have just made a big bid for something else) then the final auction price will be affected.
- *Information is not perfect*: buying a business is always going to be something of a lucky dip. The price paid will always depend on how much of a risk the various buyers are prepared to take.
- *Management makes a difference*: it is often difficult to separate the value of a business from the value of its management. One can buy one but not always the other.
- *Auctions are not open*: the fact that most auctions have to be carried out in conditions of secrecy means that some potential buyers will be excluded.

The result is that the price that a business realises on sale is often more a matter of chance than the financial value of the business.

It is for this reason that executives regularly involved in assessing the value of businesses tend to rely on instincts and rules of thumb rather than the more intellectually sound methods of valuation recommended by valuation professionals. In fact, many valuation professionals also rely on rules of thumb (such as sales multiples) and then justify their findings using more highfalutin methods such as discounted cash flow analysis.

Valuation methods

The three main methods of valuation are:

- *Discounted cash flow* (sometimes called the Capital Asset Pricing Model or CAP-M) is based on the idea that a company is worth as much as the net present value of the cash flows generated by a company for distributing around its shareholders.
- *Price multiples* compare the price per pound of the sales or profits between companies to illustrate how a business might be priced.
- *Asset-based valuations* price the balance sheet assets of a business separately to reach the value of the whole.

Discounted cash flow (DCF) valuation is theoretically the most pure. It keeps the mind focused on the actual value of the cash benefits derived from ownership rather than what other people might pay for a business. The main weakness is that it is highly dependent on forecasts. In fact in many cases it is necessary to be able to forecast more than 10 years into the future before one has a valuation which is any more accurate than a simple price multiple method. Consequently, DCF valuation tends to be used primarily within companies for the purposes of determining strategy. Consultants recommend using it as a means of assessing which course of action is most likely to build shareholder value.

Where one does not have full information about operations it is usually very difficult to carry out a DCF accurately.

Price multiples are the most widely used method of valuation. In fact, because they are so widely used, they are often the most reliable means of predicting the market price of a business. They are easy to use, and they do not require a great deal of information about the operation to be applied. Different multiples are used in different situations. Trade buyers, who tend to have a very strong idea about the profitability of businesses within their sector, often prefer to use sales multiples, although they do rely on instinct for their accuracy.

P/e (price to earnings) ratios enable one to compare the price of a pound of profit across different businesses. On the face of it they are more rigorous than sales multiples, although they do not take different accounting treatments into account, and often fail to predict what a trade buyer, who is in a position to alter the cost base of the business, might be prepared to pay. P/e ratios are the most widely used method of valuation among stockbrokers because they make it possible to compare the financial benefits of holding different shares.

Asset-based valuations are used only where the value of a business is easily expressed in terms of its assets. Where the primary assets are intangible, such as brands, copyrights, human capital, or goodwill, then asset-based valuations are less popular (or, if they are used, it is in conjunction with another valuation method). Investment trusts, property companies, mining companies, and other businesses whose assets have a clear market value are suitable for asset-based valuation.

Capital structure

The capital structure of a business will include both debt and equity. For some purposes, such as making investment or divestment decisions within a company, it is important to obtain a value of the unlevered company (ie as if it had no debt). In other circumstances, such as when one is buying a business complete with debtors and creditors, it is necessary to value the levered company.

The difference in the value of the levered and the unlevered company is not just the value of the debt. The debt will bring with it interest tax shields which have a value in themselves, and it will also impose a different risk profile on the equity. The more debt, the more risky the equity.

It would be wrong to ignore the difference between the value of the levered company and the value of the unlevered company, even in a crude valuation. However, it may be justifiable to avoid calculating the value of the interest tax shields and the additional discount for risk if one is using a crude price multiple method.

DCF valuation

DCF models aim to value a business by calculating the net present value of the free cash flows generated by it. These free cash flows are calculated as follows:

Earnings before interest and taxes (EBIT)
+ (–) non-cash expenses (revenues) eg depreciation
– cash tax payments (not including any interest tax shield)
– net cash capital expenditure
– (+) increases (decreases) in required working capital
– other cash operating expenditures not in EBIT
= **free cash flows of the unlevered business**

– post-tax cash interest and preferred stock dividends
– (+) other cash payments to (from) non-equity claimholders
= **free cash flow of the common equity**

These cash flows have to be forecast out as far as accurately possible. Every human effort has to be taken to ensure that they are as accurate as possible. One should start by analysing the business to identify the drivers of sales, and then examine what factors have affected these drivers in the past, such as the business cycle, interest rates, exchange rates, demographics and so on. The relationship between sales and gross and operating profit has to be examined, and the balance sheet ratios that help predict capital expenditure and interest payments looked at too.

The next stage is to draw up a forecast of the profit and loss account and the balance sheet for each year, with the two feeding into each other through interest payments and retained profit. Ideally one would want to forecast at least five years ahead. In some cases it may be necessary to forecast even further. These can then be checked against themselves by seeing whether the balance sheet ratios have been maintained and the profit and loss account has remained within the scope of what has historically been achieved in the industry. Finally, figures for the free cash flow can be derived.

Once the free cash flows have been calculated, they need to be discounted at the relevant rate. This rate has to take into account three factors: the opportunity cost of capital, risk and capital structure. To calculate the discount rate relevant to the opportunity cost of capital, one has to find the amount of money one would be prepared to forgo today in exchange for receiving the forecast cash flow in the future. This is a function of the interest rate:

Future cash = present cash × $(1 + r)^n$

Where r is the interest rate and n is the number of years before the future cash is generated. This equation can be rewritten as follows:

Present cash = future cash/$(1 + r)^n$

If one was 100 per cent sure of obtaining those future cash flows then $1/(1 + r)^n$ would be the only discount factor which needed to be applied. However, one is never sure of the future cash flows generated by a business and this has to be taken into account.

The way this is done is to include an additional risk discount factor. This can be calculated thanks to a modern portfolio which states that for any equity investment the:

Expected return = risk free return (ie if it were invested in treasury bonds) + βx the premium for having invested in the market,

where β is the riskiness of the equity investment relative to the market as a whole. This can also be expressed as:

Expected return = risk free return + β (market rate of return – risk free return)

The risk free return can be calculated by looking at the interest rate on long gilts. The market rate of return can be calculated from looking at long-term returns from investing in the market. For the UK, the premium for investing in the market has been variously estimated as between five per cent and six per cent. β is calculated as follows:

β_e = (covariance of return on equity e and the market return)/(variance of the market return)

This is a complex calculation, which can be easily carried out if one has access to one of the screen-based historic pricing services, but is otherwise laborious. The value of β is normally between 0 and 2.5, where a β of 0 would refer to an investment which offers the same security of a government bond, and a β of 2.5 would appropriate to some of the more questionable penny share investments.

The β calculated above is the β of the business complete with its existing level of debt. Calculating the value of the unlevered β requires two further steps. The first step is to calculate the impact that the debt has on the relative riskiness of the business. This is done by calculating the debt β or β_d:

β_d = (expected return on the business' debt – the risk free rate of return)/(expected rate of market return – the risk free rate of return)

This can then be fed into a formula for the unlevered β which is based on the weighted average of the debt β and the equity β, adjusted for the present value of the interest tax shields (calculated by discounting the value of the interest tax shields each year by the cost of the company's debt):

Let
β_u = β of the unlevered firm
β_e = β of the equity
β_d = β of the debt
E = market value of the equity*
D = market value of the debt
T = net present value of interest tax shields

$$\beta_u = \beta_e\,[(E/E + D - T)]/\,[\beta_d\,(D - T/E + D - T)]$$

*because of this circularity, it is only possible to calculate the value of an unlevered β for a quoted company, or part of a quoted company, accurately. When valuing unquoted companies it is necessary to estimate the relative proportion of the debt and equity within the capital structure, and give a weighting to the debt and equity βs accordingly.

The relevant β can then be used to determine the correct rate of return by which the cash flows have to be discounted:

Rate of return e_r = risk free rate of return + β × the premium for investing in shares rather than bonds.

So if the interest rate on long gilts is five per cent, and one is dealing with a business which is slightly more risky than the market as a whole (i.e. β = 1.2) then the relevant interest rate to use in the discounting formula is 12.2 per cent (i.e. 1.05 + 1.2 × 0.06).

This interest rate is then used to discount the forecast cash flows as follows:

Present value = free cash flow/$(1 + e_r)^n$

The value of the business is equal to the sum of the net present value of the free cash flows from now until the end of time. As it is not possible to forecast them that far into the future, the normal practice is to forecast them as far as possible and then to add a terminal valuation representing the value of the business after the forecast period.

The terminal valuation has to be calculated by an alternative method, such as a price multiple method or an asset-based method. The alternative is to agree a constant level of growth that would apply after the forecast period, whose net present value can easily be calculated.

The important thing is to ensure that not too much of the value of the business is the result of the terminal value after the forecast period. If it is, one may well be better off using another valuation method in the first place.

Price multiple models

The alternative to a discounted cash flow model for valuing a firm is a price multiple model. This does not attempt to reach an absolute value for a firm with the integrity of a DCF valuation. Instead, it provides a means of comparing the price of a firm with others in the same sector. The differed multiples used include:

- price to earnings (after tax) – the p/e ratio;
- price to operating cash flow (EBITDA);
- price to free cash flow to common shareholders – the free cash flow multiple;
- price to sales – the sales multiple;
- price to operating profit;
- price to gross margin;
- price to earnings before interest and taxes;
- price to net book value;
- price to replacement cost of net book value (ie replacement cost of the assets less market value of the liabilities);
- market value of the equity plus debt to operating cash flow.

Of these, only price earnings multiples and sales multiples are used regularly. The others are used only in special circumstances. For example, when comparing companies that are subject to different tax regimes, one might look at free cash flow multiples. Price to net book value ratios are commonly used where the assets rather than the cash flows drive the value of the company, ie in banking.

Applying a p/e ratio involves finding a proxy, or series of proxy companies, that face similar earnings growth prospects and whose price is known (either because they are quoted or because they have been involved in a recent trade sale). This is used to obtain a relevant p/e ratio for the company being valued, which can then be multiplied by that company's earnings to reach a valuation:

Market value of a business = earnings of business × p/e ratio of proxy company

Sales multiples work in the same way but using price/sales ratios rather than price/earnings.

The main weakness is that it has no objectivity in the selection of proxies. One also has to bear in mind that sales multiples do not take the capital structure of the business being valued into account. There is also a temptation to overstate the value of a business by applying p/e ratios from last year's accounts to earnings forecasts for next year without discounting for risk, inflation or the opportunity cost of holding cash.

Asset-based valuations

In many businesses the assets on the balance sheet are the main driver of value, and the assets themselves have an easily established market value. This is particularly true of the financial services sector, but can also be applied to other areas such as property, house building, and mining. In these circumstances, asset-based valuations tend to be used.

The total value of the asset, as accounted for on the balance sheet, can be added up, and liabilities deducted to reach a value of the business. Usually this value is notional: most businesses actually trade at a discount to their net asset value because of the costs associated with assessing that value. This discount can be estimated by looking at the discounts which apply to similar businesses either on the stock exchange or in recent trade sales.

5.4

Management Buy-outs – A Reality Check

Stephen Craik
KPMG Corporate Finance

There are a number of basic prerequisites to a successful management buy-out (MBO) and undertaking a feasibility check to assess how any prospective deal measures up to these criteria is an essential first step. For the adviser – who is likely to be working on a contingent fee basis – a review of these prerequisites will usually determine whether the idea will be attractive to financiers and is worth backing. A review forces the management team – for whom this will be a life-changing transaction – to take a long, hard look at the reality of what they are about to embark upon. Even for the propositions that score highly at this stage, the deal can be incredibly difficult. The management team must have the stomach for it and be prepared to make some hard decisions en route before they reap the rewards of ownership. A hard look at these prerequisites at an early stage can therefore save a great deal of time and anguish later.

Is there a real opportunity?

Often, the MBO team of a privately owned company may perceive that there is a buy-out opportunity if the owner wants to retire or simply move on to other things. If the company is part of a larger group, it may become apparent to a management team that their company no longer fits. Whatever the management's instincts may be at this stage, there is a need to explore whether there is a real opportunity. This can often be difficult for the team, for whom there are conflicts of interest, and they may not want to ask the question for fear of appearing disloyal. In addition, they clearly cannot supply external advisers with any confidential information without clearance from their parent company.

It is important at this stage for the management team, together with their advisers, to try and understand the dynamics of the situation. If the company is privately owned, what are the vendors' circumstances, do they require the money, are other family members involved etc? If it is a corporate, what is currently driving the corporate strategy, how best is the whole subject approached of whether divestment is a possibility? It is vital to establish at the outset whether this is an actual opportunity. Too often, vendors are happy to test the market place and obtain a free valuation but actually have no real intention of selling.

Many owners, both private and corporate, also have reservations about dealing exclusively with the management team. If the management team are to find themselves in an auction, what is their competitive advantage? The fact that they manage the business and have an intimate knowledge of it may not give them a sufficient advantage over, for example, a corporate acquirer who also knows the market well. A number of trade buyers may be prepared to purchase the business and integrate it within their own management structure. The MBO team need to assess how important they are to the business and whether they can defend their position against a trade acquirer.

Being able to argue a strong competitive advantage can decide how the vendor proceeds with a sale. In a recent example, a large corporate announced its intention to sell a subsidiary on the open market. The MBO team and their advisers recognised that there would be substantial interest from an overseas agent who was familiar with the business and could potentially outbid the management team. The key to that MBO, above all others, was to dissuade the vendors from taking it to the market place. Right at the outset a coherent set of arguments was put together to persuade the vendor that to take the business to the market would be detrimental and they agreed to deal exclusively with the MBO team.

Identifying issues from the outset, and developing the strategies to deal with them, can make the difference between success and failure.

Venture capitalists are spoilt for choice; if they come up against a problem with one buy-out, they are just as likely to move on to another one. For most management teams, however, there is usually only one chance. The issues may look straightforward but often it is difficult for the management team to perceive the broader picture and identify key priorities. The input of an experienced adviser can definitely help put strategies into perspective and contribute to the successful outcome of the deal.

Management team

Historically, there has been a view that if you back the right team, whatever the business or the market, you will make money. Although today's investors are far keener to review sector issues and the company they are buying into, essentially the core of any MBO is still about having the right team for the business.

The management team needs to do some navel gazing about themselves. How well do they know the sector? Have they been involved in the sector for 10–15 years or are they relatively new arrivals? When the going gets tough, the survivors are those who really understand the dynamics of their sector. Do they have a good track record in the sector and preferably in the company they want to buy?

The motivation of the buy-out team will vary and, of course, being in charge of their own destiny is often a key component. The bottom line is, of course, that they must want to make money within a reasonable timescale. Their objectives need to align with those of the venture capitalist: to create value and exit within 3–5 years. Lifestyle aspirations such as running the business until retirement, handing on a business to their children or simply protecting their jobs are not favoured by investment houses.

The configuration of the management team should also be clear. Who are the sponsors of the buy-out? Who is key to driving through the strategies and delivering value? Do they have in place all the people that they need? As part of a large organisation, for example, it is quite common to have finance or marketing handled centrally. Increasingly, not having a complete team would not prevent a deal going forward but new team members should be brought in at an early stage.

The quality of the team is crucial and hard decisions will often have to be made to ensure that the team is strong enough to achieve every goal. Is the company's financial controller, who currently reports to a group finance director, good enough to step into the finance director role after the buy-out? The interests of the company must come first, over and above personal relationships. How the team handles this part of the process is often a good indicator of whether the buy-out can be carried out successfully.

Underlying strategy

Strangely, it is often quite common for management teams not to have thought out their strategy properly. This is particularly the case with corporate buy-outs where the strategy for the stand-alone business is likely to be very different to that of the group.

What would we do with this business if we owned it? What is our strategy in the market place? Many people will often rush into the business planning process without first thinking about these issues. However, the strategy is the bedrock of the buy-out and everything else is the detail that sits on top – primarily, investors are backing the management team and their strategy to add value.

The management team must look at how they can create profit and cash flow. Can they shake out the balance sheet and create any value there? Sometimes their actions will have been constrained by the previous owner and they need to be open-minded about their options. Are there opportunities to acquire and should they be considering a consolidation play to increase profits?

It is also important to have a view on the exit route, although this has not always been the case. A number of apparently successful buy-outs during the 1980s failed to put exit criteria in place and, when the United Kingdom hit recession and the investors wanted out, there were no buyers. Thus, today, from the outset, venture capitalists are not only interested in getting into the right business, but are also considering how to get out and realise their investment. It is equally important, therefore, for the management team to have their own exit strategy. How are they going to get out? To whom are they going to sell the business?

Market place

Is the business in an attractive market place as far as the venture capitalist is concerned? Typically, the dynamics of an attractive market place are defined as one that is relatively stable, has some growth, where prospects generally look good and there are a limited number of players.

Historically, there have been some no-go areas – for example, property development, the construction industry and textiles. It is possible to do deals in these sectors but you need to be a major player for it to be a realistic option. For example, while the textile market in the United Kingdom has suffered due to cheap imports, there are a number of success stories where companies have been able to source successfully overseas and create profitable niche businesses. Businesses such as these could be possible buy-outs. However, failing businesses that have not repositioned themselves in unattractive sectors will probably not be buy-out candidates.

Whatever the sector, the closer a company is to a monopolistic position the more attractive it will be to venture capitalists – who are traditionally risk-averse. A dominant market position and good performance (preferably under the proposed management team) present the right profile for investment. Occasionally, businesses do under-perform but, if there have been any hiccups in profitability, the management team must be able to demonstrate that they were not responsible and that this was attributable to other factors, if they want to be taken seriously.

Cash-generative businesses are particularly favoured for buy-outs. After buy-out, the company will need to make repayments and there will clearly be interest costs. If a business requires high capital investment both to operate and maintain its market position, it will be potentially less attractive.

It will be rare to find a business that has all the desired attributes, but the closer you are to achieving all of them the better. One management team, with a business that had lost over £10 million in the previous year, is now successfully running its own company. They were able to demonstrate that the losses were due to a group strategy of expanding overseas, while they personally preferred to concentrate on their core business in the United Kingdom. They also held a virtually monopolistic position in a number of the markets in which they operated, all of which had sound long-term prospects.

Prospects for management buy-outs

The future for MBOs is currently rosy. The volume of transactions may be down but, for good-quality businesses, there is a vast amount of venture capital currently looking for investment.

There has been much talk about the downturn in the economic climate but recessionary environments can actually benefit some businesses. The monetary depression in the United States is actively fuelling MBO transactions in the United Kingdom as US businesses offload overseas and non-core investments to service debts in their home market. This trend looks set to continue and, as the UK recession deepens and vendor expectations about the value of their businesses are adjusted, there could well be far more activity to come.

5.5

Legal Aspects of Management Buy-outs and Acquisitions

Richard Murrall
Lee Crowder

Assets or shares?

A business may be acquired, fundamentally, in two ways, either by purchasing its assets or the corporate shell in which the assets are contained.

An asset acquisition involves the purchaser acquiring the assets that make up the business. The business is purchased as a going concern and the purchaser acquires a collection of assets such as premises, stock and plant. At the same time, the purchaser may acquire liabilities that are related to the business, such as the responsibility to satisfy contracts and, sometimes, the liability to discharge creditors.

A share acquisition involves the purchaser acquiring the shares of the company that owns the business and assets. The shares of the company are transferred. Accordingly, there is no change in the ownership of the business – the business continues to be owned by the same company and only the identity of the shareholders changes. Whatever liabilities and obligations the target company had before the acquisition will remain after the acquisition. On an asset purchase, however, the purchaser can choose (subject to the agreement of the selling company) which assets he wishes to buy and which to leave behind.

In practice, the manner in which an acquisition proceeds is often driven by the different tax treatments of a share or asset purchase. A share sale will frequently be more attractive to the shareholders of a vendor. However, there will be situations where a choice is not available – for example, where a company has a number of different businesses within the same corporate shell, only one of which is intended to be the subject of the sale. A purchaser may insist on an asset sale to ensure that it does not unwittingly acquire any of the historic liabilities of the target. All such issues can be addressed in a properly drawn set of warranties and indemnities, but some purchasers prefer not to take the risk of purchasing litigation.

Management buy-outs (MBOs) are, essentially, the purchase of a business by its management, usually through the vehicle of a new company established for this purpose and frequently with the assistance of equity capital provided by venture capitalists. Buy-outs vary in complexity, but the key feature of all MBOs is that the managers acquire a share in the ownership of their business. An MBO can proceed by way of share or asset acquisition. A buy-out team may include members who were not previously involved in the business – such hybrid being known as a BIMBO (buy-in management buy-out). A transaction where a completely new management team purchases the business is a management buy-in (MBI).

Consideration

'Consideration' is the legal term given to the payment that the purchaser makes to acquire the shares or assets of the target. The suitability of different methods of payment will depend on the circumstances of the transaction. The vendor may want cash, subject to tax issues. The purchaser may wish to defer making payment of part, perhaps contingently on the performance of the target post-completion or on verification of the value of the assets being acquired. Both parties may find the use of shares as consideration issued (or procured) by the purchaser attractive.

Types of consideration

The consideration may take one or more of the following forms:

Cash

Cash is the most common form of consideration and usually the one most attractive to the vendor, for obvious reasons. From the purchaser's point of view, cash for an acquisition may be raised in a variety of ways – for example, by borrowing (possibly using the assets of the target as security, see below), by the issue of new shares, or simply from surplus cash reserves. The purchaser may wish to defer payment of part of the price, perhaps contingently on the performance of the target company or business post-completion, or by reference to the value of the net assets acquired, or merely on the passage of time.

Shares

A purchaser that acquires shares may wish to pay for them by issuing its own shares (or those of its holding company) to the vendor. Sometimes, in such a transaction, the vendors can become very significant shareholders of the purchaser, and may be given a seat on the board. A transaction involving the issue of shares may be badged as a merger, rather than a takeover. From a vendor's point of view, the degree of risk being taken in the acceptance of shares depends much on the identity of the issuer, and the liquidity in the market of the shares being accepted. Clearly, shares of a publicly listed company will be more attractive to some vendors for this reason, although shares issued to vendors of publicly quoted companies will frequently be subject to dealing restrictions for a period after completion so as to try to maintain an orderly market in those shares. A publicly quoted stock is not guaranteed liquidity.

Where a private company issues shares, the vendor should take steps to ensure that the rights attaching to those shares (eg voting, dividends) are satisfactory.

A purchaser should also be aware that shares may not be issued at a discount, ie less than the nominal value. Also, where shares are issued at a premium, a sum equal to the premium must be credited to the company's share premium account. These two rules are equally applicable where shares are issued as payment for other shares or assets. Consequently, steps should be taken by the purchaser to obtain an accurate valuation of the property proposed to be acquired in return for the issue of shares.

Loan notes

An acquiring company may issue loan notes to the vendor for the purchase price or part of it. Loan notes are no more than an acknowledgement of the indebtedness of the purchaser to the vendor. They may be secured, or perhaps guaranteed by a third party, eg a bank. The loan note 'instrument' will set out the terms on which the loan is made. Frequently, the vendor can demand repayment of all or part at six-monthly or other intervals after a certain period from completion. Loan notes have been popular in recent years to enable vendors to (attempt) to carry forward gains made on the sale of shares to future tax years, usually for the purpose of maximising taper relief. When taper relief reaches its maximum from April 2002, the incentive for the use of loan notes will diminish for many vendors who have held the sale shares for the relevant period. It should be noted that loan notes issued to maximise taper relief should be categorised, in tax terms, as 'non-qualifying corporate bonds'.

Financial assistance

The Companies Act 1985 provides that a company may not give financial assistance to purchase its own shares. Accordingly, the rule does not apply to transactions involving only the sale of assets. Breach of this rule is a serious matter, and any director who is involved in such a transaction may face up to two years imprisonment and/or a fine. Additionally, the transaction entered into by the company is void, and the company also liable to a fine. The object of the rule against financial assistance is the protection of the creditors of the target company.

The financial assistance rule is wide-ranging and covers not only situations where the company itself gives assistance, but also any of its subsidiaries. Additionally, the assistance may occur before, at the same time, or even after the acquisition. Financial assistance includes, gifts, loans, transactions at an undervalue and charges granted over the assets of the target company.

There are a number of exceptions to this rule, of which the most useful is the relaxation available to private companies. This relaxation is known as the 'whitewash procedure' and although extremely useful in practice, companies must ensure it is followed to the letter to avoid any liability. The whitewash allows a private company to give financial assistance where either its net assets are not depleted by the giving of the assistance, or if they are depleted, if the company has sufficient distributable reserves to cover the amount of the depletion. In addition, the directors of the target (almost always the incoming directors) are to make a statutory declaration stating that they believe that the company will be able to pay its debts as they fall due for 12 months.

The agreement

Warranties and indemnities

Both share sale and asset sale agreements will almost always contain warranties. A warranty is a contractual statement or promise given by the vendor to the purchaser in respect of a particular fact relating to the target company or assets being sold. The purpose of warranties is twofold:

- They provide the purchaser with a means of obtaining information, probably of an unwelcome nature, about the target company.
- They provide the purchaser with protection against actual or contingent liabilities, losses or setbacks in the target company, typically where such matters or their scope are not apparent before completion. If a warranty transpires to be untrue, a purchaser may be able to make a claim based on the loss flowing from the breach of warranty, subject to the normal rules of mitigation of loss.

An indemnity is a contractual promise made, usually by the vendor to the purchaser, whereby the vendor agrees to hold the purchaser harmless from the consequences of the fact or circumstance giving rise to the breach of the indemnity. An indemnity is usually used where a particular risk has been identified. Comfort in relation to the tax affairs of the target are usually given on an indemnity basis. The key distinguishing feature of an indemnity, as compared to a warranty, is that the purchaser does not need to show that he has attempted to mitigate his loss. The vendor is simply obliged to pay.

Warranties in share sale agreements

A purchaser in a share sale will often seek greater warranty protection than on an asset sale. This is because the purchaser will acquire the corporate shell, complete with all the liabilities and obligations that the company had before the acquisition.

In addition, as the liabilities acquired include the target company's tax liabilities, the purchaser will wish to ensure that it is protected against unforeseen liabilities relating to tax. Such protection is customarily given on an indemnity basis, since there is frequently little prospect of mitigating a tax liability. Such indemnities are usually contained in a separate document known as a tax deed, frequently expressed to be in favour of the purchaser (rather than the target in which the liability has arisen).

Warranties in asset sale agreements

The scope of warranties given on a business acquisition does not (usually) need to be as extensive as those given on a share sale. This is because the purchaser has to a certain extent 'cherry picked' which assets he is to acquire, and liabilities do not automatically pass with assets as they do within a separate legal entity. Warranties will generally be limited to those that relate to the assets being purchased, although a purchaser may also wish to obtain comfort as to historic trading, relationships with customers etc. The scope of the warranties, as with many other aspects of the agreement, will be governed ultimately by the relative bargaining strength of the parties.

As taxation liabilities remain with the vendor, there is no need for a tax deed or extensive warranties relating to tax.

Warranties on an MBO

During the negotiation process of an MBO, the vendor will frequently argue that the scope of the warranties given should be less than would otherwise be the case since the managers will have a significant amount of knowledge relating to the business that they have been running. Indeed, the vendor may argue, often with justification, that the purchaser knows more about the target than the vendor. However, as one of the functions of warranties is to apportion risk between the purchaser and vendor, the managers will have to carefully consider whether they are happy to receive only limited warranties, and how far their knowledge of the business extends. A parent company may be responsible for much of the administration of a group including accounting, tax and payroll functions. In addition, the backers of the

MBO team may insist on a full set of warranties, if not from the vendor then from the MBO team themselves.

Disclosure letter

Disclosure letters are commonly used in both share and asset sales. The purpose of the disclosure letter is to provide information that qualifies the warranties (but not, usually, the indemnities). A vendor's liability under the warranties will be reduced or eliminated to the extent that the disclosure letter discloses the information that renders the warranty untrue. This has the benefit (for the purchaser) of enabling him to go in with his eyes open, and (for the vendor) to reduce the risk of a claim later. Significant disclosures may lead to a renegotiation of the price or even the transaction being aborted altogether. A well-advised purchaser will not accept disclosures that are general in nature or are merely expressed to contradict a warranty. Disclosures of publicly available records (eg at Companies House) may be acceptable.

Restrictive covenants

A purchaser may wish to impose restrictions on the vendor competing with the purchaser or the target business after completion. This is particularly the case where the vendor has special skills or contacts with customers. Much depends on the circumstances, of course – competition may be less of an issue in a sale by a 70 year old than by a 40-year old. In an MBO, the vendor may wish to impose restrictions on competition by the purchaser with businesses that remain under the control of the vendor, which are likely to be allied to the business being sold. The managers of the target may be well equipped to compete with such businesses. In all cases, great care should be taken in drafting such covenants. They are regarded as anti-competitive by the courts, and are interpreted strictly against the party seeking to rely upon them. If they are too wide in scope they may not be enforceable. Where a substantial payment has been made for goodwill, enforceability may be easier.

Other relevant agreements

Aside from the principal asset/share purchase agreement, consideration may need to be given to the following:

- Service agreements, which govern the contract of employment between the company and its employees (who may also be directors). A service agreement may be required or desirable to protect the positions of both the employer and the employee. In a leveraged transaction, the venture capitalist will be anxious to ensure that the terms (particularly the notice period required to be given by the employer to terminate) are not overly generous. Service agreements frequently contain restrictions on activity post-employment, as well as a so-called 'garden leave' clause, whereby an employer is entitled to require the employee not to attend work during his notice period (more effective than non-competition clauses as the employee will still be an employee while on garden leave and under a duty not to compete with the employer).

- A subscription and shareholders' agreement, which is frequently used where a venture capitalist is involved, to govern the relationship between the directors/managers, the company and the venture capitalist. The subscription agreement will set out the terms of the investment by the venture capitalist – that is, its agreement to subscribe for shares and the terms attaching to that agreement. If the venture capitalist is making any other kind of investment, eg a loan, the subscription agreement may deal with that too, although there may be a separate loan agreement. The rights attaching to the shares are usually set out in the articles of association (see below). The venture capitalists may require that the agreement should contain non-competition clauses from the management in favour of the investee company. These will be drafted so as to offer the investee company protection if there is a parting of the ways. Although traditionally also found in service agreements, their inclusion in a subscription agreement helps overcome enforceability problems as the consideration given by the venture capitalist (its agreement to subscribe for shares) will be taken into account. Undertakings will invariably be given by the management to the venture capitalist. These will include an obligation of management to provide full information about the business to the venture capitalist, including for example, an information pack every month (management accounts, sales reports, analysis etc), in addition to an annual business plan and any other information the venture capitalist might reasonably (or unreasonably!) require. Additional undertakings will be required as regards the management of the company: typically there will be a fairly extensive list of matters or actions that will require the venture capitalist's consent. These range from commercial issues such as substantial acquisitions or disposals of assets outside the ordinary course of business, to legal matters such as changes to the articles of association, issue of new shares etc. Warranties are also likely to be contained in a subscription agreement; however, in this instance the management team will give them to the venture capitalist. Any management team should be cautious that they do not expose themselves to additional liability, by giving warranties to the venture capitalists that they themselves have not obtained from the vendors, although this may, particularly in an MBO, be unavoidable.

- Articles of association. In an MBO, both the new management and the venture capitalist will usually acquire shares in the new company. The articles specify the rights attaching to the different classes of shares that the company has issued covering matters such as voting, dividends and priority to assets of the company on a winding-up. In addition, the venture capitalist is likely to insist upon other rights to protect its investment or its exit from its investment, such as provisions requiring management to sell or buy the venture capitalist out if an offer to buy the company is received which is acceptable to it. Many venture capitalists use funds that have defined closing dates: they will wish to avoid management being able to frustrate their exit. The articles will also deal with the transfer of shares in the new company including:

  (i) what happens when a shareholder wishes to transfer their shares, must they first offer them to the other shareholders?
  (ii) what happens when a shareholder leaves the company, can they keep their shares or must they transfer them and should the circumstances of the departure affect the price paid for the shares (good leaver/bad leaver)?
  (iii) how is the price to be paid for the shares transferred to be agreed or determined? (particularly relevant on a compulsory transfer).

Finally, the articles will almost always contain a right for the venture capitalist to appoint a director to represent their interests on the board. This power may be exercisable from day one, or only when the venture capitalist is concerned about the performance of the company.

Other issues to consider

Employment issues

Whether an acquisition proceeds as an asset acquisition or share acquisition can have important consequences on the liability of both purchaser and vendor to the target company's employees.

Where an acquisition proceeds by way of asset acquisition, the Transfer of Undertakings (Protection of Employment) Regulations 1981 (TUPE) apply. The effect of TUPE is to transfer the contracts of employment for all employees of the target company to the purchaser. All rights and liabilities attaching to the employees (other than in relation to occupational pension schemes) transfer to the purchaser automatically, and employees will continue to be employed on the same terms and conditions, as they were before the acquisition, unaffected by it. Any dismissal of an employee for a reason connected with the acquisition will be automatically unfair, unless the purchaser can successfully run the (difficult) argument that the dismissal was for an economic, technical or organisational reason.

Where an acquisition proceeds by way of share acquisition, TUPE does not apply. This is because, legally, there is no change in the identity of the employee's employer. Again, all rights and liabilities attaching to the employee remain the same after the acquisition, but any dismissal relating to the acquisition will not be automatically unfair. Normal rules relating to unfair dismissal and redundancy will apply.

Property issues

In both share and asset acquisitions, property issues may well be relevant, and the purchaser should ensure that his solicitors fully investigate title to any properties being acquired. If time constraints do not allow for a full investigation, the solicitors may attempt to obtain a certificate of title from the vendor's solicitor and/or warranties in respect of the properties from the vendor (essential if the property in question is being offered as security).

Environmental issues have had much greater significance for a purchaser since the introduction of the Environmental Protection Act 1990. A purchaser who is aware of any environmental issues which may potentially affect the land they are to acquire should consider undertaking a full environmental audit prior to proceeding with the deal. Warranties and indemnities should also be used in almost every matter involving property to apportion liability or risk between the parties.

As part of an asset sale, if any property is leasehold, as the identity of the leaseholder is to change, the consent of the landlord will need to be obtained in order to assign the lease to the purchaser. In the case of a share acquisition, the identity of the leaseholder remains the same (ie the company), and thus a landlord's consent may not be needed unless the terms of the lease dictate otherwise.

A purchaser who acquires property by way of asset acquisition will have the benefit of a priority period, during which they can purchase property in the knowledge that no further matters will appear on the Land Charges Register. A purchaser of shares may wish also to benefit from a priority application and will usually be able to do so either directly or indirectly (via its lender).

Pension issues

The importance of pension matters on an acquisition should never be underestimated. Indeed, the value of the target's pension funds often exceeds the consideration given by the purchaser. Pension-related considerations vary according to a number of factors. For example, is the scheme a discrete or group scheme? In the case of a discrete scheme, the target company's employees constitute the only members of the scheme, and thus the most important question is whether the scheme is adequately funded. Where a group scheme is involved, the target company's employees are part of a larger pension fund. Here, the issue to be addressed is what would be an appropriate transfer payment for the vendor's fund to make in order to provide for those target company employees transferring out of the group scheme.

Another consideration will be whether the scheme is a money purchase (defined contribution) or final salary (defined benefit) scheme. Both employee and employer usually make contributions to a money purchase scheme, although not necessarily so. The employee is not entitled to any set level of benefit on retirement. The level of benefit he receives depends upon the return on the contributions made. Accordingly, the purchaser's principal concern is to be satisfied that all contributions that the target is due to have made have been made. By contrast, a final salary scheme throws up more difficult issues, particularly where the target employees are members of a group scheme. The level of pension an employee is entitled to receive is calculated by reference to their salary at retirement age. Consequently, with such a fund, the level of contributions made has no correlation with the level of benefits to be received by the employee. It is for the target to ensure that sufficient contributions have been made, as the liability is created at the time the employee joins the scheme. Here the help of an actuary will be invaluable in order to determine whether the fund is adequately funded. If the fund is not adequately funded, the consideration for the target should be reduced accordingly in order to reflect the amount that the purchaser will be required to contribute to the scheme. Alternatively, on a transfer out from a group scheme, the issue may be addressed by negotiating a larger transfer value, although the vendor is likely to resist this.

5.6

Tax Aspects of the Purchase and Sale of Private Companies or their Businesses

Maurice Fitzpatrick and
Jay Sanghrajka
Tenon Group

This chapter sets out to address a number of the principal tax issues associated with the purchase and sale of private companies or their businesses. With this in mind, the chapter is divided into two parts. The first looks at the tax aspects in terms of purchasing a company or purchasing a business, while the second concentrates on the tax planning which an individual vendor shareholder of a company may wish to consider before selling shares in the company concerned.

Tax aspects when purchasing a company or purchasing a business

Various issues arise, the more important of which are dealt with below.

Buying shares/buying assets

In the case of a purchaser of an economic entity currently organised as a company (T Co), one of the first decisions the purchaser will have to make is whether to buy T Co, or to buy T Co's trading assets from it. The tax issues to be considered in arriving at such a decision include the following:

- If the purchaser buys T Co's assets, the purchaser may enjoy an enhanced ongoing capital allowances position as compared to that which would have continued to be enjoyed by T Co under new ownership.
- Where the purchaser has previously realised capital gains on business assets, the purchase of assets such as land and buildings or fixed plant and machinery may enable those earlier capital gains to be rolled over and tax deferred.
- Where the purchaser buys assets, the capital gains base cost of those assets (in the purchaser's hands, and in terms of any future disposal of the assets concerned) may be higher than they would have been in the event of a disposal of same assets by T Co under new ownership.
- The cost of any trading stock acquired by the purchaser will be a revenue expense.
- Stamp duty is charged at 0.5 per cent on the acquisition of shares; the purchase of assets rather than shares in T Co may achieve a stamp duty saving if a high proportion of the value of T Co is represented by assets which can pass by delivery (eg debtors and stock). However, the higher rates of stamp duty on property and goodwill (4 per cent in connection with property and goodwill costing more than £500,000) may turn this potential advantage into a disadvantage.
- The purchaser of assets avoids taking on past tax (and VAT) issues of T Co.

However, there is no such thing as a free lunch, and the flipside of the above advantages to the purchaser of assets, as opposed to the purchaser buying the shares in T Co, is that there may be certain tax disadvantages to the vendor. For example, the vendor may suffer a double effective charge to capital gains tax (once in T Co on the sale of the assets, and second on the shareholders of T Co when funds are extracted). The vendor may either resist an attempt to purchase assets rather than shares, or adjust the price to take into account what the vendor regards as his fiscal disadvantage. The VAT position of the purchase of a business, rather than of shares, may also be more complex for both parties concerned.

Tax warranties and indemnities

The purchaser of T Co will try to ensure that any hidden tax problems in T Co do not effectively become the purchaser's problem as a result of his having acquired T Co. The purchaser will normally seek to achieve this via a twin-track approach of seeking tax warranties and tax indemnities.

Tax warranties consist of a number of statements covering the tax position of T Co, such statements being included in the overall purchase and sale agreement for the shares in T Co. Essentially, the inclusion of these statements regarding T Co's tax position represents the confirmation by the vendor that there are no hidden problems in T Co's tax position. If a warranty is given and then found to be false, the purchaser can sue the vendor for the loss occasioned to the purchaser as a result of his having relied on the warranty concerned. There is an exclusion to this basic principle – namely, that in response to being asked to give a particular tax warranty (tax warranties normally run to several score pages), the vendor 'discloses' a piece of information regarding the tax issue on which the warranty is sought. Broadly, that disclosure will prevent the purchaser subsequently suing the vendor regarding the issue disclosed. As a result, the inclusion of tax warranties in the draft purchase and sale agreement almost invariably leads to the disclosure of various information regarding T Co's tax position. Indeed, that is part of the function of warranties, and the forced disclosure of various aspects to do with T Co's tax position provides the purchaser with more knowledge on this subject, knowledge that the purchaser may use in final negotiations to reduce the price.

As a long stop, the purchaser will also normally seek a deed of tax indemnity from the vendor. The effect of the indemnity is that any unprovided for tax liabilities arising on T Co in respect of any period prior to the change of ownership, are met by the vendor via the vendor keeping T Co indemnified for the liabilities concerned. The judgement then is whether the purchaser seeks to persuade the vendor to back this deed of indemnity by a bank guarantee, or indeed by an amount held in escrow.

All of the above issues are very important to the purchaser in terms of safeguarding the value of what he is buying, namely the shares in T Co, although they are all broadly rendered unnecessary if the purchaser buys assets rather than shares.

Trading losses in T Co at the time of its acquisition by the purchaser

It may be the case that T Co has trading losses available for offset against future taxable profits from the same trade at the time T Co is sold. Longstanding anti-avoidance tax legislation states that if there is a change of ownership of a company, and 'a major change in the nature or conduct of the company's trade' during any part of the period beginning three years before the date of the change of ownership, and ending three years after the date of change of ownership, the trading losses at the time of the change of ownership are forfeited.

A major change in the nature or conduct of the trade is not specifically defined, but includes a major change in the type of products dealt in or services or facilities provided in the trade, or a major change in customers, outlets or markets of the trade. Two practical problems arising are:

(i) a change sufficient to trigger the relevant anti-avoidance legislation may come about gradually over a period of years, rather than as a result of one 'big bang' event;
(ii) the overall change concerned may in fact start from the three-year period prior to the change of ownership, and may then simply be continued after the date of change of ownership.

The approach to the availability of tax losses as at the date of the change of ownership will differ from deal to deal. Often, no account at all is taken of the potential value of the tax losses, but an additional amount of consideration is then paid by the purchaser should the tax losses ultimately be useable. The best (albeit impractical) advice to the purchaser of T Co is to make no changes at all to T Co's trade in the three years after the date of the change of ownership (although even this would not protect the position should the Inland Revenue be able to argue that a major change in the nature or conduct of the trade had already taken place in the three years prior to the change of ownership). Each case has to be looked at individually and, if at all possible, changes should only be made very gradually in the three-year run-out period following the change of ownership.

Capital gains exit charge

There is one particular piece of anti-avoidance legislation that the purchaser of T Co, in circumstances where T Co is being sold out of another UK group of companies, should be aware of. This is Section 179 of TCGA 1992, which can create a nasty tax trap for the unwary.

In general terms, where an asset is transferred between one member of a UK group of companies to another fellow group member, the asset goes through on a capital gains neutral basis – in other words, at no gain/no loss in the hands of the transfer or company. However, where the transferee company (E Co) leaves the UK group concerned within six years of having received an asset from another group company, a capital gains charge is levied on E Co. Broadly, E Co has to pay corporation tax on the difference between the market value of the asset at the time E Co received it, and the original capital gains base cost of the asset concerned. Clearly, any purchaser of a company, in circumstances where the company concerned is being bought out of a UK group, needs to be aware of this anti-avoidance legislation, and ensure that the tax warranties and indemnities specifically cover it.

Tax planning which might be carried out by an individual vendor shareholder of a company

When an individual, B, sells shares in T Co, he may well be set to realise a capital gain (CG) chargeable to capital gains tax (CGT). The basic CG computation takes the proceeds of sale and compares this to the base cost of the shares, the difference being the CG. The base cost of the shares will either be (in the case of shares held as at 31 March 1982) their 31 March 1982 market value (MV) uplifted for indexation relief to April 1998 or, in the case of shares acquired since 31 March 1982, their acquisition cost together with (if appropriate) indexation relief as from date of acquisition to 5 April 1998. Indexation relief over any particular period represents the movement in the retail prices index (RPI) over that period, and indexation relief came to an end in respect of all periods subsequent to April 1998.

This basic CG may then be subject to CG retirement relief or CG taper relief, further details of which are given in Chapter 4.3.

Long before the contract to sell the shares in T Co is finalised, an exercise should be carried out to discover the 'marginal rate' of CGT which the vendor shareholder is set to pay on each pound of consideration at the margin, after taking into account all relevant reliefs including taper relief. If it is discovered that the effective marginal rate of CGT at the margin is more than 25 per cent, it may be worth considering the possibility of T Co paying a predisposal dividend to its shareholders. A cash dividend of £1 will normally be charged to higher-rate income tax in the hands of vendor shareholders at an effective tax rate of 25 per cent on the cash dividend, while the amount of the dividend will reduce the sale price of the company on a pound-for-pound basis. This exercise is by no means as simple as it sounds, since different shareholders may well face different marginal rates of CGT, as a result, for example, of having different base costs or different entitlements to retirement relief or taper relief. It may be found that it is in the interests of some shareholders to receive a pre-sale dividend but not others. There is no substitute for considering the position in detail on a shareholder-by-shareholder basis, with a view to optimising the overall fiscal position of the shareholders as a whole.

The vendor shareholder may also wish to consider taking some or all of his consideration either in shares to be issued by the acquiring company (A Co), or interest-bearing loan stock issued by A Co.

The potential advantage to the vendor shareholder is that this has the effect of deferring the CGT liability until the shares/loan stock are sold/redeemed, so that in the meantime an investment return is earned by the shareholder on the proceeds gross of the CGT liability. Several points arise:

- It will be necessary to obtain tax clearances from the Inland Revenue under Taxes Act 1988 Section 707, and TCGA 1992 Section 138, to the effect that the proposed transactions are being carried out for bona fide commercial purposes and will indeed produce the tax result desired.
- In the case of loan notes, careful consideration needs to be given to their precise form, both in commercial terms and tax terms.

Finally, if at the end of the day CGT is payable by the vendor shareholder, he may wish to consider taking advantage of a further tax relief known as enterprise investment scheme (EIS) deferral relief (EDR). Under EDR, if an amount equivalent to the CG is then reinvested in new shares in a qualifying unquoted trading company, the new shares concerned being known as 'the replacement shares', then the CGT concerned is deferred until the replacement shares themselves are sold. If an amount equivalent to one-third of the CG concerned is reinvested under EDR for example, one-third of the CGT concerned is deferred on a pro rata basis.

Conclusion

This chapter has attempted to bring out the main tax considerations that the purchaser of a company or business should consider, and has also looked briefly at some of the ways in which a vendor shareholder of shares in a company might mitigate his CGT bill. These are of course complex areas and professional advice should always be taken in connection with the tax and commercial aspects of the deal.

Part Six

Management Issues in Generating Investment

6.1

The Business Plan – Making it Fly

Shiju Varghese
Director, Strategic Development and Corporate Finance, Tenon Group

All too often businesses do themselves a disservice when planning a corporate finance transaction by failing to prepare a compelling business plan that captures the imagination of the reader. While it is not intended to give instruction in creative writing, hopefully this chapter will highlight the areas that need to be considered in preparing a business plan.

This chapter has been written for a broad audience and the recommendations below will need to be overlaid with the specific considerations that may apply to any single company. Furthermore, it is not meant to be prescriptive, nor must it be seen as comprehensive. Ultimately, every business is unique and any general guide can only hope to draw out common themes.

Although every good business plan will have an executive summary at the start that should be written last, after all the other sections of the business plan have been completed, it is also important that any financial projections are done after the business plan itself has been articulated. Do not try to write a business plan that justifies a number of ridiculously optimistic projections.

Sector

A brief summary of the development of the business and the industry sector it operates in is required. An outline explaining how the business relates to other participants in the sector and what trends affect the industry gives the reader a basis upon which to evaluate the plans.

Key elements

1. Provide a history of the development of the business:
   - Date and form of incorporation, details of founders.
   - How is the business currently financed?
   - What are the major accomplishments of the business?
2. Describe the industry in which the business operates:
   - What is the current size of the industry?
   - Who are the major participants – competitors, market leaders, suppliers – in the industry?
   - What are the critical success factors in the sector?
   - What do published forecasts say about the future growth and profile of the sector?
   - What fashions, legislation or environmental trends affect the sector?

Product/service

A full description of the product should be provided. Consider planned developments and assess any competitive products. Use charts where appropriate to compare the product with those of competitors and include photographs or drawings if that would be helpful. Do not make this section too technical, if necessary attach an appendix. Above all, describe the advantages of the product.

Key elements

1. Fully describe the product:
   - What need does it fulfil?
   - Which features make it unique? (cost? technology? versatility?)
   - How is the product perceived within the industry?
2. Discuss the development of the product:
   - How fully developed is the product? (working model? in production? in use?)

- Are there opportunities to expand the product line?
- Is the product patented or otherwise protected by copyright?

3. Discuss competitive products on the market:
   - How do they compare in quality and features with your product?
   - Why do customers buy competitors' products?
   - Which pricing strategies are pursued for these products?
   - Is it normal to pay commissions or offer discounts?
4. Research and development:
   - What are the future developments and objectives?
   - Discuss the influence of new technology.
   - What resources are required – both financial and human?
   - What are the technical risks?
   - Describe the state of competitors' technological developments and how these will affect you.
   - Consider the next-generation derivative products.
5. Financial considerations:
   - Explain your pricing strategy.
   - Indicate the required levels of stocks of raw materials and finished products.
   - What are optimal order sizes?
   - How is distribution effected?
   - Consider cash flow requirements.

Market

This section should describe the opportunities available in the market and show how your proposals will exploit them successfully. It will be helpful to prepare this section of the plan before some of the other sections, such as operations and finance, as they will be dependent on the ability of the business to penetrate and expand in the market. It is critical to show that a market exists for the products or services that you will provide. Show that you understand the market forces and have the abilities and resources to supply and publicise your products effectively. Make a realistic estimate of your potential market share based on sound assumptions and give a concise appraisal of the competition. Do not overestimate your strengths or underestimate your weaknesses. Do not unjustifiably downplay your competitors' abilities. Investors expect to obtain an in-depth understanding of why your sales goals can be achieved despite competition.

Key elements

1. Describe your customers:
    - Who are they? (individuals? manufacturers? end-users?)
    - Where are they located geographically?
    - How sensitive are they to price, quality and service?
    - Who has bought or expressed an interest in the product?
2. Describe your market:
    - How large is the market? (volume? value?)
    - How developed is the market and what is its history?
    - What is the projected growth rate for the future?
    - Identify unusual market characteristics such as barriers to entry.
    - What do published forecasts predict about the market's future?
    - What is your market share?
    - Are you aiming for particular market segments?
    - What are your plans regarding the export market?
3. Discuss your company's competition:
    - Which companies do you compete with?
    - What are their strengths and weaknesses? (financial backing? technology? market share?)
    - What are their similarities?
    - What are their marketing strategies? Consider their likely response to your product.
    - Consider the potential for new competitors to enter the market.
    - Consider competition from overseas.
4. Explain how you will achieve your sales goals:
    - Which marketing strategy will you employ?
    - How will potential customers be identified?
    - Which customers will be the target in your initial marketing effort?
    - How will you attract customers away from the competition?
    - Are advertising efforts important to your strategy?
    - Consider the size of your sales force.

Operations

The section on operations should describe how your business will provide its product successfully and efficiently. For a manufacturing operation, you should include a full description of the production process, the raw materials required and whether any particular trade skills are needed. For a service venture, the availability of skilled personnel will be a prominent feature. Be sure to highlight any competitive advantages.

Key elements

1. Describe the production process:
   - How will critical elements be controlled? (bottlenecks? quality? delivery?)
   - To what extent are you dependent on key factors – suppliers, materials, skilled labour?
   - Which make or buy decisions are involved?
   - Which raw materials are required?
   - What is your relationship with suppliers?
   - What is the production capacity? Is it sufficient for the future?
2. Discuss personnel requirements:
   - What are your employee needs? Discuss any particular trade skills needed.
   - What are your labour costs, including benefits?
   - How will you attract sufficient, suitably qualified employees?
   - What is the state of your industrial relations?
3. Evaluate your plant and equipment needs:
   - Which facilities and equipment do you require?
   - Which future additions will be required for expansion and how much will they cost?
   - Is there a need to rely on subcontractors?
4. What are your needs for premises?:
   - What are your existing premises and where are they located?
   - Are your existing premises suitable for your needs?
   - Do you need any additional premises?

Management

Investors will be particularly interested in the strength and quality of the management team, and in many cases the investment is more in the management team than in anything else. It is important to openly discuss the strengths and weaknesses of current management and show what steps will be taken to rectify any weaknesses highlighted. In addition, indicate what additional skills will be required as the venture grows. Include full profiles of key individuals and an organisation chart as appendices.

Key elements

1. Discuss the structure of the organisation:
   - How are responsibilities distributed?
   - Is management centred around one person?
   - What additions to management are anticipated?
2. Identify key management personnel and their backgrounds:
   - Who are the key managers and what have they accomplished in the past?
   - What are their goals for the organisation?
   - Is there a balance of skills among the members of the management team (marketing, research, finance, administration)?
   - What steps have been taken to ensure that key members of the management team will be retained?
   - Have any personal financial commitments been made to the business by the management team?
3. Describe the role of any outsiders in the venture:
   - Are there to be any non-executives on the board of directors? What skills will they bring to the organisation?
   - Which professionals (lawyers, accountants, bankers) does the company rely upon?
4. Include general personnel details:
   - Employment terms of key personnel.
   - Planned staff numbers.
   - Future recruitment plans.
   - Other incentives issued.
   - Qualifications and skills required.

Implementation schedule

The implementation schedule should outline all the activities required to implement the proposals set out in other sections of the business plan.

Key elements

1. The schedule should be internally consistent and co-ordinated with the financial projections and requests for finance. Typical factors should include timings for:
   - Obtaining finance.
   - Capital expenditure programme.

- Staff recruitment.
- Product testing.
- Contacting distributors.
- Obtaining orders.

2. A timetable should indicate expected completion dates and milestones.
3. Decision points in the company's growth should be identified where the choice may be made to commit further funds.

Finance required and repayment/exit

The investor will want to assess your current financial position and you will need to provide your latest audited and management accounts, together with a commentary on the trends they reflect. The investor will also be interested in forecasts of profits and cash flow, incorporating the proposals detailed elsewhere in the plan.

In addition, you should set out the amount and form of finance sought as well as a schedule for its repayment. Bear in mind that investors in start-up companies will want to see evidence of financial commitment on the part of the founders.

It is important to demonstrate that the financial projections have been subjected to careful thought. Therefore, document your assumptions explicitly and include a commentary on the financial projections. Do not include too many spreadsheets but the statements included in your plan should be clear and to the point.

Key elements

1. Include historical statements:
   - Where possible, include full financial statements (balance sheets, income statements, statements of sources and applications of funds) for the past 2–5 years.
2. Present financial projections:
   - Prepare projected income statements, balance sheets and cashflow statements for the next 3–5 years. These should be on a monthly basis for the first year and then quarterly. Include:
     - assumptions you have used in preparing the projections;
     - the impact of capital expenditure, fixed costs, and research and development costs on the cash flow;
     - a breakeven/sensitivity analysis, identifying the split between fixed and variable costs;
     - a contingency element, identified as such.

Executive summary

The executive summary should provide a brief overview of the plan. It is the most important section in that it may well determine the amount of consideration your proposal will receive by the potential investor. It must succinctly express the uniqueness and viability of your venture. Try to limit the executive summary to two pages if possible but, in any event, try to avoid exceeding four pages. Write it after the rest of the business plan is complete and ask someone who understands the business to review the summary to test its effectiveness.

Key elements

1. Describe your business and why it is unique:
   - What is your product or service?
   - Why is your market attractive?
   - Who are your customers?
   - Who are your competitors?
   - Why are your products or services preferable to those of your competitors?
   - How far has your company evolved to date?
2. Briefly state management's qualifications:
   - What is management's past success record?
   - What abilities do management bring to the venture?
   - How is ownership to be distributed?
3. Present your financial projections summary:
   - How much growth is expected?
   - What earnings are projected?
   - Over what period of time will these be achieved?
4. Indicate the amount, form and use of finance:
   - How much finance is required?
   - What form will the funding take? (equity? debt?)
   - What will the money be used for?
   - How will finance be repaid?
   - What are the risks/rewards for the investor?

Appendices

The appendices should include documentation that supports or further explains the strategies and observations noted elsewhere in the plan, for example:

- profiles of key management personnel;
- market research studies;
- photographs or drawings of the product;
- detailed technical specifications;
- organisation chart;
- letters of commitment from potential customers and suppliers;
- plant layout;
- key contracts (eg management agreements, technology rights, leases);
- magazine, newspaper and trade articles about the business and its operating environment.

6.2

Building the Management Team

Charles Russam

Russam GMS Limited

Paradoxically, the team comes last. It ought to come first. The leader comes first. Then comes the money. Financial backers look for a good idea, carefully worked out and professionally presented, together with a view on how their return will be generated and when. They look for a leader with whom they can do business – not always an easy judgement. They look at the proposition. Next they look at the team that is going to make it work. Without the idea and without the leader to drive it there is nothing to talk about. But the team can be built. If there is a team in place already it has to be assessed, if there is not one in place it has to be created. In truth, without the right team, the venture will fail to take off, let alone fly.

At the top end of the league are the large-scale acquisitions, sometimes wholly owned by the venture capital company involved. At the other end of the scale are the SMEs and start-ups, variously funded by entrepreneurs and their families, banks, 'business angels' and government-backed initiatives. All have their leaders. Leaders are entrepreneurs. They all need the right people around them to be successful. Those who really acknowledge that getting the mix of people right at the start of a new venture tend to be at the higher end, mostly having a structured management training behind them. At the smaller end, the driving force is invariably the idea or the opportunity.

In all cases, however, it is up to the advisers to assess the quality of the management team and to do something about it – and for those who set about building their team, there can be a minefield ahead. Where do you get the right-fit management team members from? How do you do it? Who do you talk to? What techniques do you use? How can you recognise good advice? How much should you pay for it?

The entrepreneur's role in team-building

Each leader needs to be treated differently as they put together the deal and the teams that are going to make them work. The notion that entrepreneurs are all extrovert and high-profile, born and not made, that they battle against great odds and adversity with burning convictions and relentless drive is a great image. Today, not all entrepreneurs are cast in that mould – but they need to be like that to a degree. Take, for example, Nigel Stephens.

After several years as vice-president, finance, of an international car rental company, Stephens decided that he wanted to do it for himself. He saw some niches that, with a different approach, could make good money. It took him about four years and a number of abortive pitches to find what he was looking for. On his own but with venture capital promises for the right deal, he eventually landed Velo. He remembers all too well 11.45 on the evening of the 23 November 1999. He remembers the way he felt – like stepping off into the unknown. He remembered all the effort, the emotional ups and downs of the previous four years and he was very conscious of the enormity and the risk of what lay ahead.

Since that time, he has taken the turnover from about £40 million to £50 million and – a slightly more meaningful statistic – the company now has about 13,500 vehicles under management for its clients. What makes it work, says Stephens, is the team that runs Velo. Getting right the tricky balance between the executives he inherited and those he brought in was crucial.

'Whatever advice you ask for, and receive, in putting the management team together, it all boils down to personal judgement in the end', says Stephens. 'Recognising this ability is an important part of the skills mix of any CEO. The inherited executives were understandably nervous about the shape of the new structure and their own roles within it and the brought-in executives clearly wanted to make their mark.' One way in which Stephens set about reconciling these two approaches was to start to reposition the culture. Developing a more open and participative style of decision-making made the whole team focus on the business outcomes, minimising any point-scoring and turf wars that might have happened – and it would appear to have worked.

In many ways, what we now seem to have is a new breed of owner-manager, very much a product of the ways in which our working world is changing. These are the main drivers:

- There is a virtual obsession with immediacy in all we do and expect.
- There is a year-on-year increase in money available for investment, although there are peaks and troughs in how individual investments are made. There are also huge fluctuations in investment sentiment from year to year. What many have seen as a 'South Sea Bubble' investment approach in the dot.com era has, in the eyes of others, been followed by the Puritan approach whereby the best thing to do with money is to stick it under your bed. Predominantly, those who invested in technology businesses are now either licking their wounds and/or having to use what money they have left as secondary financing. Good proposals are finding it hard to get funding. What is clear, however, is that the national wealth in the hands of individuals and companies has increased and something needs to be done with this money because it all demands a return.
- Round-the-clock working hours and the merging of work time with leisure time, the increase in part-time and flexible working, the broadening and expansion of the service sector, and accelerating outsourcing trends are all major features in this process of change.
- Perhaps most significantly, the personal qualities of loyalty, commitment, integrity and professional skill, which all used to be seen as integral parts of being an employee, are now being realistically seen as something an organisation buys for a period of time. Paradoxically, against the background of growing and global corporate power, the power of the individual is also growing.

Recruitment process

Personal lifestyles are changing markedly. Increasing numbers of business people are going it alone. Very active in the SME market is the

UK200 Group of practising chartered accountants, an association of some 180 small-to-medium-sized firms of chartered accountants throughout the United Kingdom. Keith White is chairman of the UK200 corporate finance panel, whose task it is to advise, support and co-ordinate the corporate finance activities of the UK200 Group. He says that of all the SME corporate finance proposals that cross the desks of himself and his colleagues what is absent most is a good team to support the entrepreneur. It is easy to say 'Get yourself a good team' but it is difficult to say just how. 'Many entrepreneurs baulk at the cost of putting together a good team and have to be persuaded that for a good idea to turn into a good business a good team is needed', is White's comment. 'Costing it into the proposal also needs taking into account the benefits of having the right professional skills in-house.' Often, UK200 member firms' partners can make good introductions. Otherwise, the would-be entrepreneur has to look elsewhere.

The process of building the management team is a minefield full of fragmented resourcing mechanisms and difficult and tortuous networking routes towards finding the right people. In practice, the process starts with the 'who do we know?' approach. This is the best way of achieving the best results. It is also the easiest way of making terrible mistakes. Knowing someone with whom you have worked before may well be the best way of assessing their skills and abilities. But is it the best and most objective way of judging their suitability for the task and challenges in hand? It is easy to assume that a new venture is little more than a re-run of what happened in the past. It is easy to go for those cosy memories. It is easy to go for the comfortable assurances of someone you have known for a long time and who may well be a personal friend.

Building the management team through professional recruitment is the most sensible option. Most venture capital companies have good contacts with search and selection firms who understand the market and, more importantly, the issues involved in recruiting into either newly acquired or established companies. The choice of approach is between search, selection or file search. Search involves pinpointing the person or the organisation and at the level where the right person might be found – and then finding a way of extracting that person. Selection is based on placing an advert in the media and choosing from those who reply. File search is a process of trawling round the agencies and sifting through a pile of CVs of those available. Availability is not always the best selection criterion!

Alastair Singleton is a senior partner with leading search and selection firm, Hanover Fox International. In his opinion, although personal career risk is a key issue in introducing someone new into a new management team, an important attribute that they look for is a blend of clear energy and an outgoing view on business.

'A new business is someone else's old business', observes Singleton. 'Had it been a real winner in its old form, it would probably not have been sold – so it has to be energy and ability that is going to make the difference!'

In recent years, however, a fourth option has begun to work well – talking with some of the interim management providers who have a specialism in this area. Russam GMS, for example, runs part of its website for this very purpose. They recognise that of the 5,500 interim managers registered with them – and others who visit their entrepreneurship web page – many have entrepreneurial aspirations of varying types and intensities, and are interested in becoming involved in new ventures. Some degree of risk is attractive to them. In general, however, the greater the risk the more difficult the resourcing process. Who is going to leave a good job for a high-risk mega-bucks promise?

One answer is that many people did exactly this in the dizzy heights of the dot.com gold rush. Most now wish that they had stayed where they were, but are reluctant to admit it. The truth is that the jury is still out and many believe that the Internet is a journey that will inevitably have many happy endings. What has happened previously is that some of those embarking on this journey accelerated too quickly and crashed. What is happening now is that those who did not crash are suitably chastened and are proceeding more modestly, and some of those who did crash have regrouped and started again, often with a revised strategy. Some have taken the view that the best approach is to go to ground until the climate changes and then dust the product down and start again.

Keeping the management team together

Nigel Kendall prefers to see his start-up as an 'online' business rather than a 'dot.com'. He is a survivor, having reshaped his business strategy and altering the focus to selling to businesses rather than consumers. He had the advantage of getting both his financial backing and his management team from family and friends. His greatest concern now, however, is how to keep his management team of about ten together when the market is unfavourable.

'If I allow the team to break up,' Kendall says, 'the disruption will be very damaging. It has taken me years to get this far.' Part of the answer, he adds, is to keep his people focused on the product. It is not the immediate money that characterises 'new economy' businesses, but it clearly has something to do with the pot of gold at the end of the rainbow! The main driver for many is the product itself. Keeping people excited about the product has to be part of the process of keeping the team together. On the matter of 'immediate money', Kendall tells a salutary story of hiring a Java programmer from an agency for £1,100 per day and, on complaining that he was not delivering what had been asked for, discovering that the IT contractor had only recently arrived from India and was earning only £45 per day himself – not a sound basis for building a management team.

One of the challenges that Kendall had to deal with was the contract – the management agreement with his key people. How do you structure an arrangement that motivates, locks people in wisely and balances short-term and long-term rewards? Clive Borthwick runs the commercial side of leading Home Counties lawyer, Taylor Walton. He starts the process by asking the leader who wants to put a share scheme (of whatever type) in place if he really wants others to make the decisions, either as well as or instead of, themselves? The superficial and instantaneous 'yes' is soon replaced by some hard thinking. Entrepreneurs want to do things their way – needing to persuade others rather than simply expecting them to follow is a difficulty. Getting past this conceptual hurdle is probably the most significant milestone in building the management team.

For the larger deals, the first port of call for many is the industry giant, 3i. For those backed by 3i, building the management team will receive heavy support. Patrick Dunne is director of marketing with specific responsibility for the management buy-in (MBI) and independent directors' programmes. He knows more than most just how crucial it is to get the right team in place. 'You need to start with the leader', he confirms when looking at a do-able deal and the entrepreneur. Mostly the leader is the entrepreneur, but where growth in the business points to the need for a CEO this can be put in place through 3i's resources. What is slightly more difficult is finding a new CEO at a later stage when – as sometimes happens – the entrepreneur CEO loses the plot.

The independent director and the management team

Dipping into their 600-strong independent directors' programme results in approximately 200 appointments each year, mostly in the form of an independent director for each investee company. 3i can then work with the entrepreneur to complete the executive team mostly by searching their MBI programme register and, where this does not identify the right people, external search firms are brought in. From the entrepreneur's point of view, the advantage of going down this route lies in the skill and experience that is brought to bear. In addition, the significant cost and time that the leader would otherwise have to devote to this process is bundled into the deal as part of the total offering.

Most entrepreneurs would not see having an independent director on board as important or a priority, preferring to focus on completing the executive team first. 'Think again' is the advice from many financial backers. Many finance providers do want their own non-executive director involved to safeguard their investment. This can be a tricky one. If the non-executive is also a director of the finance provider that approach would be understandable but conflicts of interest can arise, sometimes taking the form of serious conversations taking place out of range of the non-executive and board meetings turning into contrived set pieces. Where it works best is for non-executives to see themselves as genuinely independent with a level of objectivity and experience which is of considerable value to the board and the finance providers. A growing number of owner-managers are, however, making their own decision to bring in non-executive directors.

The best independent directors introduced by many finance providers are keen to stress the point of independence. Buckinghamshire-based Antony Ripper, for example, who has held a number of independent directorships over the past six years, including some from 3i, always says that integrity is a vital element of the job. It is a rare occasion, indeed, he stresses, when he would not express exactly the same view to the sponsor as he would to the board. Chris Bundy, from York, agrees and stresses the importance of getting to know all the members of the board. He needs to know what they think and how they think – what drives them and how they are likely to react in any given situation. Team members can fall out over strategy issues – and, indeed, diversity of opinion is important – but committed team members sometimes need rescuing before adopting an isolated position.

Traditionally, the large clearing banks have rarely nominated or asked for non-executives on the board – and, where this has happened, they have had no strong lines of communication with the non-executives. They have tended to see it as an internal matter, have been nervous at being seen as shadow directors and have relied on the loans being secured and repayable on demand. 'This is now changing', says David Eales, North London corporate business centre director of the Royal Bank of Scotland. 'We need to offer more than our competitors and our customers want to negotiate and do deals. As important as the cost of the money is the level of business support we can offer, particularly in hard times, and we are keen to find commercial ways of doing this.' The criticisms of pulling the plug unreasonably levelled at the clearers during the last recession still rankle with some borrowers and the more enlightened are now seeing their lending banks as stakeholders and are involving them more in the business process.

The cynics would recommend the local golf club to find the right independent director. At the SME end of the business spectrum, research shows that a very high proportion of non-executives are found through personal contact, while at the medium-sized and larger company end of the market, bringing in professional help is the best approach. Peter Waine of market leaders Hanson Green says that despite the potential legal downside of being a non-executive director and the widening remuneration differential between executives and non-executives, there is no shortage of good non-executive candidates. The only restricting factor, Waine adds, tends to be the number of non-executive directorships that any one executive main board director is allowed to take. There is a growing awareness that a non-executive position adds value to both boards and is a perfect form of personal development. Ultimately, the key to a successful non-executive appointment is chemistry; it is not simply the quality of the input but the manner in which it is given. The very best non-executive directors also offer curiosity and courage, in Waine's final analysis.

In an increasingly global economy dominated by knowledge and the use of knowledge, entrepreneurship is now seen by government, businesses and business people as the key to the future prosperity of the United Kingdom. There have been more ideas and business innovation in the United Kingdom since the war than in any other country in the world.

Individuals provide the dream and the spark but it is those around them and who work with them that turn that dream into reality. Build the management team – there is no other way.

Useful contacts

1. Patrick Dunne's two books – *Running Board Meetings* and *Directors' Dilemmas* – are published by Kogan Page and are available from most good book shops. 3i can be contacted on +44 (0)20 7928 3131.
2. Nigel Stephens, CEO of Velo +44 (0)1628 898088.
3. Alistair Singleton, Hanover Fox +44 (0)20 7409 1177.
4. Entrepreneurship at Russam GMS +44 (0)1582 666970.
5. Nigel Kendall +44 (0)1483 232641.
6. Clive Borthwick – Taylor Walton +44 (0)1582 731161.
7. David Eales – Royal Bank of Scotland +44 (0)20 8367 7150.
8. Interim management companies can be contacted through their professional association, the Interim Management Association, on +44 (0)20 7323 4300.
9. Peter Waine – Hanson Green +44 (0)20 7493 0837.
10. Keith White and the UK200 Corporate Finance Panel +44 (0)1865 243155.
11. Antony Ripper +44 (0)1908 584042.
12. Chris Bundy +44 (0)1904 608297.

6.3

Enterprise Management Incentive (EMI) Schemes

Maurice Fitzpatrick and
Jay Sanghrajka
Tenon Group

This chapter examines how the new Inland Revenue-approved EMI schemes (introduced in the March 2000 Budget, and subsequently amended in the March 2001 Budget) function.

Context

An Inland Revenue-approved EMI scheme is essentially a tax-generous method of giving some or all key employees of a relatively small company significant share options over the share capital of the company. In order to appreciate how tax-generous the EMI rules (as explained later) are, it is necessary to first examine the normal income tax treatment of share options.

The basic rule is that if an employee is given an option to acquire shares in his employer company (E Co), then at the time he exercises the option and acquires shares he may face an income tax liability, whether he sells the shares or not. The amount on which he will be charged income tax would be the difference between the market value of the shares at the time he acquires them on the one hand, and the price he pays for the shares under the option on the other. It will be appreciated that if the options are heavily favourable to the employee (ie if they extend over a large number of shares, or where the exercise price is at a heavy discount to the market value at the time of the exercise) this income tax liability can be quite significant. The employee's problem is that he may not have sufficient cash to pay the tax, unless he immediately sells some or all of the shares. The basic income tax rules regarding share options are therefore penal.

Somewhat more generous, but relatively restrictive, are the rules appertaining to the Inland Revenue-approved company share option (CSO) schemes, effectively introduced in 1996 and replacing the old Inland Revenue-approved executive share option schemes. Under a CSO scheme, and subject to various detailed rules, one or more employees of a company can be granted share options to acquire shares at some stage in the future, such that no income tax arises at the time the option is exercised. Broadly, the exercise price has to be equivalent to the market value of the shares at the time the option is granted and the employee concerned can only have total approved options on £30,000 of shares in total. This £30,000 limit is computed with reference to the market value of the shares at the time the option is granted. The crucial advantage of a CSO scheme over the normal share option rules described in the previous paragraph is, of course, that no tax is payable at the time the option is exercised: the only potential tax liability is essentially a capital gains tax liability on the subsequent sale of the shares, whenever that should occur.

Nonetheless, in terms of incentivising a key employee, £30,000 worth of shares is a relatively low limit. It was to address this particular difficulty that the Inland Revenue-approved EMI scheme was introduced in 2000.

Inland Revenue-approved EMI schemes

Under an Inland Revenue-approved EMI scheme a company with gross assets (as defined below) of not more than £15 million can grant options with a total 'value' of £3 million to any number of employees. There is no upper or lower limit on the number of employees who can receive options under the EMI, subject to the overriding requirements that the total value of all options granted by the company under the EMI scheme cannot exceed £3 million and that no one employee can be granted options over shares in excess of £100,000 in value.

The 'value' for this purpose is computed with reference to the market value of the shares at the time the options are granted. Essentially, EMI enables a relatively small company to grant employees a more significant value of options in a tax-generous way than under any other route.

Qualifying company

The company's gross assets must not exceed £15 million. In general terms, 'gross assets' represent the total balance sheet value of the gross assets on the company's balance sheet. The Treasury is currently consulting on the possibility of raising this limit to £30 million, but any such change will not be effective prior to 6 April 2002 at the earliest.

To qualify, the company must additionally either be:

(a) a trading company; or
(b) the holding company of a trading group.

So far as concerns (a) above, the company concerned must be carrying on its trade wholly or mainly within the United Kingdom, while the trade must not consist wholly or as to a 'substantial' part the carrying on of 'excluded activities' (see below). The term 'substantial' is not defined in the legislation but is generally taken by the Inland Revenue to mean 20 per cent or more of total activities.

In terms of (b) above, then:

(i) at least one group member must satisfy the requirements as set out above for a single trading company; and
(ii) the group as a whole must not carry out to any substantial extent (ie to the extent of more than 20 per cent of its total activities) 'non-qualifying activities'.

'Non-qualifying activities' represent the aggregate of 'excluded activities' (as set out below), and non-trading activities.

'Excluded activities' include dealing in land, the provision of financial services, property development, the provision of legal and accountancy services, farming or market gardening, forestry and woodland, and the operation of hotels or nursing homes and residential care homes. Clearly, the object of the legislation is to exclude relatively low-risk trades from benefiting from EMI status.

Eligible employee of the company which issues the options under EMI (E Co)

Broadly, the employee concerned must work for E Co for at least 25 hours per week, or, if less, 75 per cent of his overall working time. He must also not own more than 30 per cent of E Co. In computing whether or not he owns more than 30 per cent of E Co, unexercised options are ignored.

Miscellaneous provisions

The option must be capable of being exercised within ten years beginning with the date of the grant. The option must specify the exercise price of the option, and can impose performance conditions affecting the employee's entitlement to exercise the option concerned. Provided the option exercise price is no less than the market value of the shares at the time the option was granted, there is no income tax liability arising on the employee at the time of exercise of the option. In circumstances where the exercise price is less than the market value of the shares at the time the option was granted, an income tax liability can arise at the date of exercise of the option. However, the amount of income, subject to income tax, is limited to the lower of:

(a) the excess of the market value of the shares at the date the option was granted over the amount paid for the shares on exercise of the option; or
(b) the excess of the market value of the shares at the time the option was exercised over the exercise price.

There are provisions whereby replacement options can be granted in certain circumstances where E Co is taken over by another company.

Possible use of EMI options

Smaller companies may face particular difficulties in terms of attracting and retaining employees who may well be key to the development of overall shareholder value. High-calibre employees may prefer the security of working for a larger organisation or may, for that matter, be lured away by smaller competitors offering generous share option packages. Smaller companies operating in relatively narrow markets may actually wish to lure vital people away from competitors, in order to damage those competitors. In these types of context, an EMI scheme could be regarded as a key part of a smaller company's human resources strategy. The key commercial question for a company (E Co) which is considering the use of an EMI scheme to address is this: can the use of an EMI scheme boost the total value of E Co by a greater proportion than the ultimate diluting effect (on existing shareholders) when the EMI options which are exercised? Clearly, in attempting to answer this question the use of estimates comes into play, but, subject to the uncertainty caused by the use of estimates, it may frequently be found that the answer to the question is yes. If it is, the implementation of an EMI scheme will probably be crucial in terms of developing the value of E Co for its individual shareholders.

Professional advice should always be taken to maximise the benefit from EMI options.

6.4

HR Issues Arising from Acquisitions

Judy Brown

Introduction

Business leaders now realise that deals are increasingly about people. Sometimes this is because they represent a major unexpected cost discovered in due diligence, perhaps due to an unfunded pension liability, but often the risks are more subtle. For instance, two teams of people previously worked in competitor organisations and believed – or were told – that their way of doing things was different – if not better – than the competition. They are now expected to work with the former competitor team, together as one. Difficulties are bound to arise.

In fact, management and people issues are the main reason for deals failing. Survey results show this time and again. These issues are therefore critical to the deal – and they need to be taken account of as an integral part of the merger and acquisition process.

Like all other aspects of an acquisition or merger, the HR elements flow through three basic phases:

- *Before*: identifying business strategy; assessing the target; planning the deal;
- *During*: doing the deal itself; negotiating; planning for Day 1;
- *After*: making the deal work; integrating, consolidating, harmonising.

This chapter identifies the most important HR issues that are likely to arise in a deal within this basic framework, including employee demographics, benefits, terms and conditions, and performance management. However, these issues cannot be assessed in isolation. An approach of 'Smith will do the pensions issues and Jones will assess the key people' leads to incoherent strategy and scope for unnecessary risk. An integrated approach identifies areas of overlap when looking at each of the issues.

> *Reshaping the workforce is not merely an exercise calculating the redundancy cost and corresponding reduction in payroll costs. It has significant effect on the pension needs, collective agreements, employee demographics and the culture of the entity. It may affect incentive plans and even performance management systems – are these people being made redundant because of inadequate past training, will re-training be introduced so potential candidates for redundancy can fill existing vacancies elsewhere in the organisation? Only by looking at the whole picture can the questions be asked and answered sensibly.*

In the HR area there is likely to be as much, if not more, time spent on post-deal issues. Holding on to key staff, the formation of new pension schemes and other benefit arrangements, the integration of two work forces (involving harmonisation of terms and conditions), reduction in staff numbers through redundancies and assessing existing relations with a trade union are all post-deal issues which a buyer may face. Evidence shows that many deals fail because one or more of these issues is mismanaged.

> *Recent surveys have focussed on lessons learnt. Post-deal feedback consistently contains the message that early planning of the post-merger stage has a significant impact on success. Without such planning, a company cannot implement necessary changes quickly enough to achieve maximum results.*

The key to success, then, is a successful HR strategy, which we start with below. HR strategy must be aligned with the overall deal objectives and must act as a constant focus for the detailed HR issues throughout – and beyond – the deal process.

> *Unfair dismissal claims, TUPE penalties, unfunded pensions, loss of certain key, but replaceable, staff will all give rise to one-off costs of varying significance, but ill-considered or 'forced' commitments on salary or pension funding, loss of critical skills and experience, or a failure to harmonise certain systems, will mean that the business plan is never met.*

Strategy

Strategy covers the ground from today's position, to the deal, and then to the desired performance.

Ideally, the HR director will be responsible for the HR issues in the deal, but not all companies have HR directors. The CEO or Finance director could take on the responsibility personally, but only if he or she has sufficient time to devote to it. If there is no one with sufficient relevant knowledge and authority internally, then external help in this area is an option, and one most successfully taken seriously and early.

In the area of HR strategy the role involves responsibility for aligning the calibre, retention and performance of staff with the overall business and acquisition strategy – and responsibility for the associated cost.

Although individual businesses and deals are all different, the role should include:

- identification of the HR drivers in the deal;
- identification of the impact of the deal on the HR drivers;
- the extent to which the strategy requires a high or low level of integration of the businesses;
- the extent to which a fundamental change in operation is required to achieve merger/acquisition goals;
- cultural fit – the extent to which 'ways of working' and style are likely to mesh between acquirer and target businesses (see below); and
- basic communications messages.

> *Various stakeholders, particularly employees, will expect an announcement of a deal to have credible analysis running through it from a 'people' perspective, and for the messages to be conveyed in a robust and effective way. Inconsistencies, doubts and gaps in the people dimension are likely to flow through the deal beyond integration and increase the probability of failure.*

Strategy needs to take account of:

- geographic profile – the challenge of managing or understanding cultural issues, employment law and tax impacts in the target geographies can significantly affect the cost of the deal;
- sector issues, including regulatory impact – strategically, moving into another sector can involve management control issues for the acquirer, more than usual reliance on the target management team, under-estimating or missing sector differences, exacerbated culture clash, or search and selection in unfamiliar markets; and
- demographics and size of acquirer in relation to target – there may need to be regional differences, and the impact on the culture and style of the acquirer will often be underestimated.

Cultural fit

> *Cultural fit is not simply an internal people issue – the integrity of the brand and the customer's view of a business are significantly influenced by cultural factors.*

For a successful merger the culture must fit the business strategy. Culture embodies the corporate values which need to be well defined and communicated (see later under Communication and Consultation). It is also supported and moulded by tangible factors:

- employee demographics, the age, skills, motivators of management and workforce;
- contracts and agreements, written and unwritten;
- remuneration from pensions to incentive schemes; and
- performance management systems.

Cultural imbalances between the acquirer's organisation and the business it is buying should not be disregarded. Cultural issues run deep in people, and many employees leave for no reason other than the fact that they do not like the way things are being done.

Strategy can be refined as information is gathered, and it is important to refer back to the strategy throughout the deal process and assess how the deal and the business are meeting the strategic objectives.

The three stages of a deal

Before: assessment

As with all other elements of the deal, before the buyer commits to acquiring his target he needs to know what he is getting. A thorough due diligence of the people issues is an especially vital part of the assessment process, even when the acquisition is achieved by the purchase of business assets rather than shares in a company. This is because the Transfer of Undertakings (Protection & Employment) Regulations 1981 (known as 'TUPE') will likely apply.

> *The TUPE Regulations transfer, by operation of law, the employees engaged in the target business to the acquirer. The acquirer inherits their terms and conditions of employment, their accrued periods of service and all rights and obligations relating to them. Only certain pension rights are currently excluded (although this is often quite significant).*

The prudent buyer should plan for and carry out as much due diligence as possible. HR due diligence should identify, quantify and prioritise the financial and business implications associated with people in mergers and acquisitions. These include existing liabilities, one-off costs, the need for future incentives and cultural fit. This analysis is a precursor to building a successful transaction.

HR due diligence includes all of the following areas:

- understanding hierarchy, demographics, working conditions and terms and conditions of the employees and the surrounding industrial/employee relations environment;
- identifying the key people and the key skills, understanding their 'fit' with the business strategy;
- quantifying the associated pay, benefits, pensions, training, and system costs and comparing them with costs shown in the accounts and other financial statements of the target;
- estimating the likely costs resulting from the deal; and
- examining full compliance with tax, pension and legal requirements.

HR due diligence means looking at people issues in the round.

A fair amount of information is usually available early in the process as it is often in the public domain. Annual reports, press reviews, articles and in-house magazines, publicity and recruitment material all have their own story to tell.

When data are available directly from the target, a detailed and specific information request must be made. Sometimes, depending on the circumstances of the deal, and often when only general requests are made, information on people can be the most sensitive and the hardest to obtain. Partial information is useless. Press for complete information and you will probably have insights on the workforce the target never had.

Key questions to be addressed in this process are:

- What does the HR asset look like as an investment? Are there areas which affect the desirability of making an offer?
- What HR costs and risks will there be in the transaction?
- If the company is to be reshaped, how expensive will this be?
- Will the right people stay? Will people perform at the highest possible level and in line with the business strategy?
- What are the cultural issues (which can cause an ostensibly sound deal to fail)? On so-called softer issues, it is amazing what information can emerge out of simple interviews of managers which would not be apparent from written material.

> *During a due diligence exercise, an HR manager was asked why the pay rates were less than market rates and the staff turnover rate was less than the industry norm. Had this company cracked the HR retention issue with good training, or with a supportive culture? No, she said, the people weren't very good and could not command market rates and this was why, regardless of any other excuses, the results were falling off.*

This assessment provides a proper basis for determining what employees must be offered to secure their commitment in the future. It should also identify any potential ongoing cost liabilities and negative consequences that the deal could trigger (for instance the crystallisation of benefit arrangements, which have the effect of loosening handcuffs).

HR due diligence is most effective when it draws on the skills of employment lawyers, actuaries, share scheme specialists, tax experts and performance management and communications experts, who are up-to-date in their area of competence. The latest cases on who has employment rights, on pension funding transfer of value, and on the effectiveness of restrictive covenants, the latest Revenue statement on PAYE, NIC and share schemes, and up-to-date benchmark data, will all affect the outcome of the acquisition. The latest developments on the European Union (EU) proposed directive on information and consultation will impact the process of the acquisition.

During: negotiations and transition planning

Key areas of specific negotiation at the time the deal is actually done are likely to be:

- Warranty terms and disclosures on employment, pensions and employee tax matters.
- Where TUPE applies to the transaction, a specific clause allocating (usually by way of legal indemnities) the employee liabilities, account being taken of the impact of TUPE.
- Pension arrangements (as to which, see below).
- In some cases equity and other incentive plans that are disturbed by the deal, or needed to retain key staff.

The due diligence and the warranty/disclosure process are closely linked. Communication between the people who carried out the due diligence and those who are negotiating the HR warranties and indemnities is vital, otherwise problem areas which have been identified through the hard work on due diligence may never be covered legally.

A clear example of this is pensions which, after salaries, can be the single largest employee cost. It is important to establish whether the costs currently being incurred are sustainable in the future. This includes not only reviewing the underlying assumptions used in calculating the pension costs, but also understanding how pensions are to be dealt with as part of the transaction. Is the whole scheme being transferred or a transfer payment is to be made available? If it is the latter, negotiations will have to be undertaken to ensure that adequate funds are made available to meet liabilities taken on by the purchaser. The past should not, however, affect the future. Going forward, there should be no constraints on the freedom of the purchaser to put in place arrangements for the future which accord with its corporate objectives. Pensions exposure goes far beyond the review of the formal pension schemes rules – it is also necessary to establish what individuals have been promised both in employment contracts and other communications.

Separate from the agreement, the businesses must retain key people and ensure that they perform throughout the transition to a consistent standard. It is imperative to manage the gap between the idea of the deal and completion date.

- Negotiate where possible with key people.
- Plan for day one and beyond.
- Identify 'must dos' and do them.

The communication and consultation issues (particularly those which are legally required under TUPE) must be addressed on a timely basis. The longer the time between when employees first heard about the deal and the actual time of the transition, the greater the opportunity for failure through, for example, the loss of key staff.

> *Keep a focus on day-to-day HR matters. Businesses need to keep a tight review of what is going on in the 'business as usual' arena, and ensure that liability risk is not introduced through loss of focus. This may suggest a particularly cautious approach to line HR matters during transition.*

After: post-deal performance

After the deal has been closed there are still many tasks to be completed to achieve effective performance. The most important of these are discussed below (see The main HR issues). Whilst these should be planned for prior to acquisition, it is only after closing that the purchaser is able to implement.

Longer term, all of these steps need to be consolidated in the creation of development and performance goals in an effective performance management system. The performance management system is often the point at which many HR 'enablers' to business success come together – it is important therefore that consideration is given to 'complementarities' with other HR processes. Key factors for the development of an effective performance management system include:

- the values of the newly merged organisation;
- support for behaviours appropriate to the new culture;

- individual and team levers against the key value drivers for the business;
- clarity of links to pay review, bonus and skills development; and
- appropriate mix of operational management, and integration transition effort.

> *Plan for day 2 and beyond – as well as day 1. Focus on d-day may lead to a problem with longer term planning. Both transition and line teams need to maintain a forward looking orientation and continually move their working horizon forward, as far beyond day 1 as is feasible. Clear reporting and authority should be established to adapt and reflect the changing context.*

Much of the HR transition planning review flows through into the post-deal implementation phase. Here, the key is for fast, effective action. The notes below outline some ways in which the transition planning focus evolves into action.

> *Review HR systems in terms of integration requirements and compliance. HR systems strategy for the new business must be clearly articulated and action agreed. As part of this process, potential problems need to be identified quickly. Different evaluation systems running in parallel can rapidly cause discontent and, potentially, statutory risk.*

The main HR issues

Key appointments and organisation

The shape of the organisation and key appointments and the methods by which these are put into place send a strong signal about the kind of business a newly-integrated organisation will be. New appointments should clearly have the respect of stakeholders (staff, shareholders and colleagues), and so require early assessment and careful consideration.

Who will manage the business? Some deals have foundered embarrassingly publicly at this point – it is clearly an issue that needs to be addressed courageously and without delay. And it is not just one chief appointment that needs to be made. Retention of other key people may well be an issue.

Appointments should be made quickly and decisively in order to maintain leadership momentum. Delay to the appointment process can create risk – during a hiatus there is unlikely to be effective articulation of new strategies and goals. Any hiatus gives the people who are uncertain about their future the opportunity and incentive to make mischief, putting their own contribution in the rumour mill and encouraging press speculation. Expediency in the interim will inevitably diminish the ability of new management to take a strong lead when finally appointed.

A lack of contingency succession plans for leadership and key staff who do leave, or the failure to implement such plans immediately, will risk unnecessary staff turnover and will have an immediate effect on the bottom line.

For the wider workforce, plan an industrial employee relations strategy. Where unions are recognised in relation to the target, these recognitions will normally be inherited by the buyer (including an assets acquisition under TUPE). Where union recognition is voluntary derecognition is an option for the buyer. If recognition has been agreed or awarded under the statutory recognition procedures, derecognition for up to three years will not be permissible (so it is important to understand how recognition is granted). If derecognition is considered, great care is needed given employee relations, the possibility of compulsory recognition being sought and awarded and (particularly in TUPE situations or if staff reorganisations are planned) other legal considerations. If recognition is to continue, the buyer needs to prepare for dealing with the unions (within the context of its own recognition arrangements, if any).

Key skills

> *'Adverse selection', the process whereby if people have a personal choice, they make the wrong decision for the company, is symptomatic of acquisitions: the good people with valuable skills walk away, often to competitors, and the others stay. Early cash payments triggered from incentive schemes exacerbate the issue. Deferred handcuffs are sometimes used but retention without performance can be a waste of money. This needs to be explored before and during the due diligence process and action taken to minimise the waste of talent.*

In some instances, sellers may be willing to give a buyer access to staff, either to meet and discuss a senior person's or team's likely future in the new organisation, or to agree and complete new employment contracts.

This approach is not risk free. Executives who recognise that they are key can set a higher price for their services if they realise the deal is dependent upon them (although a buyer may be quite willing to pay what it takes). Confidentiality issues are also raised and, whatever executives say, they might walk away anyway. But the process allows a more thorough understanding by the buyer of what he or she will (or may not) get.

With or without these commitments, a carefully planned implementation is necessary to ensure that the key assets do not walk out the day after completion. A recent survey showed that most companies underestimate the number of people with key skills they will need after a transaction, and in the event do not retain even this too low number.

Above all, there must be careful structuring and communication of incentive arrangements at all levels within the new organisation. It also means that the employees be given, and understand, the organisational back-up necessary for them to do their jobs.

Restructuring

Restructuring includes expansion, relocation and contractions (or any combination of these).

Where continued growth is required by the acquisition, recruitment effort must be sustained. This may mean development of market facing materials and induction training programmes which should tie in with the general external marketing strategy.

HR issues in location decisions need to be considered as part of the planning process. The merger of offices/closure/relocation could make the difference between someone staying through the transition or not. More fundamentally, the sooner people are located together, the quicker they work together and the faster the business performance should improve (or at least stop declining).

Mergers are often associated with job losses, at senior level and/or across the work force more generally. At the transition planning phase the focus is likely to be on assessing the numbers and costs involved. Some planning for the process may be undertaken. Care, again, is needed where the deal is subject to TUPE, as there are extra restrictions on carrying out dismissals at the time of a TUPE transfer and there may be an ongoing process of formal worker consultation.

If there are structural changes, the cost of any redundancies, the training needs, the likelihood of equal opportunity claims, the consultation process and, possibly most importantly, the communication process must be established very quickly. Those who remain must see that a 'no redundancy' promise is kept, or if redundancies are inevitable that redundancies are handled openly and fairly, otherwise they will not perform for the business. Badly handled redundancies not only increase cash costs but also hit the top line (not to mention the headlines) if remaining employees become disaffected.

Implementation of a redundancy exercise is well regulated by the law. Key points include:

- *Collective consultation (with unions or elected employee representatives) is required in all but small-scale exercises.*
- *Determining who is selected for redundancy needs detailed consideration to avoid employee claims.*
- *Redeployment must be considered.*
- *Individual consultation must not be overlooked.*
- *The exit package needs to be constructed in light of legal requirements and benchmarked best practice.*

Harmonisation

The information on terms and conditions emerging out of the due diligence exercise and the warranty/disclosure process in the agreement negotiation phase should allow the acquirer to do a full and detailed review of employees' terms. This can help assess the implications of harmonising terms and conditions of employment after acquisition, in terms of cost, and to find the appropriate fit for benefits going forward.

Harmonising terms and conditions of employment may be desirable. Without harmonisation, two workers doing the same job can be paid differently, which can have an adverse effect on the morale of at least one of them. Generally it is rarely desirable to operate two separate terms and conditions structures within one integrated business.

However, new terms and conditions cannot simply be imposed on staff without the risk of legal challenge, or the risk of the change being ineffective, or both. This is particularly the case when changes are linked to a TUPE transfer. Where the law currently stands, staff agreement to new terms may subsequently be able to be revoked.

It may be very costly to give both workforces the best of both sets of arrangements. Reducing benefits, on the other hand, can lead to employee resistance. A more effective solution may be the introduction of a completely new set of terms for all staff, probably including a flexible benefits scheme. This allows the employer to demonstrate the cost of each benefit and lets the employee choose from a selection that includes their existing benefits at the existing level, as well as benefits which their opposite numbers from the 'other' business enjoyed before the deal. The benefits could include medical insurance, holidays and pension contributions.

It is more difficult and not always necessary to harmonise actual pension arrangements, particularly where there is a vendor who retains the pension scheme for other employees.

Implementation of a harmonisation of terms programme can be a complex process. There is often a trade-off between ease of process and achieving legal certainty without the risk of claims. However the task is approached, the manner of communicating the changes is vital.

Compensation strategy

Compensation strategy needs to be clearly established. This goes beyond just harmonisation of two pay and benefits systems. There is a need to agree the goals and methods of the compensation programme. For example, a statement of philosophy might be: 'Newco is committed to a compensation strategy of pay in the top 25 per cent of similar businesses in each country in which we employ staff.'

A fundamental issue will be to ensure that the overall compensation and benefits strategy reflects the market positioning within the strategy, and the overall philosophy and values of the new business, including effective rewards for the very best performers. The strategy will be ineffective if the costs are not understood and the employees are unaware of the proposals.

Normally the acquirer is allowed to participate in the vendor's pension arrangements for a period of time following the completion of the transaction (although some vendors insist on a clean break from the date of completion). Thus the purchaser may have some time after closing to establish new schemes.

However, employees can become extremely agitated about uncertainties surrounding their pension arrangements. Therefore even where a participation period in the vendor's scheme is agreed, pensions must be included in the transition planning and the development of the overall compensation strategy.

The new arrangements should then be consistent with that strategy, recognising that this can cause major concerns with employees, even if the changes represent an improvement in their arrangements. Careful communication is therefore imperative.

In putting in place any new pension arrangements, it will be necessary to communicate to employees:

- the structure of the new arrangements; and
- the options which they have in respect of their service benefits.

At a minimum, employees must be told that they will continue to participate in the existing arrangements for a period, during which time they will be provided details of the new pension arrangements.

Incentives

A company's incentive schemes, or lack of them, reveal the type of performance or behaviour that is rewarded. The scheme may speak to a small team, or the whole company or to individuals. Inherited schemes are unlikely to be exactly appropriate for the future: they must match the deal aims and the business plans.

The immediate concerns are

- whether the deal is going to trigger an early payment out of the existing scheme;
- whether the deal is going to make the scheme inoperable (or encourage inappropriate behaviour);
- what incentive there is for directors and employees to stay during a transition period of uncertainty;
- what incentive there is for directors and employees to support the business plan.

Share schemes are easily recognised as needing attention as the changing tax laws, the deal requirements and the company and employment law issues can raise complex puzzles to solve; and yet appropriate equity participation is one way to incentivise employees to perform in the shareholders' interests and buy them into the deal.

Bonus schemes also need attention. Performance targets may cease to be measurable, or may confer exceptional bonuses. Such schemes can often be bought out with new schemes, but some early cash will almost inevitably be necessary.

The potential for mixed messages is high particularly with retention payments. For example, if the acquisition/merger is promoted as inherently 'good for staff', then a mixed message will result if people are then apparently paid an inducement to stay. A more consistent message might focus on reward for the extra effort required to meet the challenge of bringing two businesses together whilst maintaining 'business as usual'.

In structuring new pay arrangements one must be aware that the acceptability of recognition/bonus schemes may vary between the legacy businesses, and also may vary within business units/geographies.

Non-equity incentives need not be cash compensation based. Effective retention techniques include training and particularly programmes that enhance professional development as a means of demonstrating the business' commitment to invest in the individual. Dates for such programmes could be set out ahead, providing a longer-term incentive for employees to stay.

Continued training and development

In many businesses (especially knowledge intensive businesses), development for existing and newly merged staff should remain at the core of messages going through the transition. Some 'get rights' will be:

- continued personal development/career discussions with line managers/directors;
- ensuring that the ability to shape work around career development objectives remains at least in line with each group's existing norms and expectations;
- ensuring that investment in training and development is not pushed aside by integration issues.

Communication and consultation

Where TUPE applies to the transaction, staff who are affected by the transfer have the right to be informed of the deal and consulted over the effects on them. This should happen at a collective level, that is, with the representatives of any trade union recognised in relation to the staff, or with representatives elected by the staff. The obligation relates to all affected employees, not necessarily just those who are the subject of the transfer (although in practice they may be the only ones affected). This exercise must occur prior to the sale, so the main obligation in relation to the transferring staff falls on the seller, as their employer. The buyer therefore needs to be aware of this obligation in its planning process. But the buyer has a role too: to give details of any plans it has for the staff after transfer so that this information can be fed into the consultation process. Given that it may have job cuts in mind, this can often be a delicate issue. Also, because important pension rights currently fall outside TUPE, the buyer's plans regarding pensions are invariably a key part of this information.

This collective communication process needs to be considered within the overall staff communication exercise. Prior to completion of the deal, direct communication between the buyer and the target's employees is likely to be limited, firstly because of general confidentiality issues and second because the seller is unlikely to want to lose control of staff communication until the deal is set in stone.

New business leaders will need to articulate a compelling vision and quickly translate the big messages into something relevant and strong for their own areas.

In addition to leveraging 'broadcast' communications media, there is a need to plan the building of new teams as they emerge in the new organisation. This includes active attention in a number of areas, for example:

- clear messages around the strategy, direction and operation of new teams;
- director/manager time with individuals in newly forming groups;
- routine group meeting structures for planning, surfacing concerns, gaining support for changes, and taking forward ideas for change; and
- team-building events to share development of the team as an entity.

Key messages should be timed to ensure that staff, to the greatest extent possible, hear them at the same time, if not before, the public.

COMMUNICATION IS THE KEY

Written notes/memos/e-mails:
Good for more extensive or factual information (eg organisation issues, regulatory updates, client news). Not so good for dealing with individual concerns, or gaining support for new ideas/concepts.

Voicemessage or similar 'broadcasts':
Good for progress updates (it's very quick) and important bulletins. Not so good for long or complex messages and, at the broadcast level, not especially effective as two-way communication, nor for reaching people on a personal level.

Group meetings:
Good for local additions to business-wide messages; if run on a participative/small group basis, good for surfacing concerns, gaining support for changes, and of course taking in ideas for change. Not so good if local management is unable to add much local content, or to own local responsibility for the wider change programme.

Team building events:
Good for transforming issues into solutions, around the development of a new team; clearly less effective if there are unclear goals in terms of building the team. Likely to be essential 'technology' as a new organisation and management structure emerges.

One-to-one meetings:
Most effective in dealing with individual concerns, helping individuals to link into the transition programme, and surfacing deeper issues. Likely to be a key element of retention for individuals that are 'at risk'. Clearly not easy to use for wider messages, need to take into account consistency of messages, and require a manager/director with the skills, information and authority to deal with concerns.

The battle for 'hearts and minds' (which includes morale and retention) is won on an individual level. The more business leaders and managers can do to *listen* to their employees and address their concerns, the more likely they are to win. In this process it will be particularly important to 'capture', and then dispel, myths and misperceptions (for example 'we will all have to move to their building', 'our group will be disbanded' and 'we will all have to work in another part of the country').

One of the key issues in communication is to ensure that the correct media and vehicles are used to promote communications with the target groups concerned.

Conclusion

HR issues in acquisitions are important issue which should be dealt with by important people. It is imperative to address these from the start, to identify the risks and the costs, and to look forward to how the business will succeed from the HR perspective. Treating strategic and detailed planning, thorough due diligence and effective and timely implementation as one process is more likely to deliver business success.

6.5
Effective Environmental Due Diligence

William Butterworth
RPS Group plc

Background

Until a decade ago, the evaluation of environmental liabilities and risks associated with a merger or acquisition was a reasonably rare occurrence, particularly outside the United States. Now, however, environmental due diligence is widely incorporated as part of the transaction process and has become a critical aspect of risk management and due diligence. This is particularly the case in transactions involving manufacturing businesses or where property assets form part of the deal. This requirement for environmental due diligence has come about through the introduction of more stringent environmental legislation, more rigorous regulatory enforcement, intense public interest and awareness, more transparent financial reporting and the disclosure of provisions and contingencies for environmental works as part of the corporate governance culture. Each of these factors has combined to promote the corporate adoption of a systematic approach to environmental due diligence as access to capital may be blocked in the absence of such information.

What is environmental due diligence?

Broad and strict environmental liability regimes have now been established in many jurisdictions, including most of the Americas, Europe and Australasia, and as a result buyers must protect themselves against acquiring unwanted environmental risks in commercial transactions. Therefore, the goal of environmental due diligence is simple: it is to identify all material environmental risks and liabilities of the company or the facilities that the buyer is acquiring. Once these have been identified, the best strategy for protecting against these risks can be developed and negotiated, having consideration also for the proposed exit route, whether this be, for example, a trade sale or an initial public offering (IPO).

Environmental risks represent both practical and legal challenges, quite unlike any of the other factors that have to be addressed in a merger or acquisition. From a practical perspective, environmental problems can be expensive to correct, particularly the remediation of contaminated land. Identifying the source of the contamination for which remediation is required may not be that difficult; however, identifying the parties that have been responsible for causing it and hence are liable for its clean-up can be.

Other environmental risks that are as important as identifying contaminated land are operational liabilities. The operational deficiencies of a business can result in significant capital expenditure both to comply with current operational requirements and those that may be imposed by future changes in legislation. This is particularly pertinent in Europe at present with the introduction of new legislation for pollution prevention and control for industrial facilities. Operational costs can relate to waste water treatment plants, scrubbers to control air emissions or storage areas for hazardous chemicals, and the costs can run into millions of pounds.

A third and related category of risk is human health and safety, both in terms of the indoor workplace environment and beyond the factory boundary. Workers' injuries not only lead to a risk of claims, but can also require expensive upgrades for machine guarding or other protection systems. In extreme cases, regulatory inspectors may order that critical machinery be shut down at short notice, potentially crippling operations.

These practical challenges can be legally complex to resolve and getting appropriate commercial protection for issues identified or future unknowns can involve detailed legal solutions in the form of indemnities, warranties or even insurance. It has therefore become clear to sophisticated investors that some level of environmental due diligence is needed for every transaction, even if it is simply an informed decision that, due to the nature of the business, no further action is needed to assess potential environmental, health or safety risks.

How is it done?

The environmental due diligence process needs to be bespoke to take account of the issues that are specific to the business and the type of transaction. It is also important to ensure that the findings are disclosed in an appropriate and timely manner so that any risks or identified costs can be factored into the deal negotiations. It is therefore preferable to involve environmental advisers at an early stage in the process in order that this can be facilitated. This will enable an initial evaluation of environmental risks facing the business to be made, based on a review of data room information or information that is publicly available. From this initial evaluation any major issues that could be deal-stoppers can be identified and proposals for the contractual due diligence can be established. It is important to remember at the outset that different parties involved in the deal will have differing requirements from the due diligence process. These requirements need to be considered at an early stage so that all the relevant issues are addressed adequately for those concerned.

To ensure that the contractual due diligence process is undertaken as efficiently as possible, the RPS typically recommends a staged approach comprising:

- A desk study to investigate the site history and environmental setting of the site, with recommendations for a full 'Phase I' assessment if a contaminated land use or sensitive setting are identified.
- Phase I assessment including a visual inspection of the site, discussions with facility management and environmental regulators, and a review of documents and records.
- Phase II investigations such as soil and groundwater investigations, asbestos surveys or health and safety risk assessments to quantify risks that have been identified.

- Phase III remediation work such as the remediation of soils and groundwater or the removal of asbestos.

Increasingly, contractual due diligence is becoming more complex with a greater range of factors that require assessment, including: health and safety, food hygiene, fire risks, planning considerations, building management issues (asbestos, legionella and noise) and environmental management and reporting as well as environmental compliance and contaminated land assessment. The resources available within a service provider such as the RPS Group mean that all these risk assessment capabilities can be utilised to provide a co-ordinated and comprehensive due diligence service.

Benefits

From both the buyer's and seller's perspectives, effective due diligence reduces environmental issues from poorly defined, potentially costly and uncontrollable liabilities to manageable business risks that can be incorporated into the financial model of the transaction. It can also provide the basis for establishing the appropriate risk transfer solutions for the transaction whether they are achieved through a practical, legal or insurance solution. The due diligence information should also help provide a basis for continual environmental management to ensure that risks are managed as part of the day-to-day management function and in so doing making sure that indemnities, where given, and investment value are protected.

Part Seven

Directory of Corporate Finance Service Providers

7.1
Financial Advisers

Adam & Company plc
22 Charlotte Square
Edinburgh
EH2 4DF
Tel: 0131 225 8484
Fax: 0131 225 5136

Arthur Andersen
191 West George Street
Glasgow
G2 2LB
Tel: 0141 220 2000
Fax: 0141 222 2001
Website: www.arthurandersen.com

Bank of America Securities Ltd
1 Alie Street
London
E1 8DE
Tel: 020 7634 4000
Fax: 020 7634 4374
Website: www.bankofamerica.com
Contact: Elizabeth Wood, Marketing Associate

Bank of Ireland (NIIB Group Ltd)
Donegall House
9 Donegall Square North
Belfast
BT1 5LU
Tel: 028 9023 8111
Fax: 028 9024 6241

Bank of Scotland
Uberior House
61 Grassmarket
Edinburgh
EH1 2JF
Tel: 0131 243 5867
Fax: 0131 243 5948

Bank of Wales plc
Kingsway
Cardiff
CF1 4YB
Tel: 029 2022 9922
Fax: 029 2078 7555

Bankers Trust International plc
1 Appold Street
Broadgate
London
EC2A 2HE
Tel: 020 7982 2500
Fax: 020 7283 2848

Banque Nationale de Paris
8–13 King William Street
London
EC4P 4HS
Tel: 020 7895 7070
Fax: 020 7283 2848

Barclays Bank plc
54 Lombard Street
London
EC3P 3AH
Tel: 020 7699 5000
Fax: 020 7699 2509

Barclays Stockbrokers Ltd
300 Bath Street
Tay House
Glasgow
G2 4JR
Tel: 0141 352 3000
Fax: 0141 221 4951

Bertoli Mitchell Publishing M&A
Plaza 535
Kings Road
London
SW10 0SZ
Tel: 020 7349 0424
Fax: 020 7349 0338
e-mail: mail@bertolimitchell.co.uk
Contact: William Mitchell

Beson Gregory Ltd
The Registry
Royal Mint Court
London
EC3N 4LB
Tel: 020 7488 4040
Fax: 020 7481 3762

Bridgepoint Capital Ltd
101 Finsbury Pavement
London
EC2A 1EJ
Tel: 020 7374 3500
Fax: 020 7374 3600
e-mail: info@bridcap.com
Website: www.bridgepoint-capital.com
Contact: David Shaw, Chief Executive

The British Linen Bank Ltd
4 Melville Street
Edinburgh
EH3 7NZ
Tel: 0131 243 8325
Fax: 0131 243 8324

Brown, Shipley & Co Ltd
Founders Court
Lothbury
London
EC2R 7HE
Tel: 020 7606 9833
Fax: 020 7796 4875

Business Dynamics Ltd
The Coach House
50a Blackheath Park
London
SE3 9SJ
Tel: 020 8852 6560
Fax: 020 8852 2863
e-mail: business.dynamics@btinternet.com

Chartered Trust plc
24–26 Newport Road
Cardiff
CF2 1SR
Tel: 029 2029 6000
Fax: 029 2046 1345

Charterhouse Bank Ltd
1 Paternoster Row
St. Pauls
London
EC4M 7DH
Tel: 020 7248 4000
Fax: 020 7248 1998
Website: www.charterhouse.co.uk

Chase Manhattan Bank Ltd
125 London Wall
London
EC2Y 5AJ
Tel: 020 7777 2000
Fax: 020 7777 4745

CIBC World Markets plc
Cottons Centre
Cottons Lane
London
SE1 2QL
Tel: 020 7234 6000
Fax: 020 7407 4127
Website: www.cibc.com
Contact: Mark Preston, Head of Europe

Citibank International plc
336 Strand
London
WC2R 1HB
Tel: 020 7836 1230
Fax: 020 7500 1695

Close Brothers Ltd
12 Appold Street
London
EC2A 2AA
Tel: 020 7426 4000
Fax: 020 7426 4044

Clydesdale Bank plc
40 St Vincent Place
Glasgow
G1 2HL
Tel: 0141 248 7070
Fax: 0141 223 2093

The Co-operative Bank
PO Box 101
1 Ballon Street
Manchester
M60 4EP
Tel: 0161 832 3456
Fax: 0161 829 5212

Dao Hong Bank London plc
10 Angel Court
London
EC2R 7ES
Tel: 020 7606 1616
Fax: 020 7606 2900

Davenham Trust plc
8 St John Street
Manchester
M3 4DU
Tel: 0161 832 8484
Fax: 0161 832 9164

Deloitte & Touche
Bracknell
Columbia Centre
Market Street
Bracknell
RG12 1PA
Tel: 01344 454445
Fax: 01344 422681
Website: www.deloitte.co.uk
Contact: Mike Berners Price

Cambridge
Leda House
Station Road
Cambridge
CB1 2RN
Tel: 01223 259476
Fax: 01223 259517
e-mail:
stephen.fenby@deloitte.co.uk
Website: www.deloitte.co.uk
Contact: Stephen Fenby

London
Stonecutter Court
1 Stonecutter Street
London
EC4A 4TR
Tel: 020 7936 3000
Fax: 020 7583 8517
Website: www.deloitte.co.uk

Dresdner Kleinwort Benson
20 Fenchurch Street
London
EC3P 3DB
Tel: 020 7623 8000
Fax: 020 7623 4069

Dunbar Bank plc
9–15 Sackville Street
Piccadilly
London
W1A 2JP
Tel: 020 7437 7844
Fax: 020 7437 3953

John East & Partners Ltd
Crystal Gate
28–30 Worship Street
London
EC2A 2AH
Tel: 020 7628 2200
Fax: 020 7628 4473

First Trust Bank (AIB Group Northern Ireland)
First Trust Centre
92 Ann Street
Belfast
BT1 3HH
Tel: 028 9032 5599
Fax: 028 9043 8338
Website: www.firsttrustbank.co.uk
Contact: Sharon McAuley

Robert Fleming & Co Ltd
25 Copthall Avenue
London
EC2R 7DR
Tel: 020 7638 5858
Fax: 020 7588 7219

Forward Trust Ltd
Waterman House
101–107 Chertsey Road
Woking
GU21 5BL
Tel: 0800 328 3820
Fax: 0800 328 3823

GE Capital Bank Ltd
Trent House
Torre Road
Leeds
LS99 2BD
Tel: 0113 240 4230
Fax: 0113 240 4453

Goldman Sachs International Bank
Peterborough Court
133 Fleet Street
London
EC4A 2BB
Tel: 020 7774 1000
Fax: 020 7774 4510

Granville Bank Ltd
Mint House
77 Mansell Street
London
E1 8AF
Tel: 020 7488 1212
Fax: 020 7481 3911

Greig Middleton & Co Ltd
Glasgow
155 St Vincent Street
Glasgow
G2 5NN
Tel: 0141 240 4000
Fax: 0141 221 6578

London
30 Lombard Street
London
EC3V 9EN
Tel: 020 7655 4000
Fax: 020 7655 4100

Guinness Mahon & Co Ltd
32 St Mary at Hill
London
EC3P 3AJ
Tel: 020 7623 9333
Fax: 020 7283 4823

Harton Securities Ltd
6 Lombard Street
Abingdon
Oxfordshire
OX14 5SD
Tel: 01235 535000
Fax: 01235 555796

Hawkpoint Partners
4 Great St. Helens
London
EC3A 6HA
Tel: 020 7665 4500
Fax: 020 7665 4600
e-mail: annette.mason-waters@hawkpoint.com
Website: www.hawkpoint.com
Contact: Annette Mason-Waters

HSBC Investment Bank plc
Vintners Place
68 Upper Thames Street
London
EC4V 3BJ
Tel: 020 7336 9000
Fax: 020 7623 5768

IBI Corporate Finance
Donegall House
7 Donegall Square North
Belfast
BT1 5LU
Tel: 028 9024 6241
Fax: 028 9023 7921

Investec Bank (UK) Ltd
2 Gresham Street
London
EC2V 7QP
Tel: 020 7597 4013

Investec Henderson Crosthwaite
Corporate Finance
2 Gresham Street
London
EC2V 7QP
Tel: 020 7597 5970
Fax: 020 7597 5120

JP Morgan & Co Inc
60 Victoria Embankment
London
EC4Y 0JP
Tel: 020 7600 2300
Fax: 020 7325 8399

Julian Hodge Bank Ltd
10 Windsor Place
Cardiff
CF1 3BX
Tel: 029 2037 1726
Fax: 029 2034 4061
e-mail: info@jhb.co.uk
Website: www.julianhodgebank.com
Contact: James Penman, Group Marketing Manager

Kleinwort Benson Ltd
PO Box 560
20 Fenchurch Street
London
EC3P 3DB
Tel: 020 7623 8000
Fax: 020 7475 5994

KPMG Corporate Finance
8 Salisbury Square
London
EC4Y 8BB
Tel: 020 7311 1000
Fax: 020 7311 8748

Lazard Brothers & Co Ltd
21 Moorfields
London
EC2P 2HT
Tel: 020 7588 2721
Fax: 020 7628 2485

Lloyds Bowmaker Ltd
Finance House
51 Holdenhurst Road
Bournemouth
BH8 8EP
Tel: 01202 299777
Fax: 01202 299486

Lloyds TSB Scotland plc
Head Office
PO Box 177
Henry Duncan House
120 George Street
Edinburgh
EH2 4LH
Tel: 0131 260 0888
Fax: 0131 260 0300
e-mail: mark.prentice@lloydstsb.co.uk
Website: www.lloydstsb.com
Contact: Mark Prentice, Head of Corporate Banking

Matlock Bank Ltd
1 Connaught Place
London
W2 2DY
Tel: 020 7402 5500
Fax: 020 7298 0002

Merrill Lynch International Bank Ltd
Ropemaker Place
25 Ropemaker Street
London
EC2Y 9LY
Tel: 020 7628 1000
Fax: 020 7867 2867

Midland Bank plc
Poultry
London
EC2P 2BX
Tel: 020 7260 8000
Fax: 020 7336 9500

Mizuho International plc
Bracken House
One Friday Street
London
EC4M 9JA
Tel: 020 7236 1090
Fax: 020 7236 0484
e-mail: m.robertson@uk.mizuho-sc.com
Website: www.mizuho-sc.com
Contact: Michael Robertson

Morgan Grenfell & Co Ltd
6 Bishopsgate
London
EC2N 4DA
Tel: 020 7588 4545
Fax: 020 7545 7130

Naborro Wells & Co Ltd
Saddlers House
Gutter Lane
Cheapside
London
EC2V 6H5
Tel: 020 7710 7400
Fax: 020 7710 7401
e-mail: enquiries@nabarro-wells.co.uk
Website: www.nabarro-wells.co.uk

Nationsbank Europe Ltd
New Broad Street House
35 New Broad Street
London
EC2M 1NH
Tel: 020 7638 8888
Fax: 020 7282 2201

NMB-Heller
Enterprise House
Bancroft Road
Reigate
RH2 7RT
Tel: 01737 841200
Fax: 01737 841350

Noble Grossart Ltd
48 Queen Street
Edinburgh
EH2 3NR
Tel: 0131 266 7011
Fax: 0131 266 6032

Nomura Bank International plc
1 St Martin's le Grand
London
EC1A 4NP
Tel: 020 7521 2000
Fax: 020 7521 3699

Northern Bank Executor and Trustee Company Ltd
Causeway House
14 Howard Street
Belfast
BT2 7EB
Tel: 028 9033 2334
Fax: 028 9089 3413

PKF (formerly Pannell Kerr Foster)
Birmingham
New Guild House
45 Great Charles Street
Queensway
Birmingham
B3 2LX
Tel: 0121 212 2222
Fax: 0121 212 2300
e-mail: info.birmingham@uk.pkf.com
Website: www.pkf.co.uk
Contact: Sarah Holmes, Marketing Co-ordinator

Glasgow
78 Carlton Place
Glasgow
G5 9TH
Tel: 0141 429 5900
Fax: 0141 429 5901
e-mail: info.glasgow@uk.pkf.com
Website: www.pkf.co.uk
Contact: Charles Barnett; Graeme Cassells

London
New Garden House
78 Hatton Garden
London
EC1N 8JA
Tel: 020 7831 7393
Fax: 020 7405 6736
Website: www.pkf.co.uk

PricewaterhouseCoopers
32 London Bridge Street
London
SE1 9SY
Tel: 020 7939 3000
Fax: 020 7378 0647

Rathbone Investment Management Ltd
Port of Liverpool Buildings
Pier Head
Liverpool
L3 1NW
Tel: 0151 236 6666
Fax: 0151 243 7001

Rea Brothers Ltd
Aldermans House
Aldermans Walk
London
EC2M 3XR
Tel: 020 7623 1155
Fax: 020 7623 2694

NM Rothschild & Sons Ltd
New Court
St Swithin's Lane
London
EC4P 4DU
Tel: 020 7280 5000
Fax: 020 7929 1643
e-mail: salena.smith@rothschild.co.uk
Website: www.nmrothschild.com
Contact: Salena Smith

Royal Bank of Canada Europe Ltd
71 Queen Victoria Street
London
EC4V 4DE
Tel: 020 7489 1177
Fax: 020 7329 6144

The Royal Bank of Scotland plc
38 Moseley Street
Manchester
M60 2BE
Tel: 0161 236 8585
Fax: 0161 228 7625

SBC Warburg
1–2 Finsbury Avenue
London
EC2M 2PP
Tel: 020 7606 1066
Fax: 020 7568 0901

Schroder Leasing Ltd
Townsend House
160 Northolt Road
Harrow
HA2 0PG
Tel: 020 8422 7101
Fax: 020 8422 4402

J Henry Schroeder & Co Ltd
120 Cheapside
London
EC2V 6DS
Tel: 020 7658 6000
Fax: 020 7658 6459

Secure Trust Bank plc
Paston House
Arlseton Wall
Solihull
B90 4LH
Tel: 0500 207070
Website: www.securetrustbank.com

Shore Capital & Corporate Ltd
Bond Street House
14 Clifford Street
London
W1S 4JU
Tel: 020 7408 4090
Fax: 020 7408 4091
e-mail: info@shorecap.co.uk
Website: www.shorecap.co.uk
Contact: Graham Shore; Alex Borrelli

Singer & Friedlander Ltd
21 New Street
Bishopsgate
London
EC2M 4HR
Tel: 020 7623 3000
Fax: 020 7929 5338

Smith & Williamson
1 Riding House Street
London
W1A 3AS
Tel: 020 7637 5377
Fax: 020 7631 0741
e-mail: rjk@smith.williamson.co.uk
Website:
www.smith.williamson.co.uk
Contact: Robert Kidson

Solomon Hare Corporate Finance
Oakfield House
Oakfield Grove
Clifton
Bristol
BS8 2BN
Tel: 0117 933 3344
Fax: 0117 933 3345
e-mail: finlay-
mcpherson@solomonhare.co.uk
Contact: Finlay McPherson

Standard Bank London Ltd
5th Floor
Cannon Bridge House
25 Dowgate Hill
London
EC4R 2SB
Tel: 020 7815 3000
Fax: 020 7815 3098
e-mail:
stephen.naude@standardbank.com
Website: www.standardbank.com
Contact: Steve Naude

Standard Chartered Bank
1 Aldermanbury Square
London
EC2V 7SB
Tel: 020 7280 7500
Fax: 020 7280 7636

Tenon
Salisbury House
31 Finsbury Circus
London
EC2M 5SQ
Tel: 020 7628 2040
Fax: 020 7628 7531
Website: www.tenongroup.com

Also in Basingstoke, Birmingham, Brighton, Chelmsford, Eastleigh, Edinburgh, Falkirk, Fareham, Glasgow, Guildford, Inverness, Kirkaldy, Manchester, Newcastle upon Tyne, Perth, South Shields, Southampton, Sterling, Sunderland, Swindon, Windsor, Yeovil

TMG Corporate Finance
5 Oxford Court
Manchester
M2 3WQ
Tel: 0161 242 8800
Fax: 0161 242 8801
Email: enquiries@tm-group.co.uk
Website: www.tm-group.co.uk
Contact: Philip Travis

Tokai Bank Europe plc
1 Exchange Square
London
EC2A 2JL
Tel: 020 7638 6030
Fax: 020 7457 2736
Website: www.tbeuk.com
Contact: Peter Vincent, General Manager

Toronto-Dominion Bank Europe Ltd
Triton Court
14–18 Finsbury Square
London
EC2A 1DB
Tel: 020 7282 8226
Fax: 020 7638 0006

West Merchant Bank Ltd
33–36 Gracechurch Street
London
EC3V 0AX
Tel: 020 7623 8711
Fax: 020 7626 1610

Wintrust Securities Ltd
21 College Hill
London
EC4R 2RP
Tel: 020 7236 2360
Fax: 020 7236 3842

Yorkshire Bank plc
4 Victoria Place
Manor Road
Leeds
LS11 5AE
Tel: 0113 200 1200
Fax: 0113 246 7882

7.2

Legal Advisers

This section contains details of legal advisers involved in merger and acquisition deals and includes an indication of the smallest and largest consideration value of these M & A deals during the last two years. For reasons of confidentiality, exact figures have not been published, but the values have been divided into the following five bands:

Band A: £0–5 million
Band B: £6–10 million
Band C: £11–20 million
Band D: £21–100 million
Band E: over £100 million

Actons
2 King Street
Nottingham
NG1 2AX
Tel: 0115 910 0200
Fax: 0115 910 0290
Contact: J.C. Britten

Addleshaw Booth & Co
Leeds
Sovereign House
PO Box 8
Sovereign Street
Leeds
LS1 1HQ
Tel: 0113 209 2000
Fax: 0113 209 2060
e-mail: csl@addleshaw-booth.co.uk
Website: www.addleshaw-booth.co.uk
Contact: Sean Lippell, Head of Corporate Finance; Tim Wheldon
M & A range: A-E

London
60 Cannon Street
London
EC4N 6NP
Tel: 020 7982 5000
Fax: 020 7982 5060
e-mail: tmb@addleshaw-booth.co.uk
Website: www.addleshaw-booth.co.uk
Contact: Tim Bee; John Hiscock
M & A range: A-E

Manchester
100 Barbirolli Square
Manchester
M2 3AB
Tel: 0161 934 6000
Fax: 0161 934 6060
e-mail: jrs@addleshaw-booth.co.uk
Website: www.addleshaw-booth.co.uk
Contact: Jonathan Shorrock; Darryl Cooke
M & A range: A-E

Allen & Overy
One New Change
London
EC4M 9QQ
Tel: 020 7330 3000
Fax: 020 7330 9999
Contact: Guy Beringer; Alan Paul; Richard Cranfield
M & A range: A-E

Ashurst Morris Crisp
Broadwalk House
5 Appold Street
London
EC2A 2HA
Tel: 020 7638 1111
Fax: 020 7972 7990
Contact: Adrian Knight
M & A range: A-E

SJ Berwin & Co
222 Grays Inn Road
London
WC1X 8HB
Tel: 020 7533 2222
Fax: 020 7533 2000
Contact: John Daghlian
M & A range: A-E

Bevan Ashford Solicitors
35 Colston Avenue
Bristol
BS1 4TT
Tel: 0117 923 0111
Fax: 0117 929 1865
Contact: John Townsend
M & A range: A-D

Bircham & Co
1 Dean Farrar Street
London
SW1H 0DY
Tel: 020 7222 8044
Fax: 020 7222 3480
Contact: John Turnball
M & A range: A-C

Bird & Bird
90 Fetter Lane
London
EC4A 1JP
Tel: 020 7415 6000
Fax: 020 7415 6111
Contact: Charles Crostwaite; Chris Barrett
M & A range: A-E

Birketts Solicitors
24–26 Museum Street
Ipswich
Suffolk
IP1 1HZ
Tel: 01473 232300
Fax: 01473 230524
e-mail: mail@birketts.co.uk
Website: www.birketts.co.uk
Contact: Bob Wright
M & A range: A-C

Blake Lapthorn
Kings Court
21 Brunswick Place
Southampton
Hampshire
SO15 2AQ
Tel: 023 8063 1823
Fax: 023 8022 6294
Website: www.blakelapthorn.co.uk
Contact: Kathryn Shimmin
M & A range: A-D

Blandy & Blandy
One Friar Street
Reading
RG1 1DA
Tel: 0118 958 7111
Fax: 0118 951 6850
e-mail: philip_tranter@blandy.co.uk
Website: www.blandy.co.uk
Contact: Philip Tranter; David Few
M & A range: A-D

Boodle Hatfield
61 Brook Street
London
W1Y 2BL
Tel: 020 7629 7411
Fax: 020 7629 2621
Contact: Jonathan Brooks; Chris Putt
M & A range: A-D

Brabner Holden Banks Wilson
Liverpool
1 Dale Street
Liverpool
L2 2ET
Tel: 0151 236 5821
Fax: 0151 227 3185
Contact: Tony Harper
M & A range: A-D

Preston
7–8 Chapel Street
Preston
PR1 8AN
Tel: 01772 823921
Fax: 01772 201918

Bristows
3 Lincoln's Inn Fields
London
WC2A 3AA
Tel: 020 7400 8000
Fax: 020 7400 8050
Contact: Paul Cooke; John Lace;
Mark Hawes
M & A range: A-D

Brodies
15 Atholl Crescent
Edinburgh
EH3 8HA
Tel: 0131 228 3777
Fax: 0131 228 3878
Contact: William Drummond
M & A range: A-D

Brough Skerrett
99 Charterhouse Street
London
EC1M 6NQ
Tel: 020 7253 5505
Fax: 020 7253 5525
Contact: Gordon Brough
M & A range: A-D

Browne Jacobsen Solicitors
44 Castle Gate
Nottingham
NG1 7BJ
Tel: 0115 950 0055
Fax: 0115 947 5246
Contact: Rob Metcalfe; David Tilley
M & A range: A-E

Burges Salmon
Narrow Quay House
Narrow Quay
Bristol
BS1 4AH
Tel: 0117 939 2000
Fax: 0117 902 4400
e-mail: email@burges-salmon.com
Website: www.burges-salmon.co.uk
Contact: Christopher Godfrey
M & A range: A-E

Cameron McKenna
Mitre House
160 Aldersgate Street
London
EC1A 4DD
Tel: 020 7367 3000
Fax: 020 7362 2000
Contact: Richard Price
M & A range: A-E

Cartwrights
Marsh House
11 Marsh Street
Bristol
BS99 7BB
Tel: 0117 929 3601
Fax: 0117 926 2403
Contact: Chris Mitcher
M & A range: A-E

Charles Russell
8–10 New Fetter Lane
London
EC4A 1RS
Tel: 020 7203 5000
Fax: 020 7203 0200
Contact: James Holder; Simon Gilbert
M & A range: A-E

Clarke Willmott & Clarke
Bristol
The Waterfront
Welsh Back
Bristol
BS1 4SB
Tel: 0117 941 6600
Fax: 0117 941 6622
Contact: David Emmanuel
M & A range: A-C

Somerset
Blackbrook Gate
Blackbrook Park Avenue
Taunton
TA1 2PG
Tel: 01823 442266
Fax: 01823 443300
e-mail: nlindsay@cw-c.co.uk
Website: www.cw-c.co.uk
Contact: Nigel Lindsay
M & A range: A-C

Clarks Solicitors
Great Western House
Station Road
Reading
RG1 1SX
Tel: 0118 958 5321
Fax: 0118 960 4611
Contact: Richard Lee
M & A range: A-C

Clyde & Co
Beaufort House
Chertsey Street
Guildford
Surrey
GU1 4HA
Tel: 01483 555555
Fax: 01483 567330
Contact: Andrew Holderness
M & A range: A-E

Cobbetts
Ship Canal House
King Street
Manchester
M2 4WB
Tel: 0161 833 3333
Fax: 0161 833 3030
Contact: Robert Turnbull
M & A range: A-E

Collyer-Bristow
4 Bedford Row
London
WC1R 4DF
Tel: 020 7242 7363
Fax: 020 7405 0555
Contact: John Bailey
M & A range: A-D

Davenport Lyons
1 Old Burlington Street
London
W1X 2NL
Tel: 020 7468 2600
Fax: 020 7437 8216
Contact: Michael Hatchwell
M & A range: A-D

Davies Wallis Foyster
Liverpool
5 Castle Street
Liverpool
L2 4XE
Tel: 0151 236 6226
Fax: 0151 236 3088
Contact: Mark O'Connor
M & A range: A-E

Manchester
Harvester House
37 Peter Street
Manchester
M2 5GB
Tel: 0161 228 3702
Fax: 0161 835 2407
Contact: Pete Warburton
M & A range: A-E

Denton Wilde Sapte
Five Chancery Lane
Cliffords Inn
London
EC4A 1BU
Tel: 020 7242 1212
Fax: 020 7404 0087
e-mail: bs@dentonwildesapte.com
Website:
www.dentonwildesapte.com
Contact: Tony Grant
M & A range: A-E

Dickinson Dees
St Ann's Wharf
112 Quayside
Newcastle upon Tyne
NE99 1SB
Tel: 0191 279 9000
Fax: 0191 279 9100
Contact: John Flynn
M & A range: A-E

Dickson Minto WS
Royal London House
22–25 Finsbury Square
London
EC2A 1DX
Tel: 020 7628 4455
Fax: 020 7628 0027
Contact: Alastair Dickson
M & A range: C-E

Dundas & Wilson
Saltire Court
20 Castle Terrace
Edinburgh
EH1 2EN
Tel: 0131 228 8000
Fax: 0131 228 8888
Contact: Chris R. Campbell
M & A range: A-E

Edwards Geldard
Dumfries House
Dumfries Place
Cardiff
CF1 4YF
Tel: 029 2023 8239
Fax: 029 2023 7268
Contact: Jeff Pearson
M & A range: A-D

Eversheds
Birmingham
115 Colmore Row
Birmingham
B3 3AL
Tel: 0121 232 1000
Fax: 0121 232 1900
Website: www.eversheds.com
Contact: Peter McHugh
M & A range: A-E

Bristol
11–12 Queen Square
Bristol
BS1 4NT
Tel: 0117 929 9555
Fax: 0117 929 2766
M & A range: A-E

Cambridge
Daedalus House
Station Road
Cambridge
CB1 2RE
Tel: 01223 355933
Fax: 01223 460266
M & A range: A-E

Cardiff
Fitzalan House
Fitzalan Road
Cardiff
CF24 0EE
Tel: 029 2047 1147
Fax: 029 2046 4347
Website: www.eversheds.com
Contact: Paul Lowe
M & A range: A-E

Derby
11 St James Court
Friar Gate
Derby
DE1 1BT
Tel: 01332 360992
Fax: 01332 371469
e-mail: derby@eversheds.com
Website: www.eversheds.com
Contact: Richard Oakes, Director of Marketing
M & A range: A-E

Ipswich
Francisan House
Princes Street
Ipswich
IP1 1UR
Tel: 01473 284428
Fax: 01473 233566
M & A range: A-E

Leeds
Cloth Hall Court
Infirmary Street
Leeds
LS1 2JB
Tel: 0113 243 0391
Fax: 0113 245 6188
M & A range: A-E

London
Senator House
85 Queen Victoria Street
London
EC4V 4JL
Tel: 020 7919 4500
Fax: 020 7919 4919
e-mail: martinissitt@eversheds.com
Website: www.eversheds.com
Contact: Martin Issitt
M & A range: A-E

Manchester
London Scottish House
24 Mount Street
Manchester
M2 3DB
Tel: 0161 832 6666
Fax: 0161 832 5337
M & A range: A-E

Newcastle
Sun Alliance House
35 Mosley Street
Newcastle upon Tyne
NE1 1XX
Tel: 0191 261 1661
Fax: 0191 261 8270
M & A range: A-E

Norwich
Holland Court
The Close
Norwich
NR1 4DX
Tel: 01603 272727
Fax: 01603 610535
M & A range: A-E

Nottingham
1 Royal Standard Place
Nottingham
NG1 6FZ
Tel: 0115 960 7000
Fax: 0115 950 7111
e-mail: nottingham@eversheds.com
Website: www.eversheds.com
Contact: Richard Oakes, Director of Marketing
M & A range: A-E

Farrer & Co
66 Lincoln's Inn Fields
London
WC2A 3LH
Tel: 020 7242 2022
Fax: 020 7242 9899
e-mail: jt@farrer.co.uk
Website: www.farrer.co.uk
Contact: James Thorne
M & A range: A-D

Fennemores
200 Silbury Boulevard
Central Milton Keynes
MK9 1LL
Tel: 01908 678241
Fax: 01908 665985
Website: www.fennemores.co.uk
Contact: Chris Robinson
M & A range: A-D

Finers Solicitors
179 Great Portland Street
London
W1N 6LS
Tel: 020 7323 4000
Fax: 020 7344 5602
Contact: Peter Day
M & A range: A-D

Fox Williams
City Gate House
39–45 Finsbury Square
London
EC2A 1UU
Tel: 020 7628 2000
Fax: 020 7628 2100
e-mail: mail@foxwilliams.co.uk
Website: www.foxwilliams.co.uk
Contact: Paul Osborne, Head of Corporate Department
M & A range: A-E

William Fry Solicitors
Fitzwilton House
Wilton Place
Dublin 2
Ireland
Tel: +353 1 639 5000
Fax: +353 1 639 5333
e-mail: centreal.mail@williamfry.ie
Website: www.williamfry.ie
Contact: Karen O'Leary, Marketing Manager
M & A range: A-E

Furley Page
39 St Margaret's Street
Canterbury
Kent
CT1 2TX
Tel: 01227 763939
Fax: 01227 762829
e-mail: cbw@furleypage.co.uk
Website: www.furleypage.co.uk
Contact: Christopher B. Wacher
M & A range: A-D
Document Exchange: DX5301 Canterbury

Fyfe Oreland WS
Orchard Brae House
30 Queensferry Road
Edinburgh
EH4 2HG
Tel: 0131 343 2500
Fax: 0131 343 3166
e-mail: mail@fyfeireland.com
Website: www.fyfeireland.com
Contact: David Lindgren
M & A range: A-C

George Green
195 High Street
Cradley Heath
West Midlands
B64 5HW
Tel: 01384 410410
Fax: 01384 634237
Contact: RA Parry
M & A range: A-C

Gold Mann & Co
80 Fleet Street
London
EC4Y 1NA
Tel: 020 7822 2800
Fax: 020 7822 2822
Contact: Mark Hartley
M & A range: A-E

Gordons Wright & Wright
14 Piccadilly
Bradford
West Yorkshire
BD1 3LX
Tel: 01274 202202
Fax: 01274 202100
Contact: Tim Ratcliffe, Managing Partner
M & A range: A-D

Greenwoods Solicitors
Monkstone House
City Road
Peterborough
PE1 1JE
Tel: 01733 887700
Fax: 01733 424900
e-mail: mail@greenwoods.co.uk
Website: www.greenwoods.co.uk
Contact: Shelagh Smith
M & A range: A-D

Halliwell Landau
St James' Court
30 Brown Street
Manchester
M2 2JF
Tel: 0161 835 3003
Fax: 0161 835 2994
Contact: Alec Craig
M & A range: A-E

Hammond Suddards Edge
Birmingham
Rutland House
148 Edmund Street
Birmingham
B3 2JR
Tel: 0121 222 3000
Fax: 0121 222 3001
e-mail: david.hull@hammondsuddardsedge.co.uk
Website: www.hammondsuddardsedge.com
Contact: David J Hull, Partner
M & A range: A-E

Bradford
Pennine House
Lender Services
39–45 Well Street
Bradford
BD1 5NU
Tel: 01274 764400
Fax: 01274 730484
e-mail: feedback@hammondsuddardsedge.com
Website: www.hammondsuddardsedge.com

Leeds
2 Park Lane
Leeds
LS3 1ES
Tel: 0113 284 7000
Fax: 0113 284 7001
e-mail: enquiries@hammondsuddardsedge.com
Website: www.hammondsuddardsedge.com

Leicester
Regent Court
Regent Street
Leicester
LE1 7BR
Tel: 0116 247 0123
Fax: 0116 247 0030
e-mail: david.west@edge.co.uk
Contact: David West
M & A range: A-E

London
7 Devonshire Square
Cutler's Gardens
London
EC2M 4YH
Tel: 020 7655 1000
Fax: 020 7655 1001
Contact: Richard Burns
M & A range: A-E

Harbottle & Lewis
Hanover House
14 Hanover Square
London
W1R 0BE
Tel: 020 7667 5000
Fax: 020 7667 5100
Contact: Mark Bertram
M & A range: A-E

Harvey Ingram Owston
20 New Wall
Leicester
LE1 6TX
Tel: 0116 254 5454
Fax: 0116 255 4559
e-mail: hio@hio.co.uk
Website: www.hio.co.uk
Contact: Carley Ferguson
M & A range: A-D

Herbert Smith
Exchange House
Primrose Street
London
EC2 2HS
Tel: 020 7374 8000
Fax: 020 7374 0888
e-mail:
caroline.goodall@herbertsmith.com
Website: www.herbertsmith.com
Contact: Caroline Goodall
M & A range: D-E

Hobson Audley
7 Pilgrim Street
London
EC4V 6LB
Tel: 020 7450 4500
Fax: 020 7450 4545
Website: www.hobsonaudley.co.uk
Contact: Gerald Hobson; Max Audley
M & A range: A-E

Howard Kennedy
19 Cavendish Square
London
W1A 2AW
Tel: 020 7546 8851
Fax: 020 7664 4451
e-mail:
a.banes@howardkennedy.com
Website: www.howardkennedy.com
Contact: Alan Banes
M & A range: A-D

Hughes Watton
69 Eccleston Square
London
SW1V 1PJ
Tel: 020 7416 7600
Fax: 020 7416 7601
Contact: John Watton
M & A range: A-B

Andrew M Jackson & Co
PO Box 47
Essex House
Manor Street
Hull
HU1 1XH
Tel: 01482 325242
Fax: 01482 212974
Contact: John F Hammersley
M & A range: A-D

Jones Day Beavis & Pogue
Bucklersbury House
3 Queen Victoria Street
London
EC4N 8NA
Tel: 020 7236 3939
Fax: 020 7236 1113
Contact: Katie Dickinson
M & A range: A-E

Kent Jones and Done
Churchill House
Regent Road
Stoke on Trent
ST1 3RQ
Tel: 01782 202020
Fax: 01782 202040
e-mail: mail@kjd.co.uk
Contact: Peter Ellis
M & A range: A-C

Kidd Rapinet
14–15 Craven Street
London
WC2N 5AD
Tel: 020 7925 0303
Fax: 020 7925 0334
e-mail: pwild@krlondon.co.uk
Website: www.kiddrapinet.co.uk
Contact: Philip Wild; Chris Henniker
M & A range: A-D

Kimbell & Co Solicitors
463 Silbury Court
Silbury Boulevard
Milton Keynes
MK9 2HJ
Tel: 01908 668555
Fax: 01908 674344
Contact: Stephen Kimbell, Senior Partner
M & A range: A-D

Kuit Steinart Levy
3 St Mary's Parsonage
Manchester
M3 2RD
Tel: 0161 832 3434
Fax: 0161 832 6650
e-mail: ksllaw@kuits.com, weblegal@kuits.com
Contact: Robert Levy
M & A range: A-E

Ledingham Chalmers
1 Golden Square
Aberdeen
AB10 1HA
Tel: 01224 408408
Fax: 01224 408404
e-mail: john.rutherford@ledingham chalmers.com
Website:
www.ledinghamchalmers.com
Contact: John Rutherford
M & A range: A-D

Lee Crowder
39 Newhall Street
Birmingham
B3 3YD
Tel: 0121 237 2507
Fax: 0121 236 4710
e-mail: greg.emms@leecrowder.co.uk
Contact: Gregory T Emms

Lewis Silkin
12 Gough Square
London
EC4A 3DW
Tel: 020 7074 8004
Fax: 020 7832 1200
e-mail:
clare.grayston@lewissilkin.com
Website: www.lewissilkin.com
Contact: Clare Grayston, Partner
M & A range: A-E

Linklaters & Alliance
One Silk Street
London
EC2Y 8HQ
Tel: 020 7456 2000
Fax: 020 7456 2222
Contact: Anthony Cann
M & A range: A-E

Linnells Solicitors
Greyfriars Court
Paradise Square
Oxford
OX1 1BB
Tel: 01865 248607
Fax: 01865 728445
Contact: Edward Lee
M & A range: A-B

Lovells
65 Holborn Viaduct
London
EC1A 2DY
Tel: 020 7296 2000
Fax: 020 7296 2001
Website: www.lovells.com
Contact: Hugh Nineham
M & A range: A-E

Lupton Fawcett
Yorkshire House
Greek Street
Leeds
LS1 5SX
Tel: 0113 280 2000
Fax: 0113 245 6782
Contact: Bob Harrap
M & A range: A-D

McCann Fitzgerald
2 Harbourmaster Place
International Financial Services Centre
Dublin 1
Ireland
Tel: +353 1 829 0000
Fax: +353 1 829 0010
e-mail: postmaster@mccann-fitzgerald.ie
Website: www.mccann-fitzgerald.ie
Contact: Barry Devereux; William Earley; Fergus Armstrong; Paul Heffernan
M & A range: A-E

MacFarlanes
10 Norwich Street
London
EC4A 1BD
Tel: 020 7831 9222
Fax: 020 7831 9607
Website: www.macfarlanes.com
Contact: Penny Rutterford
M & A range: A-E

McGrigor Donald
Belfast
2 Donegall Square East
Belfast
BT1 5HB
Tel: 028 9027 8800
Fax: 028 9027 8881
e-mail:
richard.masters@mcgrigors.com
Website: www.mcgrigors.com
Contact: Richard Masters; Kerry O'Hara
M & A range: A-E

Edinburgh
Erskine House
68–73 Queen Street
Edinburgh
EH2 4NF
Tel: 0131 226 7777
Fax: 0131 226 7700
Contact: Colin Gray
M & A range: A-E

Glasgow
Pacific House
70 Wellington Street
Glasgow
G2 6SB
Tel: 0141 248 6677
Fax: 0141 204 1351 / 221 1390
Contact: Colin Gray
M & A range: A-E

London
63 Queen Victoria Street
London
EC4N 4ST
Tel: 020 7329 3299
Fax: 020 7239 4000
Contact: Colin Gray
M & A range: A-E

Maclay Murray & Spens Solicitors
Glasgow (Head Office)
151 St Vincent Street
Glasgow
G2 5NJ
Tel: 0141 248 5011
Fax: 0141 248 5819
e-mail:
mps@maclaymurrayspens.co.uk
Website:
www.maclaymurrayspens.co.uk
Contact: Magnus Swanson
M & A range: A-E

Edinburgh
3 Glenfinlas Street
Edinburgh
EH3 6AQ
Tel: 0131 226 5196
Fax: 0131 226 3174
e-mail:
gecs@maclaymurrayspens.co.uk
Website:
www.maclaymurrayspens.co.uk
Contact: Graeme Sloan
M & A range: A-E

London
10 Foster Lane
London
EC2V 6HR
Tel: 020 7606 6130
Fax: 020 7600 0992
Contact: David Cooke
M & A range: A-E

MacRoberts Solicitors
152 Bath Street
Glasgow
G2 4TB
Tel: 0141 332 9988
Fax: 0141 332 8886
Contact: James McGinn
M & A range: A-D

Manches & Co
81 Aldwych
London
WC2B 4RP
Tel: 020 7404 4433
Fax: 020 7430 1133
Contact: Christopher Owen
M & A range: A-D

Masons
30 Aylesbury Street
London
EC1R 0ER
Tel: 020 7490 4000
Fax: 020 7490 2545
Contact: Russell Booker
M & A range: A-E

Memery Crystal
31 Southampton Row
London
WC1B 5HT
Tel: 020 7242 5905
Fax: 020 7242 2058
e-mail: info@memerycrystal.com
Website: www.memerycrystal.com
Contact: Lesley Gregory
M & A range: A-E

Mills & Reeve Solicitors
NB: The offices based in Cambridge and Norwich undertake the majority of M&A work.

Birmingham
Midland House
132 Hagley Road
Edgbaston
Birmingham
B16 9NN
Tel: 0121 454 4000
Fax: 0121 456 3631

Cambridge
Francis House
112 Hills Road
Cambridge
CB2 1PH
Tel: 01223 364422
Fax: 01223 355848
e-mail: glynne.stanfield@mills-reeve.com
Website: www.mills-reeve.com
Contact: Glynne Stanfield
M & A range: A-E

Cardiff
Temple Court
Cathedral Road
Cardiff
CF1 9HA
Tel: 029 2078 6440
Fax: 029 2078 6441

Norwich
Francis House
3–7 Redwell Street
Norwich
NR2 4TJ
Tel: 01603 693225
Fax: 01603 633027
e-mail: bryony.falkus@mills-reeve.com
Contact: Bryony Falkus
M & A range: A-E

Morgan Cole
Cardiff
Bradley Court
Park Place
Cardiff
CF1 3DP
Tel: 029 2038 5385
Fax: 029 2038 5300
Contact: Duncan Macintosh
M & A range: A-E

London
167 Fleet Street
London
EC4A 2JB
Tel: 020 7822 8000
Fax: 020 7822 8222
e-mail: graeme.guthrie@morgan-cole.com
Website: www.morgan-cole.com
Contact: Graeme Guthrie
M & A range: A-E

Oxford
Buxton Court
3 West Way
Oxford
OX2 0SZ
Tel: 01865 262600
Fax: 01865 721367
e-mail: vanessa.williams@morgan-cole.com
Website: www.morgan-cole.com
Contact: Vanessa Williams
M & A range: A-E

Reading
Apex Plaza
Forbury Road
Reading
RG1 1AX
Tel: 0118 955 3000
Fax: 0118 939 3210
Contact: Bruce Potter
M & A range: A-E

Swansea
Princess House
Princess Way
Swansea
SA1 3LJ
Tel: 01792 634634
Fax: 01792 634500
e-mail: peter.jones@morgan-cole.com
Website: www.morgan-cole.com
Contact: Peter Jones
M & A range: A-E

Robert Muckle Solicitors
Norham House
12 New Bridge Street West
Newcastle upon Tyne
NE1 8AS
Tel: 0191 232 4402
Fax: 0191 261 6954
Contact: Ian Gilthorpe
M & A range: A-C

Nabarro Nathanson
Lacon House
84 Theobold's Road
London
W1X 8RW
Tel: 020 7524 6434
Fax: 020 7524 6524
e-mail: d.reynolds@nabarro.com
Website: www.nabarro.com
Contact: Derek Reynolds
M & A range: A-E

Nicholson Graham & Jones
110 Cannon Street
London
EC4N 6AR
Tel: 020 7648 9000
Fax: 020 7648 9001
e-mail: info@ngj.co.uk
Website: www.ngj.co.uk
Contact: Maurice Court
M & A range: A-E

Norton Rose
Kempson House
35–37 Camomile Street
London
EC3A 7AN
Tel: 020 7283 6000
Fax: 020 7283 6500
Contact: Barbara Stephenson, Corporate Finance Partner
M & A range: A-E

Osborne Clarke
Bristol
50 Queen Charlotte Street
Bristol
BS1 4HE
Tel: 0117 923 5280
Fax: 0117 927 9209
Contact: Simon Beswick
M & A range: A-E

London
Hillgate House
26 Old Bailey
London
EC4M 7HW
Tel: 020 7809 1000
Fax: 020 7809 1005
Contact: Andrew Saul
M & A range: A-E

Reading
Apex Plaza
Forbury Road
Reading
RG1 1AX
Tel: 0118 925 2000
Fax: 0118 925 0038
e-mail:
andrew.gowans@osbourneclarke.com
Website: www.osbourneclarke.com
Contact: Andrew Gowans
M & A range: A-E

Paisner & Co
Bouverie House
154 Fleet Street
London
EC4A 2DQ
Tel: 020 7353 0299
Fax: 020 7583 8621
Contact: David Collins
M & A range: A-E

Pannone & Partners Solicitors
123 Deansgate
Manchester
M3 2BU
Tel: 0161 909 3000
Fax: 0161 909 4444
Contact: Soren Tattam
M & A range: A-D

Paull & Williamsons
Investment House
6 Union Row
Aberdeen
AB10 1DQ
Tel: 01224 621621
Fax: 01224 640446
e-mail: sbarrie@paull-williamsons.co.uk
Website: www.paull-williamsons.co.uk
Contact: Sidney Barrie
M & A range: A-E

Penningtons
Godalming
Highfield
Brighton Road
Godalming
GU7 1NS
Tel: 01483 791800
Fax: 01483 424177
e-mail: peilejr@penningtons.co.uk
Website: www.penningtons.co.uk
Contact: Robin Peile
M & A range: A-D

London
Bucklersbury House
83 Cannon Street
London
ECN 8PE
Tel: 020 7457 3000
Fax: 020 7457 3240
Contact: Ron Allsopp
M & A range: A-E

Pinsent Curtis Biddle
Birmingham
3 Colmore Circus
Birmingham
B4 6BH
Tel: 0121 200 1050
Fax: 0121 626 1040
e-mail:
andrew.eastgate@pinsents.com
Website: www.pinsents.com
Contact: Clare Turnbull
M & A range: A-E

Leeds
1 Park Row
Leeds
LS1 SAB
Tel: 0113 244 5000
Fax: 0113 244 8000
Contact: Clare Turnbull
M & A range: A-E

London
Dashwood House
69 Old Broad Street
London
EC2M 1NR
Tel: 020 7418 7000
Fax: 020 7418 7050
e-mail:
alan.greenaugh@pinsents.com
Website: www.pinsents.com
Contact: Clare Turnbull
M & A range: A-E

Radcliffes
5 Great College Street
London
SW1P 3SJ
Tel: 020 7222 7040
Fax: 020 7222 6208
Contact: Rupert Lescher
M & A range: A-D

Reed Smith Warner Cranston
Pickfords Wharf
Clink Street
London
SE1 9DG
Tel: 020 7403 2900
Fax: 020 7403 4221
e-mail: ifagelson@reedsmith.co.uk
Website: www.reedsmith.co.uk
Contact: Ian Fagelson
M & A range: A-E

Reynolds Porter Chamberlain
Chichester House
278–282 High Holborn
London
WC1V 7HA
Tel: 020 7242 2877
Fax: 020 7242 1431
Contact: Tim Anderson; Jonathan Watmough
M & A range: A-E

Richards Butler
Beaufort House
15 St Botolph Street
London
EC3A 7EE
Tel: 020 7247 6555
Fax: 020 7247 5091
Contact: David Boutcher
M & A range: A-E

Rowe & Maw
20 Blackfriars Lane
London
EC4V 6HD
Tel: 020 7248 4282
Fax: 020 7248 2009
Website: www.roweandmaw.co.uk
Contact: Christopher Pullen
M & A range: A-E

Salans Hertzfeld & Heilbronn HRK
Clements House
14–18 Gresham Street
London
EC2V 7NN
Tel: 020 7509 6000
Fax: 020 7726 6191
e-mail: london@salans.com; penoch@salans.com; sfinch@salans.com; rthomas@salans.com
Website: www.salans.com
Contact: Philip Enoch; Stephen Finch; Richard Thomas
M & A range: A-E

Shakespeares
10 Bennetts Hill
Birmingham
B2 5RS
Tel: 0121 632 4199
Fax: 0121 643 2257
e-mail: info@shakespeares.co.uk
Contact: Charles Flint; Jill Kennedy; Tony Jones
M & A range: A-D

Shepherd & Wedderburn WS
Saltire Court
20 Castle Terrace
Edinburgh
EH1 2ET
Tel: 0131 228 9900
Fax: 0131 228 1222
Contact: James Will
M & A range: A-E

Shoosmiths
Banbury
52–54 The Green
Banbury
Oxon
OX16 9AB
Tel: 01295 267971
Fax: 01295 267751
e-mail:
john.spratt@shoosmiths.co.uk
Website: www.shoosmiths.co.uk
Contact: John Spratt
Hitendra Patel
M & A range: C

Northampton
The Lakes
Bedford Road
Northampton
NN4 7SH
Tel: 01604 543000
Fax: 01604 543543
Contact: Kit O'Grady
M & A range: A-D

Nottingham
Lock House
Castle Meadow Road
Nottingham
NG2 1AG
Tel: 0115 906 5000
Fax: 0115 906 5001
Contact: Oliver Brookshaw
M & A range: A-E

Reading
Regents Gate
Crown Street
Reading
Berkshire
RG1 2PQ
Tel: 0118 965 8765
Fax: 0118 965 8700
e-mail:
dean.drew@shoosmiths.co.uk
Website: www.shoosmiths.co.uk
Contact: Dean Drew
M & A range: A-E

Rugby
Bloxam Court
Corporation Street
Rugby
CV21 2DU
Tel: 01788 573111
Fax: 01788 536651
Contact: David Cranfield; Chris Hill
M & A range: A-B

Simmons & Simmons
City Point
One Ropemaker Street
London
EC2Y 9SS
Tel: 020 7628 2020
Fax: 020 7628 2070
Website: www.simmons-simmons.com
Contact: Stuart Evans, Partner, Head of Corporate Finance
M & A range: E

Simmons & Simmons has advised on M&A deals over the last two years worth approximately £96 billion – this includes UK, European and International deals.

Slaughter & May
35 Basinghall Street
London
EC2V 5DB
Tel: 020 7600 1200
Fax: 020 7726 0038
Contact: Stephen Cooke
M & A range: A-E

Speechly Bircham
6 St Andrew Street
London
EC4A 3LX
Tel: 020 7427 6400
Fax: 020 7427 6600
e-mail: marketing@speechlys.com
Website: www.speechlybircham.com
Contact: Oonagh Hunt
M & A range: C-D

Stephenson Harwood
1 St Paul's Churchyard
London
EC4M 8SH
Tel: 020 7329 4422
Fax: 020 7606 0822
Website: www.shlegal.com
Contact: Judith Shepherd
M & A range: A-E

Taylor Joynson Garrett
Carmelite
50 Victoria Embankment
Blackfriars
London
EC4Y 0DX
Tel: 020 7300 7000
Fax: 020 7300 7100
e-mail: enquiries@tjg.co.uk
Website: www.tjg.co.uk
Contact: Lisa Tooley
M & A range: A-E

Taylor Vinters
Merlin Place
Milton Road
Cambridge
CB4 0DP
Tel: 01223 423444
Fax: 01223 425456
Website: www.taylor-vinters.co.uk
M & A range: A-D

Taylor Walton Solicitors
36–44 Alma Street
Luton
LU1 2PL
Tel: 01582 731161
Fax: 01582 457900
Contact: MG Pettit
M & A range: A-D

Theodore Goddard
150 Aldersgate Street
London
EC1A 4EJ
Tel: 020 7606 8855
Fax: 020 7606 4390
e-mail: info@theodoregoddard.co.uk
Website: www.theodoregoddard.com
Contact: Joanna Whalley
M & A range: A-E

TLT Solicitors
1 Redcliff Street
Bristol
BS99 7JZ
Tel: 0117 917 7777
Fax: 0117 917 7778
Website: www.tltsolicitors.com
Contact: David Pester
M & A range: A-D

Tods Murray WS
66 Queen Street
Edinburgh
EH2 4NE
Tel: 0131 226 4771
Fax: 0131 225 3676
e-mail: maildesk@todsmurray.co.uk
Contact: David N Dunsire
M & A range: A-E

Travers Smith Braithwaite
10 Snow Hill
London
EC1A 2AL
Tel: 020 7248 9133
Fax: 020 7236 3728
Contact: Christopher Bell, Chris Hale
M & A range: A-E

Veale Wasbrough
Orchard Court
Orchard Lane
Bristol
BS1 5DS
Tel: 0117 925 2020
Fax: 0117 925 2025
Contact: David Worthington
M & A range: A-E

Watson, Farley & Williams
15 Appold Street
London
EC2A 2HB
Tel: 020 7814 8000
Fax: 020 7814 8141 / 8142
Contact: Ian Fagelson
M & A range: A-E

Wilde Sapte
1 Fleet Place
London
EC4M 7WS
Tel: 020 7246 7000
Fax: 020 7246 7777
Contact: Steven Blakeley, Managing Partner
M & A range: A-E

Withers
12 Gough Square
London
EC4A 3DW
Tel: 020 7936 1000
Fax: 020 7936 2589
Contact: Hugh Devlin
M & A range: A-D

Wragge & Co
55 Colmore Row
Birmingham
B3 2AS
Tel: 0121 233 1000
Fax: 0121 214 1099
e-mail: mail@wragge.com
Website: www.wragge.com
Contact: David Vaughan
M & A range: A-E

7.3
Private Equity Sources

This section contains details of private equity sources and includes an indication of their smallest and largest investment deals of the last two years. For reasons of confidentiality, exact figures have not been published but equity values have been divided into the following five bands:

Band A: £0–5 million
Band B: £6–10 million
Band C: £11–20 million
Band D: £21–100 million
Band E: over £100 million

Aberdeen Asset Managers Ltd
1 Albyn Place
Aberdeen
AB10 1YG
Tel: 01224 631999
Fax: 01224 425916
Website: www.aberdeen-asset.com
Contact: Hugh Little, Director
Investment range: A

Aberdeen Murray Johnstone Private Equity
London
One Bow Churchyard
London
EC4M 9HH
Tel: 020 463 6452
Fax: 020 463 6595
e-mail: private.equity@aberdeen-asset.com
Website: www.aberdeen-asset.co.uk
Contact: Tony Dickin
Investment range: A-C

Leeds
3 The Embankment
Sovereign Street
Leeds
LS1 4BJ
Tel: 0113 242 2644
Fax: 0113 242 2640
Contact: Sarah Pullan
Investment range: A-C

Abingworth Management Ltd
38 Jermyn Street
London
SW1Y 6DN
Tel: 020 7534 1500
Fax: 020 7287 0480
Contact: J. Abell
Investment range: A

Private equity provided for biotechnological/healthcare companies only

ABN Amro Development Capital
7 Hanover Square
London
W1R 9HE
Tel: 020 7495 2525
Fax: 020 7491 2050
Contact: Simon Havers
Investment range: B-C

Advent Venture Partners
25 Buckingham Gate
London
SW1E 6LD
Tel: 020 7630 9811
Fax: 020 7828 1474
e-mail: info@adventventures.com
Website: www.adventventures.com
Contact: Dr Jerry Benjamin; Dr Shahzad Malik, Healthcare; Peter Baines; Martin McNair, IT
Investment range: A-B

Albemarle Private Equity Ltd
1 Albemarle Street
London
W1X 3HF
Tel: 020 7491 9555
Fax: 020 7491 7245
Contact: Graham Barnes; Mark Hallala; Andrew Moy; Roy Parker; David Wills
Investment range: A-B

Alta Berkeley Venture Partners
9–10 Savile Row
London
W1X 1AF
Tel: 020 7734 4884
Fax: 020 7734 6711
Investment range: A

Altium Capital Ltd
30 St James's Square
London
SW1
Tel: 020 7484 4040
Fax: 020 7484 4010
Contact: Stephen Georgiadis, Director
Investment range: A-E

Amadeus Capital Partners Ltd
2 Mount Pleasant
Cambridge
CB3 0RN
Tel: 01223 578365
Fax: 01223 578488
Investment range: A

Barclays Ventures
Charles House
5–11 Regent Street
London
SW1Y 4LR
Tel: 020 7445 5900
Fax: 020 7445 5909
Contact: Jeremy Morgan; Liz Jones; Anji Gopal
Investment range: A

Baring Private Equity Partners Ltd
33 Cavendish Square
London
W1G 0BQ
Tel: 020 7290 5000
Fax: 020 7290 5025
Contact: Roger Gill; Mark Hawkesworth
Investment range: A-C

BC Partners Ltd
105 Piccadilly
London
W1J 7NJ
Tel: 020 7408 1282
Fax: 020 7493 1368
e-mail: info@bcpartners.com
Website: www.bcpartners.com
Investment range: D-E

Bridgepoint Capital
101 Finsbury Pavement
London
EC2A 1EJ
Tel: 020 7374 3500
Fax: 020 7374 3600
Website: www.bridgepoint-capital.com
Contact: David Shaw, Chief Executive
Investment range: A-E

Candover Investments plc
20 Old Bailey
London
EC4M 7LN
Tel: 020 7489 9848
Fax: 020 7248 5483
Contact: Stephen Curran, Chief Executive
Investment range: C-D

Cinven Ltd
Pinners Hall
105–108 Old Broad Street
London
EC2N 1EH
Tel: 020 7661 3333
Fax: 020 7256 2225
e-mail: info@cinven.com
Website: www.cinven.com
Investment range: D-E

Close Brothers Private Equity Ltd
12 Appold Street
London
EC2A 2AW
Tel: 020 7426 4000
Fax: 020 7426 4004
Contact: Simon Wildig
Investment range: B-C

Credit Suisse First Boston Private Equity
1 Cabot Square
London
E14 4QJ
Tel: 020 7888 3239
Fax: 020 7888 3477
Contact: Alec D'Janoeff
Investment range: A-E

Derbyshire Enterprise Board
95 Sheffield Road
Chesterfield
Derbyshire
S41 7JH
Tel: 01246 207390
Fax: 01246 221080
Contact: Andrew Street
Investment range: A

Electra Partners Ltd
65 Kingsway
London
WC2 6QT
Tel: 020 7831 6464
Fax: 020 7404 1533
e-mail: jsm@electraeurope.com
Website: www.electraeurope.com
Contact: Judy Marsden
Investment range: D-E

Enterprise Equity (NI) Ltd
78a Dublin Road
Belfast
BT2 7HP
Tel: 028 9024 2500
Fax: 028 9024 2487
Contact: Hal Wilson
Investment range: A

Equity Ventures Ltd
107 Promenade
Cheltenham
Gloucestershire
GL50 1NW
Tel: 01242 255544
Fax: 01242 255599
Contact: David Tallboys;
R Lindemann
Investment range: A

ETCapital Ltd
Cambridge
St John's Innovation Centre
Cowley Road
Cambridge
CB4 0WS
Tel: 01223 422010
Fax: 01223 422011
Website: www.etcapital.com
Investment range: A

Oxford
Oxford Centre for Innovation
Mill Street
Oxford
OX2 0JX
Tel: 01865 811118
e-mail: james@etcapital.com
Website: www.etcapital.com
Contact: James Mallinson
Investment range: A

Foreign & Colonial Ventures Ltd
Berkeley Square House
Berkeley Square
London
W1X 5PA
Tel: 020 7825 5300
Fax: 020 7825 5399
Contact: Stephen Cavell
Investment range: A-B

GE Equity
Clarges House
6–12 Clarges Street
London
W1Y 8DH
Tel: 020 7302 6000
Fax: 020 7302 6936
Contact: Mark Muth, Director
Investment range: A-D

Granville Baird Capital Partners
5th Floor
Walsingham House
35 Seething Lane
London
EC3N 4AH
Tel: 020 7488 1212
Fax: 020 7481 3911
Website: www.gbcp.co.uk
Contact: Mike Fell; Chris Harper; Nigel Guy
Investment range: A-C

Gresham Trust plc
1 South Place
London
EC2M 2GT
Tel: 020 7309 5000
Fax: 020 7374 0707
Contact: Paul Marson-Smith
Investment range: A-D

HSBC Private Equity Ltd
Vintners Place
68 Upper Thames Street
London
EC4V 3BJ
Tel: 020 7336 9955
Fax: 020 7336 9961
Contact: Chris Masterson
Investment range: A-D

HSBC Ventures (UK) Ltd
36 Poultry
London
EC2R 8AJ
Tel: 020 7260 7935
Fax: 020 7260 6767
Website: www.hsbc.com
Contact: John Brandon, Managing Director; Paul Chambers, Tom Chaloner, Jason Gould, Les Goble (Directors); Jon Stradling, Gary Stehrenberger (Investment Managers)
Investment range: A

Investment amount typically £250k to £2m but able to lead syndicates for larger transactions

Innvotec Ltd
1 Castle Lane
London
SW1E 6DN
Tel: 020 7630 6990
Fax: 020 7828 8232
Contact: Peter Dohrn
Investment range: A

LICA Development Capital Ltd
102 Jermyn Street
London
SW1Y 6EE
Tel: 020 7839 7707
Fax: 020 7839 4363
Contact: Stephen Hill; Paul Sheriff
Investment range: A-B

Lloyds TSB Development Capital
50 Grosvenor Street
London
W1X 9FH
Tel: 020 7499 1500
Fax: 020 7647 2000
Contact: Julian Carr
Investment range: A-D

LTG Development Capital Ltd
Chelsea House
West Gate
London
W5 1DR
Tel: 020 8991 4500
Fax: 020 8991 1678
Contact: Michael Rosehill
Investment range: A

Mercury Asset Management Ltd
33 King William Street
London
EC4R 9AS
Tel: 020 7203 5729
Fax: 020 7203 5833
Contact: Helen Lewis
Investment range: A-D

Merlin Ventures Ltd
67–68 Jermyn Street
London
SW1Y 6NY
Tel: 020 7976 1211
Fax: 020 7976 1444
Investment range: A

Midland Enterprise Fund for the South East
The Cadmus Organisation Ltd,
King Business Centre
Reeds Lane
Sayers Common
West Sussex
BN6 9LS
Tel: 01273 835455
Fax: 01273 835466
Contact: Howard Matthews
Investment range: A

Midven Ltd
PO Box 66
33 Bennetts Hill
Birmingham
B2 5RJ
Tel: 0121 616 1133
Fax: 0121 616 2223
e-mail: midven@aol.com
Contact: John O'Neill; Tony Stott
Investment range: A

Morgan Grenfell Development Capital Ltd
23 Great Winchester Street
London
EC2P 2AX
Tel: 020 7545 8000
Fax: 020 7545 5282
Contact: Susan Deacon
Investment range: C-E

Murray Johnstone Private Equity Ltd

Birmingham
1 Cornwall Street
Birmingham
B3 2JN
Tel: 0121 236 1222
Fax: 0121 233 4628
Contact: Harry Jeavons-Fellowes
Investment range: A-C

Glasgow
7 West Nile Street
Glasgow
G1 2PX
Tel: 0141 226 3131
Fax: 0141 248 5636
Contact: Neil MacFadyen
Investment range: A-C

Manchester
55 Spring Gardens
Manchester
M2 2BY
Tel: 0161 236 2288
Fax: 0161 236 5539
Contact: Gary Tipper
Investment range: A-C

NatWest Development Capital Ltd
21 Castle Gate
Nottingham
NG1 7AQ
Tel: 0115 959 0049
Fax: 0115 938 8400
e-mail:
david.lambert@nwdevcap.co.uk
Contact: David Lambert
Investment range: A-B

NatWest IT Fund
PO Box 12264
7th Floor
1 Princes Street
London
EC2R 8PB
Tel: 020 7390 1754
Fax: 020 7390 1123
Contact: Peter Smaill
Investment range: A

Northern Enterprise Ltd
6th Floor, Cale Cross House
156 Pilgrim Street
Newcastle upon Tyne
NE1 6SU
Tel: 0191 233 1892
Fax: 0191 233 1891
e-mail: enquiries@nel.co.uk
Contact: BS Hensby; M Hird;
DK Wilson
Investment range: A

Northern Venture Managers Ltd
30–31 Friar Street
Reading
RG1 1DX
Tel: 0118 951 7000
Fax: 0191 244 6001 2
e-mail: tim.levett@nvm.co.uk
Website: www.nvm.co.uk
Contact: Tim Levett
Investment range: A

PI Capital
7 Old Park Lane
London
W1K 1QR
Tel: 020 7629 9949
Fax: 020 7491 1015
e-mail: pi@picapital.co.uk
Website: www.picapital.co.uk
Contact: David Alexander
Investment range: A

Primary Capital Ltd
9 King Street
London
EC2V 8EA
Tel: 020 7600 9400
Fax: 020 7600 9401
e-mail:
primary@primaryeurope.com
Website: www.primaryeurope.com
Contact: Charles Gonszor
Investment range: A

Quester Capital Management Ltd
29 Queen Anne's Gate
London
SW1H 9BU
Tel: 020 7222 5472
Fax: 020 7222 5250
e-mail: john.spooner@quester.co.uk
Website: www.quester.co.uk
Contact: John Spooner
Investment range: A

Royal Bank Private Equity Ltd
Capital Building
12–13 St Andrew Square
Edinburgh
EH2 2AF
Tel: 0131 523 3333
Fax: 0131 523 9330
e-mail: info@rbpe.co.uk
Contact: David Giffin
Investment range: D-E

Sand Aire Private Equity
101 Wigmore Street
London
W1H 9AB
Tel: 020 7290 5200
Fax: 020 7495 0240
e-mail:
private.equity@sandaire.co.uk
Website: www.sandaire.co.uk
Contact: Rupert Bell; John Hudson;
David Williams; Giles Derry;
Jonathan Slow
Investment range: B

Seed Capital Ltd
Magdalen Centre
Oxford Science Park
Oxford
OX4 4GA
Tel: 01865 784466
Fax: 01865 784430
e-mail:
luciusc@seedcapital.demon.co.uk
Website: www.oxfordtechnology.com
Contact: Lucius Cary
Investment range: A

Thompson Clive & Partners Ltd
24 Old Bond Street
London
W1S 4AW
Tel: 020 7491 4809
Fax: 020 7493 9172
e-mail: cef@tcvc.com
Website: www.tcvc.com
Contact: Charles Fitzherbert
Investment range: A-B

3i plc
91 Waterloo Road
London
SE1 8XP
Tel: 020 7928 3131
Fax: 020 7928 0058
Website: www.3i.com
Contact: Patrick Dunne
Investment range: A-D

Tufton Capital Ltd
Albemarle House
1 Albemarle Street
London
W1X 3HF
Tel: 020 7529 7800
Fax: 020 7539 7801
Investment range: A

UK Steel Enterprise Ltd (Formerly British Steel (Industry) Ltd)
The Innovation Centre
217 Portobello
Sheffield
S1 4DP
Tel: 0114 273 1612
Fax: 0114 270 1390
Contact: Keith Williams
Investment range: A

Wales Fund Managers Ltd
Cedar House
Greenwood Close
Cardiff Gate Business Park
Cardiff
CF23 8RD
Tel: 029 2054 6250
Fax: 029 2054 6251
e-mail: info@wfml.co.uk
Website: www.wfml.co.uk
Contact: Richard Harbottle
Investment range: A

West Lothian Venture Fund
Geddes House
Kirkton North
Livingston
EH54 6GU
Tel: 01506 415144
Fax: 01506 415145
e-mail:
investment@wlventures.co.uk
Website: www.wlventures.co.uk
Contact: Kathy Greenwood
Investment range: A

West Midlands Enterprise Ltd
Wellington House
31–34 Waterloo Street
Birmingham
B2 5TJ
Tel: 0121 236 8855
Fax: 0121 233 3942
Contact: Peter Collings
Investment range: A

Yorkshire Fund Managers Ltd (Part of the Yorkshire Enterprise Group)
St Martin's House
210–212 Chapeltown Road
Leeds
LS7 4HZ
Tel: 0113 294 5050
Fax: 0113 294 5002
Contact: David Gee
Investment range: A

7.4

Stockbrokers and Market-makers

This section contains details of stockbrokers that deal with flotations and includes an indication of their smallest and largest flotations over the last two years. For reasons of confidentiality, exact figures have not been published but the amounts raised have been divided into the following five bands:

Band A: £0–5 million
Band B: £6–10 million
Band C: £11–20 million
Band D: £21–100 million
Band E: over £100 million

Nominated AIM advisers and brokers have been specified as such.

Austin Friars Securities Ltd
Austin Friars House
2–6 Austin Friars
London
EC2N 2HE
Tel: 020 7256 7897
Fax: 020 7256 6346
Contact: Peter Rickett; Harmon Hardy
Flotation range: A

Beeson Gregory Ltd
The Registry
Royal Mint Court
London
EC3N 4LB
Tel: 020 7488 4040
Fax: 020 7481 3762
Contact: AD Bartlett
Flotation range: A-D
AIM adviser & broker

Bloxham Stockbrokers
IFSC
2–3 Exchange Place
Dublin 1
Ireland
Tel: +353 1611 9200
Fax: +353 1829 1877
Contact: Peter O'Carroll; Angus McDonnell; John Maguire
Flotation range: A-C

Brewin Dolphin Securities Ltd
PO Box 512
National House
36 St Ann Street
Manchester
M60 2EP
Tel: 0161 839 4222
Fax: 0161 832 1672
e-mail: corporatefinance@brewin.co.uk
Website: www.brewindolphin.co.uk
Contact: Mark Brady
Flotation range: A-D
AIM adviser & broker

Brown Shipley Corporate Finance
London
Founders Court
Lothbury
London
EC2R 7HE
Tel: 020 7282 3270
Fax: 020 7796 4875
e-mail: corpfin@brownshipley.com
Website: www.brownshipley.com
Contact: Andrew Smith; Tim Feather; Martin Eales; Ruari McGirr
Flotation range: A-D

Manchester
1 King Street
Manchester
M2 6AW
Tel: 0161 214 6540
Fax: 0161 214 6541
Contact: Philip Johnson
Flotation range: A-D

Canaccord Capital (Europe) Ltd
27 Upper Brook Street
Mayfair
London
W1Y 1PD
Tel: 020 7518 7333
Fax: 020 7518 7334
Contact: T Hoare; P Reynolds
Flotation range: A-D
AIM adviser & broker

Charterhouse Securities Ltd
1 Paternoster Row
St Paul's
London
EC4M 7DH
Tel: 020 7248 4000
Fax: 020 7334 3601
Website: www.charterhouse.co.uk
Flotation range: C-D

Collins Stewart (CI) Ltd
PO Box 8
TSB House, Le Truchot
St Peter's Port
Guernsey (CI)
GY1 4AE
Tel: 01481 726511
Fax: 01481 700476
Contact: Andrew Duquemin
Flotation range: A-B

Also specialists in Channel Island Stock Exchange listing work

Credit Lyonnaise Securities
Broadwalk House
5 Appold Street
London
EC2A 2DA
Tel: 020 7588 4000
Fax: 020 7588 0278
Website: www.creditlyonnaise.com
Contact: Simon Bennett
Flotation range: C-E
AIM adviser & broker

Credit Suisse First Boston, De Zoete & Bevan Ltd
1 Cabot Square
London
E14 4QJ
Tel: 020 7888 6010
Fax: 020 7888 6017
Contact: Nicholas Brigstocke
Flotation range: B-E

Davy Stockbrokers
Davy House
49 Dawson Street
Dublin 2
Ireland
Tel: +353 1679 7788
Fax: +353 1679 1423
Website: www.davy.ie
Contact: Kyran McLaughlin
Flotation range: D-E

Dresdner Kleinwort Wasserstein
20 Fenchurch Street
London
EC3P 3DB
Tel: 020 7623 8000
Fax: 020 7623 4069
Website: www.drkw.com
Flotation range: D-E
AIM adviser & broker

Durlacher Ltd
4 Chiswell Street
London
EC1Y 4UP
Tel: 020 7459 3600
Fax: 020 7628 2749
e-mail: info@durlacher.com
Website: www.durlacher.com
Contact: GH Chamberlain
Flotation range: A-B
AIM broker

Fiske & Co Ltd
Salisbury House
London Wall
London
EC2M 5QS
Tel: 020 7638 4681
Fax: 020 7256 5365
Contact: CF Harrison
Flotation range: A-C
AIM broker

Goldman Sachs International
Peterborough Court
133 Fleet Street
London
EC4A 2BB
Tel: 020 7774 1000
Fax: 020 7774 1550
Contact: Andrew Learoyd
Flotation range: D-E

Goodbody Corporate Finance
Ballsbridge Park
Ballsbridge
Dublin 4
Ireland
Tel: +353 1667 0420
Fax: +353 1667 0410
Contact: Kevin Keating; Brian O'Kelly; Mark O'Donovan
Flotation range: A-B
AIM broker

Hawkpoint Partners Ltd
Crosby Court
4 Great St Helens
London
EC3A 6HA
Tel: 020 7665 4500
Fax: 020 7665 4600
Contact: Annette Mason-Waters

Henderson Crosthwaite Institutional Brokers Ltd
2 Gresham Street
London
EC2 7PE
Tel: 020 7623 9333
Fax: 020 7283 4823
Contact: Clive Richardson
Flotation range: A-E
AIM adviser & broker

Hoare Govett Ltd
4 Broadgate
London
EC2M 7LE
Tel: 020 7601 0101
Fax: 020 7374 7064
Contact: Nigel Mills

HSBC Securities
Thames Exchange
10 Queen Street Place
London
EC4R 1BL
Tel: 020 7621 0011
Fax: 020 7621 0496
Contact: Krishna Patel

Insinger Townsley
44 Worship Street
London
EC2A 2JT
Tel: 020 7377 6161
Fax: 020 7655 6897
e-mail: infouk@insinger.com
Website: www.insinger.com
Contact: Richard Jeffee; Simon Fox; Harley Kagan
Flotation range: A-D
AIM broker

Investec Henderson Crosthwaite
32 St Mary at Hill
London
EC3P 3AJ
Tel: 020 7772 7084
Fax: 020 7772 7112
Contact: M Stranks; J Greenall
Flotation range: B-D
AIM adviser & broker

Keith, Bayley, Rogers & Co
Ebbark House
93–95 Borough High Street
London
SE1 1NL
Tel: 020 7827 9988
Fax: 020 7403 3536
e-mail: corpfin@kbr.uk.com
Contact: AH Drummon; D Crowhurst
Flotation range: A-C
AIM adviser & broker

Marshall Securities Ltd
Crusader House
145–157 St John Street
London
EC1V 4RE
Tel: 020 7490 3788
Fax: 020 7490 3787
Contact: John Webb
Flotation range: D
AIM adviser & broker

NCB Stockbrokers Ltd
IFSC
3 George's Dock
Dublin 1
Ireland
Tel: +353 1611 5611
Fax: +353 1611 5766
Contact: John Conroy
Flotation range: A-D
AIM broker

Numis Securities Ltd
Cheapside House
138 Cheapside
London
EC2V 6LH
Tel: 020 7776 1500
Fax: 020 7776 1555
e-mail: mail@numiscorp.com
Website: www.numiscorp.com
Contact: Charles Crick
Flotation range: C-D
AIM adviser & broker

Old Mutual Securities
(Incorporating Albert E Sharp
Securities and Greig Middleton)
Birmingham
Temple Court
35 Bull Street
Birmingham
B4 6ES
Tel: 0121 710 4500
Fax: 0121 710 4599
Contact: John Folliott Vaughan
Flotation range: B-D
AIM adviser & broker

London
30 Lombard Street
London
EC3V 9EN
Tel: 020 7489 4600
Fax: 020 7489 4619
Contact: John Folliott Vaughan
Flotation range: B-D
AIM adviser & broker

Manchester
37 King Street
Manchester
M2 7AT
Tel: 0161 817 9000
Fax: 0161 819 2114
Website: www.omsecurities.co.uk
Contact: Kevin Wilson; Mark Watts
Flotation range: B-E
AIM adviser & broker

Peel Hunt plc
62 Threadneedle Street
London
EC2R 8HP
Tel: 020 7418 8900
Fax: 020 7972 0112
Contact: C Holdsworth Hunt
Flotation range: A-E
AIM adviser & broker

Rowan Dartington & Co Ltd
Colston Tower
Colston Street
Bristol
BS1 4RD
Tel: 0117 925 3377
Fax: 0117 927 2067
Website: www.rowan-dartington.co.uk
Contact: Barrie Newton
Flotation range: D
AIM adviser & broker

Seymour Pierce Ltd
29–30 Cornhill
London
EC3V 3NF
Tel: 020 7648 8700
Fax: 020 7648 8724
e-mail:
enquiries@seymourpierce.com
Contact: Richard Feigen
Flotation range: A-D
AIM adviser & broker

SG Securities (London) Ltd
Exchange House
Primrose Street
London
EC2A 2DD
Tel: 020 7522 1075
Fax: 020 7588 6144
Contact: Andrew Dawber
Flotation range: B-E
AIM adviser & broker

Shore Capital Stockbrokers Ltd
1 Maddox Street
London
W1R 9WA
Tel: 020 7734 7292
Fax: 020 7734 7635
Contact: Graham Shore; Jonathan Elstein
Flotation range: A-C
AIM adviser & broker

Charles Stanley & Co Ltd
London
25 Luke Street
London
EC2A 4AR
e-mail: charles.dampney@charles-stanley.co.uk
Website: www.charles-stanley.co.uk
Contact: Charles Dampney
Flotation range: B-D

Lewes
24–25 Cliffe High Street
Lewes
East Sussex
BN7 2AH
Tel: 01273 486244
Fax: 01273 486225
Website: www.charles-stanley.co.uk

Sutherlands Ltd
Dashwood House
69 Old Broad Street
London
EC2M 1NX
Tel: 020 7628 2030
Fax: 020 7628 2090
Contact: Trevor Inglis
Flotation range: B-D
AIM broker

Teather & Greenwood Ltd
Beaufort House
15 St Botolph Street
London
EC3A 7QR
Tel: 020 7426 9000
Fax: 020 7247 9092/1504
e-mail: timdeathers.com
Website: www.teathers.com
Contact: Tim Davis, Marketing Director
Flotation range: A-E

UBS Warburg (Investment Banking Division of UBS AG)
1 Finsbury Avenue
London
EC2M 2PG
Tel: 020 7567 8000
Fax: 020 7568 4353
Contact: Michael Lacey-Solymar
Flotation range: E

WestLB Panmure Ltd
New Broad Street House
35 New Broad Stret
London
EC2M 1SQ
Tel: 020 7638 4010
Fax: 020 7588 5297
Contact: Keith Anderson
Flotation range: C-E

WH Ireland Ltd
11 St James's Square
Manchester
M2 6WH
Tel: 0161 832 6644
Fax: 0161 661 9098
Contact: David W Youngman
Flotation range: A-B
AIM broker

Williams de Broe plc
6 Broadgate
London
EC2M 2RP
Tel: 020 7588 7511
Fax: 020 7588 8860
Contact: Tim Worlledge
Flotation range: A-D

Official List adviser & broker and AIM adviser & broker

Contributors' Contact Details

Bertoli Mitchell
Plaza 535
Kings Road
London
SW10 0SZ
Tel: 020 7349 0424
Fax: 020 7349 0339
Contact: Chris Gasson

Judy Brown
44 Bewdley Street
London
N1 1HD
Tel: 020 7609 3970

Forward Trust Ltd
Waterman House
101–107 Chertsey Road
Woking
GU21 5BL
Tel: 0800 328 3820
Fax: 0800 328 3823

KPMG Corporate Finance
1 The Embankment
Neville Street
Leeds
LS1 1DW
Tel: 0113 231 3000
Fax: 0113 231 3129
Contact: Sue Nelson

Lee Crowder
39 Newhall Street
Birmingham
B3 3YD
Tel: 0121 237 2507
Fax: 0121 236 4710
e-mail: greg.emms@leecrowder.co.uk
Contact: Gregory T Emms

Lloyds TSB Development Capital
45 Old Bond Street
London
W1S 4QT
Tel: 020 7647 2006
Contact: Michael Joseph

NMB-Heller
Enterprise House
Bancroft Road
Reigate
RH2 7RT
Tel: 01737 841200
Fax: 01737 841350

Old Mutual Securities
Old Mutual Place
2 Lambeth Hill
London
EC4V 4GG
Tel: 020 7002 4600
Fax: 020 7002 4619
Contact: Guy Peters, Corporate Finance

Royal & SunAlliance ProFin
Leadenhall Court
1 Leadenhall Street
London
EC3V 1PP
Tel: 020 7337 5952
Website: www.profin.royalsun.com
Contact: Keith Baxter

RPS Group plc
10 Queen Street
Mayfair
London
W1J 5PF
Tel: 020 7499 7007
Contact: William Butterworth

Russam GMS Ltd
48 High Street North
Dunstable
LU6 1LA
Tel: 01582 666970
Website: www.russam-gms.co.uk
Contact: Charles Russam

Small Business Service
Department of Trade and Industry
1 Victoria Street
London
SW1H 0ET
Tel: 020 7215 5000
Contact: Adrian Piper

Tenon Corporate Transactions
Salisbury House
31 Finsbury Circus
London
EC2M 5SQ
Tel: 020 7448 8120
Fax: 020 7448 8122
Email:
Shiju.Varghese@tenongroup.com
Website: www.tenongroup.com
Contact: Shiju J Varghese

TMG Corporate Finance
5 Oxford Court
Manchester
M2 3WQ
Tel: 0161 242 8800
Fax: 0161242 8801
Email: enquiries@tm-group.co.uk
Website: www.tm-group.co.uk
Contact: Philip Travis

Index of Advertisers

Printed in Dunstable, United Kingdom

88181323R00199